3 —
X co

The Problem of War

Les systèmes ont leurs fanatiques: la science n'en a jamais, elle qui use les systèmes et qui, peu à peu, les remplace dans ce qui admet à la longue une construction scientifique.—ANTOINE-AUGUSTIN COURNOT

The Problem of
WAR
in Nineteenth Century
Economic Thought

By **EDMUND SILBERNER**

TRANSLATED BY ALEXANDER H. KRAPPE

PRINCETON UNIVERSITY PRESS, PRINCETON
NEW JERSEY, 1946

To Mina and Norbert Feith

PREFACE

THOSE interested in the problem of war as it appears in the economic thought of modern times are quite aware of the fact that there exists no historical account of the subject. We attempted to fill this serious gap in the history of economic doctrines by our study "War in Economic Thought from the Sixteenth to the Eighteenth Century" (*La guerre dans la pensée économique du XVIe au XVIIIe siècle* [*Études sur l'histoire des théories économiques*, vol. VII, Paris, Librairie du Recueil Sirey, 1939]). The present volume, though constituting an independent unit, continues this study by bringing it down to the end of the nineteenth century.

For the orientation of the reader a brief outline of the contents of the present work may prove useful. It attempts to analyze the ideas of nineteenth century economists on the following questions: What is the relationship between the economic* and war? What part has war played in the economic evolution of mankind? What are the economic causes and effects of war? What is the influence of foreign commerce on international relations? Are colonies of economic advantage to the mother country? What is the best economic policy from the viewpoint of national defense? Should economic policy be subordinated to politics? What are the economic conditions of a durable peace? What economic policy is most conducive to international concord? Is military disarmament economically advantageous? Is permanent peace possible? If so, does it require any special international organization? Are social reforms indispensable to world peace? These questions, in so far as they were the subject of study by nineteenth century economists, will chiefly occupy our attention.

The present work is divided into three books devoted to nineteenth century liberalism, protectionism, and socialism

* TRANSLATOR'S NOTE: Throughout the present work we propose to translate the French term *l'économique* as *the economic* wherever it is difficult to find a wholly satisfactory English equivalent.

respectively. This division would seem the most appropriate for our purpose. In order to characterize better the leading economists of this period, and to facilitate the reading of those interested only in some of them, the chapters are devoted to the analysis of particular economists and not to the historical study of a general idea or concept. Such a division inevitably entails some repetition; but this drawback, of relatively little importance, is far outweighed by the advantage of bringing out the shades and variants of the same fundamental idea as expressed by different authors—variants which are frequently of considerable interest.

We begin our survey with a study of the English classics: Malthus, Ricardo, James Mill, MacCulloch, and John Stuart Mill. We examine next the ideas of the members of the French liberal school, particularly those of Jean-Baptiste Say, Bastiat, and Molinari. We then pass to the study of the protectionists with special emphasis on List and the followers of the German historical school: Roscher, Knies, Lorenz von Stein, Schäffle, and Schmoller. The next chapter is devoted to the followers of the historical method outside of Germany: Levasseur, Cliffe Leslie, Thorold Rogers, Laveleye, and Cunningham. Finally we examine Saint-Simon and his sect, the idealist socialists (especially Owen, Fourier, Considérant, Pecqueur, and Vidal), and the materialist socialism of Marx and Engels.

In the present work we shall study English, French, and German economic literature. It is not our purpose to review systematically the economic literature of other languages. None the less, such works by Italian and Spanish economists as have been accessible to us will be mentioned briefly.

We have confined ourselves to the nineteenth century and have ventured to go beyond it only in the case of some authors whose literary career did not come to a close until the twentieth century. This time limit would seem fairly well chosen, since in our field the beginning of the twentieth century opens up a new period, marked by the theories of economic imperialism. These have already been the subject of a number of studies, a few of which are mentioned in the last chapter.

Since this book is largely informative in character—its purpose being to analyze and elucidate the ideas of nineteenth century economists on war—we have not hesitated to quote extensively from the most significant works of that period. We realize fully that in so doing we have added somewhat to the ponderousness of our work, but we hope that this defect will be offset by its increased usefulness; for it is often true that an historical work is more valuable because of the documents quoted than because of the author's own comments.

This study is meant as a contribution to the history of economic doctrines. While in most publications in this field it is customary to sketch an historical picture of the period studied, we have preferred, in principle, to follow a different course. Only on rare occasions do we think it necessary to make a few observations on the social environment in which the ideas of our authors have taken shape. If we adopt this course the reason is certainly not ignorance of the influence exercised by the social environment upon the formation and development of ideas; it is rather the simple fact that this influence has already been studied by a large number of competent writers. It has been pointed out in more than one manual dealing with the history of economic thought, books which are easily available to the reader.

Although the present work was prepared in several libraries,† a few rare publications have remained inaccessible to the writer. None the less he hopes that nothing essential has been omitted from his bibliography. A list of the sources (both primary and auxiliary) drawn upon for this study will be found at the end of the book. In the foot-

† The author mentions particularly the university libraries of Geneva, Vienna, Havana, and Princeton, the Sociéte de Lecture in Geneva, the Bibliothèque Nationale (Paris), the Bibliothek der Arbeiterkammer in Vienna, the Library of the Institute for Advanced Study (Princeton), and the New York Public Library, to the staffs of all of which he owes a lasting debt of gratitude.

notes, publications quoted accessorily will be referred to simply by author's name and date of publication, which will enable the reader to find the title in the Bibliography.

Work on this volume was begun at the beginning of 1940 in Geneva. It was near its completion when, in the fall of 1941, I was obliged to interrupt it for nearly one year and a half. It was then resumed and completed at The Institute for Advanced Study, at Princeton.

I am deeply indebted to Professor William E. Rappard for his sincere friendship, constructive criticism, and untiring interest in the progress of my work.

Further acknowledgments are made to Professor Edward M. Earle for his interest in seeing the volume completed and printed; to those of my former students at the University of Geneva who discussed with me several of its chapters; to the anonymous reader of the Princeton University Press for his critical reading of the whole manuscript; to Mr. Datus C. Smith, Jr., Director of the Press who has been helpful in many ways; to Miss Gladys Fornell of Princeton University Press for editorial aid; and to the American Council of Learned Societies for assistance in the translation of the work.

Last, but not least, I owe thanks to my wife for having cheerfully taken upon herself the monotonous task of typing and retyping the entire manuscript.

E. S.

Princeton, New Jersey
February, 1944.

CONTENTS

xi

CONTENTS

BOOK ONE. The Classical School

A S is well known, the classical school is of English origin; but its influence upon nineteenth century economic thought has made itself felt in all countries of the continent. Nowhere, however, was it as pronounced and as lasting as in France, and in no other country did liberals pay as much attention to the problem of war. Hence the division of Book One into two parts devoted respectively to the English classics and to the French liberals.

The English classical school of the nineteenth century opens with the works of two illustrious economists—Thomas Robert Malthus and David Ricardo. Among the latter's successors, James Mill and John Ramsay MacCulloch take first rank. With John Stuart Mill the classical school reaches its apogee, while John Elliot Cairnes, an author of considerable renown, and Henry Fawcett, less well known, may be considered as the last representatives of this school.

In the French liberal school Jean-Baptiste Say stands foremost. In Frédéric Bastiat it finds its most eloquent and fervent defender, while Pellegrino Rossi, Michel Chevalier, Henri Baudrillart, and Frédéric Passy represent it also very successfully. Gustave de Molinari is its last famous adherent in the nineteenth century.

In the following pages we propose to analyze the ideas of these economists in so far as they bear on war in its relationship to economics. Though none of these authors, with one exception (Molinari), covers the entire problem, each of them, following his own tastes and preferences, studies certain of its aspects.

1

Malthus considers chiefly the demographic side of war. Ricardo analyzes certain economic and financial problems bearing on armed conflicts between nations. James Mill deals more especially with the relationship between economic progress and war. MacCulloch discusses autarky, freedom of trade, and the pacifist mission of political economy, while John Stuart Mill focuses his attention on the Navigation Acts and upon the relation between trade and peace. Cairnes expresses his opinion on militarism, and Fawcett anticipates some form of total economic war.

Jean-Baptiste Say develops a new system, Industrialism, and applies it to the solution of the problem of war. Bastiat insists particularly upon universal concord; Passy sanctifies, as it were, the doctrine of free trade. Rossi, Chevalier, and Baudrillart are interested in the question whether or not political economy can solve the problem of war. Molinari develops a theory on the greatness and decline of war and works out the project of an international peace organization.

Part One. English Classics

I. MALTHUS

THE most renowned English economist at the beginning of the nineteenth century, Thomas Robert Malthus,[1] studies the demographic phase of war in his famous *Essay on the Principle of Population*. The first (anonymous) edition[2] contains some observations on armed conflict, but they are little more than *obiter dicta* of small importance. In 1803 Malthus published a second edition of his *Essay*, considerably enlarged and appreciably modified, this time under his own name: it met with outstanding success. Four further editions appeared during his lifetime. While the first edition does not profess to inquire into the problem of war, in the subsequent editions considerable space is devoted to it.

The economic aspect of war is analyzed in his *Principles of Political Economy* (1820); but his studies on the corn laws, too, supply some data on his attitude toward the problem of war.

1. The Principle of Population and War

Without attempting to outline, in this connection, the theory of Malthus in its entirety, let us recall briefly his famous principle of population. For it is to be noted that the observations of the English economist on war are closely linked with this principle.

---

[1] Intending in early youth to become a clergyman, Malthus (1766-1834) enrolled in Jesus College, Cambridge, from which he was graduated in 1788. Having taken orders, he became a curate at the small parish of Albury. A reading of Adam Smith's *Wealth of Nations* and of Hume's *Essays* determined his vocation as an economist. The stir produced by the second edition of his *Essay* (1803) and Pitt's patronage led to his being appointed, in 1805, professor of history and political economy at Haileybury College, which had just then been founded with a view to providing training for the civil servants of the British East India Company. On Malthus's life cf. Bonar, 1924.

[2] *First Essay on Population* (1798), pp. 42, 109.

3

Malthus is convinced that population, when unchecked, goes on doubling itself every twenty-five years, or increases in a geometrical ratio. On the other hand, the means of subsistence, under circumstances the most favorable, cannot be made to increase faster than in an arithmetical ratio. The resulting deficit in food supply can never be covered. As a matter of fact, two types of checks hold population down within the limits imposed by the quantity of available food: the positive and the preventive check.

When men multiply too much in relation to the available food supply, this phenomenon is only of short duration. The insufficiency of the means of subsistence brings about famines and epidemics resulting in an increased death rate. It is also the cause of cannibalism, infanticide, the killing of old people and, above all, of war. In this painful manner the balance between population and the food supply is restored. Thus an insufficient food supply acts as a positive check on the surplus population.

A nation might adapt the increase of its population to the increase of the food supply by a less painful means, namely moral restraint which, in Malthus's view, means abstention from marriage combined with chastity. This preventive check he warmly recommends to those whose income is insufficient for the support of children, hence, chiefly, to the working classes. According to him, moral restraint is the only means for improving the condition of the poor.

"The object of those who really wish to better the condition of the lower classes of society must be to raise the relative proportion between the price of labour and the price of provisions, so as to enable the labourer to command a larger share of the necessaries and comforts of life. We have hitherto principally attempted to attain this end by encouraging the married poor, and consequently increasing the number of labourers, and overstocking the market with a commodity which we still say that we wish to be dear. It would seem to have required no great spirit of divination to foretell the certain failure of such a plan of proceeding. There is nothing however like experience. It has been tried in many different countries and for many hundred years, and the success has always been answerable to the nature of the scheme. It is really time now to try something else.

"When it was found that oxygen or pure vital air would not cure consumption as was expected, but rather aggravated the symptoms, trial was made of an air of the most opposite kind. I wish we had acted with the same philosophical spirit in our attempts to cure the disease of poverty; and having found that the pouring in of fresh supplies of labour only tended to aggravate the symptoms, had tried what would be the effect of withholding a little these supplies."[3]

War is one of the checks to an increase in population. Its effectiveness as such is seen particularly clearly in the case of primitive peoples, whose boundary disputes are productive of unending conflicts. In these continual wars and plundering raids large numbers of men are bound to perish. There is a permanent state of hostility between tribe and tribe, and the mere increase of one tribe is regarded by its neighbors as an act of aggression, for the simple reason that it requires an increased territory. A war resulting from this cause can come to an end only when, through serious losses, the population balance is restored or when the weaker party is exterminated.

Such conflicts are particularly frequent among pastoral peoples. The grazing lands utilized by a given tribe in a certain season of the year are only a small portion of its possessions. In the course of the whole year it successively occupies a vast extent of territory. Since this entire area is absolutely necessary for its subsistence and is therefore regarded as its own exclusive property, every trespass, even in its remotest part, is thought a just cause for war.

Among the nations of antiquity, particularly Greece and Rome, the losses in population resulting from armed con-

[3] Malthus, *An Essay on the Principle of Population*, 6th ed., bk. IV, chap. iii (vol. II, pp. 289 f.).

flicts were no less serious: their wars were continuous and bloody.[4]

The losses in men produced by the struggle for space and food are tremendous. With other factors war thus contributes to hold the population within certain limits and operates as an effective check. This repressive action upon population reaches a climax when, in addition, war stops or slows up the development of industry, especially that branch which contributes to an increase in the food supply.

On the other hand, wars do not greatly depopulate countries in which labor and industry are hardly touched by hostilities. This is particularly the case in modern times, since armed conflicts now seem to exercise less influence than formerly upon the production of the means of subsistence. For this reason war, though the chief cause of depopulation among savage tribes, is less destructive among modern civilized peoples, and this holds true even for the unfortunate revolutionary wars.[5] None the less, if a nation does not increase the quantity of its food supply, its population cannot multiply even in time of peace.

The natural increase of society, Malthus concludes, has been constantly and effectively restrained by a number of repressive checks: and "as it seems evident that no improved form of government, no plans of emigration, no benevolent institutions, and no degree or direction of national industry can prevent the continued action of a great check to population in some form or other, it follows that we must submit to it as an inevitable law of nature. . . ."[6]

Thus the only choice left to men is to determine which of the various checks is the least prejudicial to virtue and to happiness. Now, if we are to believe Malthus, all checks to population are reducible to three, viz., moral restraint, vice, and misery. If this point of view is correct, the choice cannot be subject to doubt: in fact, Malthus recommends moral restraint. By reducing the number of workers, it will

---

[4] Cf. *ibid.*, bk. i, chaps. viii, iv, vii, xiii, xiv.
[5] Cf. *ibid.*, bk. ii, chap. xiii (vol. i, p. 534).
[6] *Ibid.*, bk. iv, chap. i (vol. ii, p. 255).

in due course raise the price of labor; it thus constitutes the only means available to man for improving the condition of the poor and bringing about a general betterment in the social status of a nation.[7]

An application of the system of moral restraint would assure the greatest advantages to humanity. International relations would improve quite as much as the internal economy of each nation: "It might fairly be expected that war, that great pest of the human race, would, under such circumstances, soon cease to extend its ravages so widely and so frequently as it does at present."[8]

No doubt, one of the most ancient and most important causes of war is lack of living space and food; and greatly as the circumstances of mankind have changed in the course of its long history, the same cause still continues to operate and to produce, though in a smaller degree, the same results. The ambition of princes would want instruments of destruction if the distress of the lower classes did not drive them under their standards. A recruiting sergeant always prays for a bad harvest and lack of employment, or in other words a redundant population.[9]

This last point calls for some explanation. At a time when large armies were composed of mercenaries, Malthus naturally made some reference to this system. However, he by no means implies that moral constraint would prevent only wars of mercenaries. On the contrary, in his thought it is quite able to eliminate one of the chief causes of war in general, irrespective of the type of armies used. He states this opinion quite clearly in a text (cited below) in which he insists once more on the happy effect of moral constraint upon the internal and external peace of nations. While increasing the defensive power of peoples, it would at the same time make them averse to aggression.

In a society such as the one imagined by Malthus, all of whose members would endeavor to attain happiness by

[7] *Ibid.*, vol. ii, p. 256.
[8] *Ibid.*, bk. iv, chap. ii (vol. ii, p. 278).
[9] *Ibid.*

obedience to a moral code derived from an understanding of nature and sanctioned by Revelation, it is clear that individuals unable to provide for offspring would not contract marriages: ". . . the prevention of a redundant population, in this way, would remove one of the principal encouragements to offensive war; and at the same time tend powerfully to eradicate those two fatal political disorders, internal tyranny and internal tumult, which mutually produce each other."[10]

Malthus continues: "Indisposed to war of offence, in a war of defence such a society would be strong as a rock of adamant. Where every family possessed the necessaries of life in plenty, and a decent portion of its comforts and conveniences, there could not exist that hope of change, or at best that melancholy and disheartening indifference to it, which sometimes prompts the lower classes of people to say, 'Let what will come, we cannot be worse off than we are now.' Every heart and hand would be united to repel an invader, when each individual felt the value of the solid advantages which he enjoyed, and a prospect of change presented only a prospect of being deprived of them."[11]

2. Economic Effects of the Transition from War to Peace

The peace of 1815 was followed in England by an economic crisis which hit the working class particularly hard. In the last section of his *Principles* (1820) Malthus examines this distress and tries to find its cause.

He recalls to begin with that, in the course of the Napoleonic wars, England's economic condition was favorable, and led to a vast increase in her population: "During nearly the whole of the war, owing to the union of great powers of production with great consumption and demand, the prodigious destruction of capital by the government was much more than recovered. To doubt this would be to shut

10 *Ibid.*, bk. iv, chap. ii (vol. ii, pp. 280-281).
11 *Ibid.*, p. 281.

our eyes to the comparative state of the country in 1792 and 1813."[12]

The economic condition thus did not deteriorate while the war was on and distress was not then rife. The depression set in later, after the conclusion of peace. Malthus then raises the question as to why the transition from war to peace could bring about such a sudden change.

This stagnation so widely felt and so bitterly complained of after the end of the war seems to him unexplainable on the assumption that the power of production constitutes the only element of wealth and that, as a result, an increase in the means of production is equivalent to an increase in wealth. For there can be no doubt that the powers of production increased as a result of the cessation of hostilities and that more people and more capital could be employed in productive labor; but in spite of this obvious increase worry and distress were rampant where one would have expected ease and plenty.

How is this phenomenon to be explained? For a sustained increase in wealth an increase in the productive powers does not suffice: demand, too, must rise. Unfortunately, the signing of the peace of 1815 had a contrary effect, a general and prolonged decrease in the demand for goods as compared with the available supply. This slump is explained by the fact that after the cessation of hostilities the taxpayers began to save a large part of the money they had formerly paid to the State in the form of war taxes, abolished at the conclusion of peace. These savings decreased consumption and, consequently, the demand for goods, thus bringing about the depression. The belligerent States had been spending the taxes raised, thus producing a demand for labor and commodities which was both greater and more certain than that of private individuals who, at the return of peace, recovered possession of this income. Since this difference in spending lasted for quite some time, it is easy to understand that the effects produced by the transition

12 Malthus, *Principles*, chap. vii, sect. 10 (ed. 1821), p. 381.

from war to peace likewise made themselves felt for a considerable period.[13]

For this reason Malthus does not think it wise to raise the supplies of a long and expensive war within the year, as recommended by Ricardo, for example. When war becomes inevitable, it is necessary to regulate the expenses so as to make them tolerable for the nation while the war is on, and to avoid as much as possible too great a contraction of demand at the conclusion of peace.[14]

The effects of the transition from war to peace vary from country to country, depending upon the circumstances of each. The transition in wealthy countries is different from the one in poor ones: the latter are relieved by the return of peace, the former, on the contrary, languish. In general, "those States which have suffered the most by the war have suffered the least by the peace."[15] Malthus arrives at this conclusion by the following reasoning:

"In the countries where a great pressure has fallen upon moderate or scanty powers of production, it is hardly possible to suppose that their wealth should not have been stopped in its progress during the war, or perhaps rendered positively retrograde. Such countries must have found relief from that diminution of consumption, which now allows them to accumulate capital, without which no state can permanently increase in wealth.

"But in those countries, where the pressure of the war found great powers of production, and seemed to create much greater; where accumulation, instead of being checked, was accelerated, and where the vast consumption of commodities was followed by supplies which occasioned a more rapid increase of wealth than was ever known before, the effect of peace would be very different. In such countries it is natural to suppose that a great diminution of consumption and demand would decidedly check the progress of wealth, and occasion very general and severe distress, both to capitalists and the labouring classes. Eng-

---

13 *Ibid.*, pp. 385-386.   14 *Ibid.*, pp. 388 and 402.
15 *Ibid.*, p. 387.

land and America come the nearest to the countries of this latter description. They suffered the least by the war, or rather were enriched by it, and they are now suffering the most by the peace."[16]

According to Malthus it is impossible not to regard as deplorable an age in which peace seems to have been a source of distress for the country. Should one conclude from this that for certain nations war is economically preferable to peace? Certainly not, for the advantages involved are only temporary and purchased at the price of prolonged sufferings which are the harder to bear the wealthier a country growing richer by war happens to be.

War artificially swells demand whose sudden reduction at the conclusion of peace produces misery which is the more acute the higher the degree of development attained by the industry of a country. To put it differently, this danger consists in an abrupt disturbance of the equilibrium of supply and demand, of production and consumption.

Nothing is more harmful to mankind than a sudden upswing in population after two or three years of abundance, an upswing which is bound to end at the first return of scarcity or even as a result of some years of moderate harvests. The sudden but short-lived increase in the demand for labor in the course of a war produces a like effect. Hence "it is obviously the duty of all governments, if they have any regard for the happiness of their subjects, to avoid all wars and excessive expenditure as far as it is possible."[17]

In their speculations, theorists are inclined to overlook the depressions because they are but transitional periods. None the less, in human life these periods recur rather frequently and have a certain duration. They are particularly hard on the workers; for while in times of prosperity the capitalists accumulate reserves which go far toward securing them against the future, this is unfortunately not true for the working classes. Though the latter doubtless

[16] *Ibid.*   [17] *Ibid.*, p. 402.

do share in the general prosperity, they share even more in the general adversity. They suffer the most serious distress in periods of low wages but are not sufficiently compensated by periods of high wages. These fluctuations are always bound to be more harmful than useful to them. Consequently "with a view to the happiness of the great mass of society, it should be our object, as far as possible, to maintain peace, and an equable expenditure."[18]

Malthus makes no apology for the profession of arms. As is well known, he regards certain classes of unproductive consumers as indispensable, not only for the government, the protection, the health, and the education of a nation but also to bring into play the activity necessary for the full development of its physical resources. Among these classes he mentions soldiers, judges, lawyers, clergymen, officials, and servants. These classes, by buying up the surplus of the goods produced by the workers, prevent general overproduction. Though he was certainly not bellicose, such a view might have led him to glorify the army, as did Büsch and Dohm, for example, two German economists of the second half of the eighteenth century. However, such was not his attitude. Far from singing the praise of the armed forces, he contents himself with ranging them among the unproductive classes.[19] His ideal society, such as would result from a general acceptance of moral constraint, is necessarily peaceful: it is too weak for aggression but very strong in defense.

3. *Agrarian Protection*

Free trade would be of considerable advantage to the world; but it offers no remedy against economic sufferings and against war: such is the view of Malthus who, moreover, does not believe in the feasibility of a perfect freedom of trade though this ideal should be approached as closely as possible.[20]

18 *Ibid.*, p. 403.
19 Malthus, *Principles*, chap. vii, sect. 9, p. 369. On Büsch and Dohm cf. Silberner (1939), p. 157.
20 Malthus, *Essay*, bk. iii, chap. xii (vol. ii, p. 210).

In agricultural policy he deems it necessary to recommend a number of measures far remote from the principle of free trade. He advocates duties on the importation of cereals, justified, in his view, by the danger incurred by any grain-importing country of being cut off from its foodstuffs in time of war. Furthermore, foreign wheat may always be withheld from an importing country, particularly when the exporting countries themselves have not enough. To these arguments of an economic and political order in favor of agrarian protection he adds others drawn from the field of social policies. Agriculture makes for the health of a nation and for the stability of its national life.[21]

Agricultural autarky is possible for any nation possessed of an extensive territory of average fertility. Such a nation may easily support on the products of its own soil "a population fully sufficient to maintain its rank in wealth and power among the countries with which it has relations either of commerce or of war."[22]

For all these reasons, Malthus declares, "it may not appear impolitic artificially to maintain a more equal balance between the agricultural and commercial classes by restricting the importation of foreign corn, and making agriculture keep pace with manufactures."[23]

In his *Observations* (1814) Malthus sums up the arguments for and against agrarian protectionism. He recalls that in the course of a long war economic dependence on foreign countries may cause serious distress to a nation. There is always a danger of being cut off from one's foreign grain supply, though this peril is not very serious for a great and wealthy country. Quite true, an exporting country has a powerful economic interest in selling its cereals even to a nation with which it is at war; but it is well to remember that States are moved by passions rather than by interest.[24]

There are thus valid reasons for making a country in-

21 *Ibid.*, pp. 203-204, 191. 22 *Ibid.*, p. 189.
23 *Ibid.*, p. 191.
24 *Observations*, p. 23. Cf. also *The Grounds* (1815), p. 47.

dependent of foreign wheat, and this independence may be highly desirable: it is of much the same nature as the Navigation Acts. In view of the general situation of Europe, Malthus recommends it highly to English statesmen.[25] In his reservations to an all-out free trade policy he is thus largely swayed by the danger of war which renders international commerce very unstable.

4. Malthusianism and Peace

According to Malthus, the economic function of war is to restore, in common with other positive checks, the balance between population and the means of subsistence.[26] The primitive and ancient peoples were driven to war by lack of living space and food. In Malthus's view the same causes are still operative in the case of modern nations.

In asserting that war has its chief cause in an excess of population as compared with the means of subsistence, he really expresses two quite distinct ideas: he points out the principal cause of armed conflict, that is, misery, and at the same time the reasons responsible for the latter. This distinction is important. For even if one rejects his principle of population—which has proved untenable—one may reasonably attribute to the misery of the masses a large share of responsibility among the factors making for war. The least one can say is that it conspicuously favors armed conflict. It is thus a great merit of Malthus to have formulated and developed the idea of this interdependence between war and the underlying material conditions.

None the less, he linked this idea altogether too closely

[25] Malthus, *The Grounds*, pp. 47-48.

[26] Sismondi shares the same viewpoint: "comme la peste, la guerre et la famine maintiennent le niveau entre les générations naissantes et la nourriture que la terre peut leur fournir" (*Nouveaux principes*, bk. vi, chap. vii, vol. ii, p. 248). Though opposed to bellicism (cf. *ibid.*, pp. 245, 249), he attributes to war still another function. By absorbing the production surplus resulting from technological progress and from the under-consumption of the population, military expenses and war, as well as luxury, were perhaps necessary ("étaient peut-être nécessaires") to restore the economic equilibrium, particularly the equilibrium of production and consumption (*ibid.*, p. 248).

to his famous principle of population, which he proclaimed without a thorough and objective preliminary inquiry. His principle of population was formulated a priori and erected on arbitrary basic assumptions. Quite true, in the second edition of his *Essay* Malthus did add a detailed historical account absent from the first; but this very procedure shows that his theory, far from being based on demographic facts, was preconceived.

Malthus considers misery as the chief cause of war. Logically he should then admit that the elimination of misery would lead to a considerable reduction of armed conflicts, if not to their complete eradication. Economic progress—if by that we mean the continual improvement of the material conditions of the working classes—would thus seem to constitute the road leading to world peace. Malthus's principle of population, however, prevents him from recognizing in economic progress the remedy looked for. To express it differently, this principle forces him to find economic progress exclusively in a reduction in the number of the working population. To accomplish this only one means would be infallible, namely "moral restraint," which in turn could be carried out solely in a "really virtuous society."[27]

In the pursuit of peace Malthus assigns no function to the State. It suffices that the latter does not incite to war; the rest is the task of individual citizens. In short, to suppress the essential cause of war, the lack of balance between population and its means of subsistence, and to establish peaceful relations between nations, no international organization is required. Individual effort is both necessary and sufficient for the establishment of world peace.

[27] Malthus, *Essay*, bk. iv, chap. ii (vol. ii, p. 282).

II. RICARDO

IT is at first blush astonishing that David Ricardo,[1] who witnessed the innumerable military conflicts of the Revolution and the Empire, should have left no systematic account on the relationship of war and economics. It is possible, however, to fill this gap by grouping the relevant texts scattered through his work.

Ricardo brings out his position on the various aspects of war in several of his writings: *Essay on the Influence of a Low Price of Corn on the Profits of Stock* (1815), *Proposals for an Economical and Secure Currency* (1816), *Essay on the Funding System* (1820), *Principles of Political Economy* (3rd ed., 1821), and *On Protection to Agriculture* (1822). His correspondence with Malthus and Trower, and his notes on Bentham, discovered by the writer in Geneva in 1935 and published by him under the title *Un manuscrit inédit de David Ricardo sur le problème monétaire* (pp. 233 f.), also contain some interesting observations on war.

He analyzes at some length the economic effects brought about by abrupt changes in international trade, the relationship between free trade and national defense, the effect of war on wages, and the financing of war. But he is very brief on the causes of war, contenting himself with remarking, in a posthumous work (*Observations on Parliamentary Reform*), that it is private interests that make for war.

1 The son of a very wealthy Dutch Jew, a member of the London Stock Exchange, Ricardo (1772-1823), at the close of an elementary education, became a banker, starting his career, at the age of fourteen, in his father's office. After his conversion (about 1793) he became estranged from his father and set up a business of his own. By the time he was twenty-five years old he was already wealthy. A reading of Adam Smith led him to the study of political economy, and his writings had immediate success. In 1819 he was elected to Parliament. A close friendship united him with Jeremy Bentham, Malthus, James Mill, and MacCulloch. Cf. Hollander, 1910.

1. Sudden changes in the Channels of Trade

Ricardo devotes a chapter of his *Principles* to the economic effects which follow abrupt changes in international trade routes. In connection with this problem he pays particular attention to the consequences of armed conflicts.

A war breaking out after a long period of peace, he observes, produces considerable distress in industry and agriculture. Much the same holds true when a long war is followed by peace. In consequence of such events capital is shifted from one industry to others settling in branches which new circumstances have made more profitable. During this movement much fixed capital lies idle or is even destroyed, and there is unemployment. The duration of this distress will be longer or shorter, depending upon the degree of reluctance which most men feel to abandon the particular industry in which they ordinarily invest their funds. This calamity is frequently prolonged as a result of restrictions and prohibitions which are the fruit of absurd jealousies existing between the different States of the commercial commonwealth.

In rich and powerful countries a large part of the capital is invested in machines, while in poor ones there is proportionately less fixed and more circulating capital. The distress brought about by an abrupt change in trade routes will thus be felt more in rich countries, since it is less easy to withdraw fixed than circulating capital from their ordinary uses. It is often impossible to utilize in one branch of industry machines constructed for another. But the clothing, the food, and the lodging of a worker are of service to him in any kind of work, which is as much as to say that he may receive the same food, clothing, and lodging, though he may be engaged in an altogether different occupation.

Agriculture is by no means safe from such contingencies, though it is less subject to the fluctuations of the market. By interrupting international trade, war frequently prevents grain imports. The importing country is therefore compelled, while the war lasts, to invest an unusual quantity of capital in agriculture, with a view to making itself independent of foreign countries. On the other hand, at the close of hostilities, when the checks to grain import disappear, a competition disastrous for the domestic producer sets in, which involves the loss of a considerable part of his capital.

The best economic policy would be, for the State, at the close of the war and for a limited number of years afterwards, to put a special import tax on foreign corn. This tax, the amount of which should periodically decrease, would permit the domestic producer gradually to withdraw his capital from agriculture. True enough, this measure would raise the price of wheat for a certain number of years following the conclusion of peace. It would, however, prevent an excessive rise in the price of cereals during the war and the resulting interruption of imports.

If the farmers, by investing their funds in agriculture while the war is on, were running a risk of financial ruin at the close of hostilities, they would not wish thus to endanger their capital. They would demand, in addition to their ordinary profit, an indemnity for the risk they run after the war as a result of a sudden influx of corn. This would lead to a rise in the price of cereals at a time when the consumer needs them most. This rise would be due not only to the superior cost of growing corn at home but also to the insurance premium which the consumers would be obliged to pay to the farmers to indemnify them for the peculiar risk incurred by their investing additional capital in agriculture. It would thus be advisable, for a short period, to put an import duty on cereals.[2]

Its adoption, as an emergency measure in time of war, according to Ricardo, does not alter the principle of free trade, to which he remains faithful. It is simply an extraordinary measure of very limited duration. To prevent an excessive rise in farm prices during the war, one might eventually introduce an exceptional import duty on cereals, to be levied for a short period *after the war*. By this

2 Ricardo, *Principles*, chap. xix, pp. 160-162.

18

temporary measure Ricardo intends to obviate a *real* danger of the nation at war, while in his view *preventive* protectionism applied in anticipation of a war, would, because of its permanent character, pervert the entire economic life of the nation. It is then clear that the remedy proposed by him differs fundamentally from the usual protectionist measures.

As a matter of fact, he proposes this expedient for the very reason that he does not aim at an agricultural autarky: he does not wish to make the country independent of foreign grain so that the nation might at every moment be prepared for war. For to him war is not the supreme goal to which industrial or agricultural policies must be subordinated. It is simply an accident to be met by emergency measures. Ricardo is convinced that even after the outbreak of a conflict a nation has time enough to adapt its agriculture to the exigencies of war. In the following section we shall see that his reasoning is based on the economic and military position of contemporary England.

2. *Free Trade and National Defense*

Like all classics, Ricardo admits the superiority of free trade over protectionism. Freedom of trade, he thinks, allows each country to devote its capital and its labor to the most useful enterprises. He is of the opinion of Adam Smith for whom economic freedom is fully able to vouchsafe the greatest possible abundance to all nations.

"Under a system of perfectly free commerce, each country naturally devotes its capital and labour to such employments as are most beneficial to each. This pursuit of individual advantage is admirably connected with the universal good of the whole. By stimulating industry, by rewarding ingenuity, and by using most efficaciously the peculiar powers bestowed by nature, it distributes labour most effectively and most economically: while, by increasing the general mass of productions, it diffuses general benefit, and binds together, by one common tie of interest and inter-

19

course, the universal society of nations throughout the civilized world."[3]

To Ricardo the principles of free trade appear so evident that he expects final victory for them. They are, in his view, so powerful that every day they are winning new adherents. The English economist notes with satisfaction that the liberal philosophy is making rapid progress even among those who clung most obstinately to the old mercantilist prejudices.[4]

In this he finds the surest proof of the doctrinal and political power of free trade. The general adoption of economic freedom would thus be merely a matter of time. In all his observations on war and peace, his starting point is the liberal criterion which seems to him not only superior to all others but also bound to triumph in short order.

The prohibition of foreign goods is harmful even to the country taking such a measure. Whatever the policies followed by other nations, the national interest is clear: it is to buy goods where they are cheapest.[5] It is thus not surprising to find Ricardo recommending free trade to his own country, even when there is no reciprocity.

If foreign nations are not sufficiently enlightened to adopt the liberal system, if they persist in following their policies of prohibition and of excessive duties on British goods, this is no reason why England should not set them a fine example and go ahead to her own benefit. Instead of countering their trade barriers by erecting similar ones, she should do all in her power to do away as quickly as possible with the last vestiges of a policy as absurd as it is harmful. The pecuniary advantages accruing from such a system would soon engage other States to adopt it in turn, and "no long period would elapse before the general prosperity would be seen to be best promoted by each country falling naturally into the most advantageous employment of its capital, talents, and industry."[6]

[3] *Ibid.*, chap. vii, pp. 75-76.   [4] Cf. Ricardo, *Proposals*, sect. 4, p. 407.
[5] Cf. Ricardo in Hansard, vol. XLI, p. 1208.
[6] Ricardo, *Proposals*, sect. 4, p. 408.

Certain partisans of economic liberalism are of opinion that, in spite of all the advantages of the liberal system, England should favor and protect domestic agriculture because the danger of war forces her to make herself independent of foreign grain supply. Ricardo is not convinced by this argument and refutes it in his *Essay on the Influence of a Low Price of Corn on the Profits of Stock.*

He poses the problem in these terms: Would, if war should break out, a coalition of continental powers be sufficient to cut off all English food supplies from abroad? If England were to import wheat regularly, foreign countries would immediately enlarge their wheat acreage in view of the new export possibilities. Considering the vast size of English wheat consumption, it is clear that, if the continent were to supply a large part of this consumption, the interruption of these exports would mean for it the most ruinous commercial distress. For this reason no sovereign and no coalition of sovereigns would venture to provoke such a catastrophe. What is more, if the monarchs were to decree such a prohibition of exports to England, the chances are that no nation would submit to such a decree.

England would always be able, even in time of war, to buy up wheat in neutral countries. If worst came to worst, she would have to pay a very high price. These purchases, added to the normal stock, would suffice to tide her over until she had bestowed the necessary capital and labor on her own land, with a view to future production.

No doubt, such changes in production would have very serious inconveniences. Ricardo, however, is convinced that, in spite of war, foreign countries would continue to pour into the British market the cereals they have grown for this very purpose. Even Bonaparte, at a time when his hate for England had reached a climax and when he prohibited all trade with her, permitted the exportation of wheat to England by licenses, when prices in Great Britain were high as a result of a bad harvest. Moreover, a war does not break out all of a sudden: one sees it coming and should therefore be able to take due precautions.[7]

In short, in his view there would be no danger whatsoever for England in being, as it were, tributary to foreign countries for the larger part of her food supply. Once her demand is constant and uniform, as it would inevitably become under the system of free trade, foreign countries would produce immense quantities of wheat for the British market. Those countries would have no less interest in selling their cereals to England than the latter would have in buying them.

Ricardo further believes that, were England to export grain, she would not dare stop these exports in time of war, thereby exposing her farmers and landlords to general ruin. In spite of all feelings of enmity which animate belligerents, and in spite of their desire to inflict suffering upon the foe by depriving him of part of his means of subsistence, he is convinced that the English would give up their feeling of revenge under such conditions. Since British policies would take this course, he concludes that, in like circumstances, the policies of other nations would be no different and that Great Britain would never be deprived of her foreign food supplies.[8]

Thus it is not necessary to promulgate laws for the protection of agriculture for the sole purpose of obviating an evil which might never come up, and to waste, year after year, considerable sums to conjure up a danger which is most improbable.[9]

Ricardo thus gives a negative answer to the question whether, in spite of all the advantages of free trade, the permanent danger of war does not impose upon the nation the duty of following protectionist policies at least in certain cases. Considering the superiority of contemporary England over the continent, he does not even examine the

[7] Ricardo, *An Essay on the Influence* (1815), pp. 382-383.
[8] Ricardo, *On Protection*, conclusion, p. 494.
[9] Ricardo, *An Essay on the Influence*, p. 383. It is to be noted that Malthus, in contrast to Ricardo, does not attempt to minimize this peril (cf. above, chap. i, sect. 3).

eventual necessity of industrial protectionism with reference to future war. He merely analyzes the possibility of
protective tariffs for agriculture but finds them, as we just
saw, quite superfluous.

To understand Ricardo's thought, it is useful to recall
that England did not then largely depend upon foreign
agriculture. On the other hand, her naval hegemony was
already established and vouchsafed importation by sea.
England's economic structure and her naval power thus
suffice to explain this confident attitude of our author. If
he admits, as he does in the case of Great Britain, that
other European countries need not feel threatened by famine in the course of a war, the reason is that, when he
wrote, the European continent was even more agricultural
than England. Notwithstanding its importance, the problem of food supplies, at that time, was much less complex
than it was to become subsequently.

Ricardo's free-trade philosophy can be understood only
against the background of British economy at the beginning of the nineteenth century. Her economic power enabled her to stand foreign competition without danger.
Her industry was sufficiently developed to supply the needs
of national defense. Essential foreign imports, required to
cover the deficit of agricultural production, were not exposed, thanks to the powerful British navy, to interruptions
in time of war. In proclaiming the superiority of freedom
of commerce, Ricardo could thus be certain of not endangering the national defense of his country. He had no reason to fear an economic or military weakening of Britain.
In this connection he frankly expresses the British point
of view, i.e., his opinions are in complete harmony with
the national interests of Great Britain.

On the other hand, he completely neglects the interests
of States whose foreign trade is not immune from interruptions in time of war. Yet such interruptions, if prolonged
over a considerable period, might ruin the economic life
of a country and make its defense impossible. Ricardo,
however, does not examine the necessity, for these States,

to follow, in time of peace, economic policies calculated to increase their military power and thus to ward off all danger of foreign aggression.

What amazes the modern reader is the confidence with which Ricardo considers the possibility of continued trade relations between belligerents. His forecasts are of course based on the trade tradition of the preceding centuries. In those days war was an almost exclusively military matter. The economic factors, though naturally present, played a much smaller role than they do in the period of "total war," when as complete an interruption as possible of trade relations between belligerents is the rule. Total war, in both the military and economic sense, was as yet unknown.

3. War and the Working Classes

In the third edition of his *Principles* (1821) Ricardo adds a new chapter on machines, in which he examines, among other things, the influence of war upon wages and population.

The idea there developed will be better understood after a preliminary observation.

Ricardo is of opinion that that part of the net income which a wealthy man spends on luxuries does not necessarily increase the *additional* demand for labor. For example, in buying carpets or furniture one acquires objects through the possession of which it is impossible to create an *additional* demand for labor; for their owner cannot feed workers with these goods. But if the same wealthy man instead acquires food, he is able to maintain additional servants by this means. (To simplify matters, he may pay them wages and leave it to them to buy their provisions themselves.) In proportion as the number of servants engaged by him increases, the labor supply decreases in the market.

In other words, the net income spent on servants creates an additional demand for labor. This additional demand depends then on the manner in which the rich man spends his net income, that is, whether he spends it on luxuries or on servants. Since workers are always interested in an increased demand for labor, they must, in Ricardo's view, naturally desire that as much of the revenue as possible be diverted from expenditures on luxuries and devoted to the upkeep of servants.

Ricardo does not deduce from this a general rule to the effect that it would be more profitable to the working class if the income were spent as much as possible on services rather than on goods. Senior[10] is evidently wrong in suggesting such an interpretation. For in the analysis referred to, Ricardo thinks only of the effects of expenses of one special category, namely expenses on luxuries. However, as for that part of the income which is set aside for the accumulation of capital, it increases the demand for labor and, according to him, is therefore favorable to the working class.

Ricardo concludes that the produce of the additional taxes imposed upon the richer classes during war, being chiefly expended upon soldiers and sailors, furnishes the subsistence for a larger number of persons than if it were left with its original owners; for in that case it would very probably be spent, at least in part, on luxuries which cannot be consumed by workers.

As a result war, paid for with the net income, would increase the demand for labor. All other things being equal, it would thus favor a rise in wages and a growth of population.

Let us now quote Ricardo himself: "A country engaged in war, and which is under the necessity of maintaining large fleets and armies, employs a great many more men than will be employed when the war terminates, and the annual expenses which it brings with it, cease.

"If I were not called upon for a tax of £500 during the war, and which is expended on men in the situations of soldiers and sailors, I might probably expend that portion of my income on furniture, clothes, books, etc., and whether

10 *An Outline of the Science of Political Economy* (1836), ed. 1938, p. 171.

it was expended in the one way or in the other, there would be the same quantity of labour employed in production; for the food and clothing of the soldier and sailor would require the same amount of industry to produce it as the more luxurious commodities; but in the case of the war, there would be the additional demand for men as soldiers and sailors; and, consequently, a war which is supported out of the revenue, and not from the capital of a country, is favourable to the increase of population.

"At the termination of the war, when part of my revenue reverts to me, and is employed as before in the purchase of wine, furniture, or other luxuries, the population which it before supported, and which the war called into existence, will become redundant, and by its effect on the rest of the population, and its competition with it for employment, will sink the value of wages, and very materially deteriorate the condition of the labouring classes."[11]

Should we conclude then that since in Ricardo's view war, at least in certain respects, is favorable to the working class wage earners might be reasonably expected to desire it in order to better their condition? Should we conclude that war seems to him to be a means susceptible of effectively increasing population? At first sight one might be tempted indeed to interpret the passage in this sense. Such an interpretation would, however, be wholly erroneous.

As is well known, Ricardo's writing, though very concise in style, is rather difficult to understand, for he frequently makes certain mental reservations, without mentioning them explicitly, simply because he considers them self-evident and known to the reader. Though his reasoning is perfectly logical, the intelligibility of his writings is none the less impaired. He frequently implies certain preliminary conditions without expressly saying so and thus clearing up all possible misunderstanding. Many mistakes

---

[11] *Principles*, chap. xxxi, p. 240. Cf. MacCulloch, *Principles*, pt. iii, chap. ii, sect. 4, pp. 443-444, with an interpretation of the above quoted text.

in the interpretation of his writings could have been avoided had his analyses been less brief.

This observation holds true also for the case under discussion. Let us point out, first, that Ricardo excludes from his examination all wars paid for, not with the net income, but with the capital; for such wars are evidently harmful to the entire population and particularly to the working class. As for wars paid for with the income, which is the only type of war examined by him, he does not believe that, taken by and large, they are necessarily conducive to a rise in wages and an increase in population. He does not consider the problem as a whole, that is to say, the total effect of this type of war upon the working classes and the population. He simply concludes that, *leaving out of account all disturbing factors* (a clause always implied by him), wars paid for with the net income favor a rise in wages and the growth of population. This conclusion is indeed logical: all other conditions being equal, war, by increasing the number of soldiers, reduces the labor supply and consequently tends to increase wages and hence the birth rate. But all this leaves out of account other factors operating in an opposite sense.

Ricardo could not be ignorant of the presence of many disturbing causes counteracting the tendency just discussed, such as, for example, the loss of life on the battle field, an increased death rate, epidemics, famines, and high food prices not compensated for by the rise in wages. The question is whether these disturbing factors outweigh the tendency pointed out by Ricardo. He does not say. But the logical answer one might expect of him would be that the result looked for depends on the specific circumstances of each particular war: The action of these factors may or may not prevail. None the less, it is useful to repeat once more that he does not attempt to study the whole complex of these questions. In his analysis he contents himself with the examination of one angle of the problem and arrives at the conclusion that, in certain respects, wars defrayed with the net income (leaving out of account factors operating in a contrary sense) favor the working classes and a growth of population.

Knowing Ricardo's deep sympathy for the working classes we cannot admit that he could have believed that by and large war, even if defrayed exclusively by the net income, can be effectively advantageous to them. In a somewhat superficial critique of the above quoted text, Senior observes that "War is mischievous to every class in the community; but to none is it such a curse as to the labourers."[12] In view of his general opinions, we may safely say that Ricardo would without hesitation have subscribed to this formula. One might add also that he never said the opposite while pointing out the presence of a certain tendency of wars defrayed by the net income to compensate for the harm caused by war in general.

Such an interpretation of our author seems the more well-founded when we consider his assertion that wars defrayed by the net income lead to a growth of population. Can this mean anything else but a tendency to increase the population in spite of the loss of life caused by armed conflicts, that is, to express it differently, a tendency to offset, to a certain extent, the reduction in population which is one of the effects of war?

To say that war is advantageous to the working classes because it decreases the supply of labor in proportion to its demand implies a more general idea, namely, that any calamity eliminating a large portion of the wage earners is favorable to the interests of this class because, all other factors being equal, the condition of those of its members which will survive is bound to be improved. It may be affirmed, however, without a tendentious interpretation of his writings, that this could not be Ricardo's conclusion.

12 Senior, *An Outline*, p. 173. For a similar view cf. Carey, *Principles of Political Economy* (1838), vol. II, p. 347. Cf. also Senior, *The Law of Nations* (1843), pp. 154 and 156.

4. The Financing of Wars

(A) LOANS OR TAXES?

The funded debt of Great Britain rose from some 240 millions of pounds sterling, in 1792, to more than a billion in 1816.[13] The continual increase of the British public debt at the beginning of the nineteenth century does not leave Ricardo indifferent. Already in his *Principles* he shows interest in the problem of financing wars. Visibly inspired by Adam Smith, he is opposed to the financing of wars by loans, which he does not regard as the best method for covering the extraordinary expenditures of the State. Loans, in his view, are conducive to making a nation less thrifty and to keeping it in the dark about its true situation. So he advocates another system, that of providing for the cost of the war by means of an income tax to be levied while the conflict is on. The practical carrying into effect of such a system, which had been proposed a long time before him by Postlethwayt and Adam Smith, leaves him however skeptical: "We have, I fear," he says, "neither wisdom enough, nor virtue enough, to adopt it."[14]

He reverts to the subject in his *Essay on the Funding System* (1820), where he develops it more systematically. He sketches, to begin with, the origin and progress of the sinking fund, adding some observations on the effectiveness of this financial institution. He then tries to discover the best mode of providing for the annual expenditure of Great Britain both in war and peace. It would go beyond the scope of the present work were we to attempt a complete analysis of this important treatise, which belongs rather to the field of public finance. We shall limit ourselves instead to the parts dealing with war.

Let us now follow Ricardo's reasoning on the basis of his own example. Let us suppose that a country, completely free from debt, is all of a sudden thrown into a war requir-

[13] R. Hamilton, *An Inquiry* (1818), pp. 320-332.
[14] *Principles*, chap. xvii, p. 149. On Postlethwayt and Smith cf. Silberner (1939), pp. 78, 248-249.

ing an additional expenditure of twenty millions. There are three modes of providing for this supplementary expenditure. The State may (1) impose new taxes to the amount of twenty millions, from which the country would be totally freed on the return of peace; (2) borrow this sum without amortizing it (if the rate of interest, for example, is five per cent, the perpetual charge would be one million a year); (3) borrow the twenty millions and provide, in addition to the interest, a sinking fund which, accumulating at compound interest, would finally equal the debt. Thus the war debt will disappear after a certain time and with it the taxes levied to pay it. Reverting to the example cited (twenty millions at five per cent), if 200,000 are added annually to the million paid by way of interest, twenty millions may be accumulated in forty-five years from the end of the war. By thus imposing annually, for a debt of twenty millions, new taxes amounting to 1,200,000, it will be possible to redeem the total debt in forty-five years, and then to repeal the whole of the taxes to which war gave rise.

Ricardo thinks the first of these three modes is certainly the most advantageous. Undoubtedly the burden resting upon the country during the war would be great; but it would be removed at the conclusion of peace. What is more, *such a means would be an effective precaution against unnecessary wars*: "When the pressure of the war is felt at once, without mitigation, we shall be less disposed wantonly to engage in an expensive contest, and if engaged in it, we shall be sooner disposed to get out of it, unless it be a contest for some great national interest."[15]

In point of economy there is no real difference between the three means mentioned, for twenty millions in one payment, one million per annum forever, or 1,200,000 for forty-five years have exactly the same value. None the less, the influence exerted by these different systems on the taxpayers is quite different. The latter are in general too much inclined to believe that the war is burdensome only in pro-

15 Ricardo, *Essay on the Funding System*, p. 539.

portion to what they at the moment are called to pay for it in taxes, without worrying about their probable duration.

It would be difficult to persuade a man who possesses, for example, 20,000 pounds sterling, that a perpetual tax of fifty pounds annually is as heavy as a single tax of 1,000 pounds. The reason is that he expects the fifty pounds to be really paid by posterity: his heirs will bear the load. However, there is no difference whatever, so far as the heirs are concerned, whether they collect an inheritance of 20,000 pounds burdened with an annual debt of fifty pounds, or an inheritance of 19,000 pounds without it. True enough, an individual will find it easier to pay fifty pounds annually than to pay 1,000 pounds in a lump sum. In general, people draw a sharp distinction between an annual tax of fifty pounds and a definite tax of 1,000 pounds. If a man were obliged to pay an income tax of 1,000 pounds, he would probably endeavor to save the whole of it from his income; but he would not do so were he merely obliged to meet the interest of a government loan by means of an annual payment of fifty pounds.

War taxes are then more economical because they induce the taxpayers to save up to the total amount of the war expenditures, so that the national capital can be left intact. Contrariwise, under the system of war loans which induces them to save only to the amount of the interest of such expenditures, the national capital is reduced.[16]

The most common objection to war taxes is that taxpayers who never dispose of large sums of money, could pay them only with difficulty. Ricardo believes, however, that they would make very serious efforts to set aside savings out of their income for the payment of these taxes. But even supposing this to be unfeasible, nothing would prevent them from selling part of their property for money or from borrowing it at interest. The ease with which the State floats its loans proves that there are people willing to lend their capital. If this giant borrower, i.e., the State,

16 *Ibid.*, p. 540. Cf. also *Letters of Ricardo to Malthus*, p. 39.

were removed from the money market, enormous sums would with one stroke be made available to private borrowers. With the money borrowed by the latter, war taxes could be paid easily, and the State would no longer be under a necessity of borrowing money from private persons to cover the cost of a war.

What does a State loan really mean? Simplifying the problem, one may say that creditor A advances money to the State, while taxpayer B provides the State with the means to pay the interest owed by the State to creditor A. In the case of a levy of war taxes, A would still advance money, though not to the State but to the hard pressed taxpayer, and B would still be paying the interest, but with this difference that he would pay it directly to A, while in the former case he pays it first to the State, which then transmits it to A. In either case A advances the money, while B pays the interest. Still, the war tax has the advantage pointed out above.

These war taxes would be very high, and it might be objected that they would fall exclusively on property, while smaller taxes are distributed more equally among all classes. True, answers Ricardo; but there is no remedy for it, for wage earners can never pay heavy taxes, which therefore necessarily fall upon the capitalist and landholder.[17]

In fact, Ricardo thinks that in the last analysis all taxes fall upon profit and rent, since wages do not rise above the minimum subsistence level. In a footnote he adds however that "perhaps this is expressed too strongly, as more is generally allotted to the labourer under the name of wages than the absolutely necessary expenses of production. In that case a part of the net produce of the country is received by the labourer, and may be saved or expended by him; or it may enable him to contribute to the defence of the country."[18]

The greatest advantage of extraordinary war taxes would

[17] Ricardo, *Essay on the Funding System*, p. 540.
[18] *Principles*, chap. xxvi, p. 210.

be that of interfering only temporarily with the economic activity of the country. At the conclusion of peace it would no longer be necessary to levy new taxes to cover the interest charges of the public debt. One would thus avoid injudicious, badly calculated, and badly applied taxes which are a serious cause of economic disorder. A whole army of tax collectors who now burden the budget, could be dismissed. There would be no charges for the management of debt. It might perhaps even be possible to do away with two great sources of demoralization, the customs and excise.[19]

In short, from every point of view the public finances and economic life would profit from the disappearance of funded debts. According to Ricardo it is better to combat difficulties at the time they come up and to keep the country free from permanent encumbrances the crushing load of which is felt only when the evil has grown beyond repair.

(B) SINKING FUND AND POLICY OF AGGRESSION

Ricardo is opposed to the system of funds allegedly meant to amortize the public debt but in reality a pretext used by the State to get hold of vast resources for purposes which have nothing to do with the payment of debts and which are in most cases plain aggression. In advocating the sinking fund the ministers indulge in highly patriotic phrases: foreign powers, they assert, will be afraid to insult or provoke an adversary possessed of powerful resources. But for the ministers this argument amounts to saying that they regard the sinking fund as a war fund pure and simple, which they expect to use on the first occasion of an armed conflict. They advocate the sinking fund only because they may divert it from its defensive purpose, as indeed they have been doing ever since. They use it for war and for paying the interest on new debts. The larger this fund is, the more it is likely to stimulate the ambition and the arrogance of the government, which

[19] Ricardo, *Essay on the Funding System*, p. 541.

will promptly plunge the country into unnecessary wars.

Now, Ricardo's effort is wholly exerted in a contrary sense, namely to prevent the government from having at its disposal considerable funds which are generally difficult to control and which permit it to embark on a policy of aggression. This tendency comes out in a polemical page against Lord Vansittart (1766-1851), then Chancellor of the Exchequer. Vansittart had said, in 1813, that the advantage of his new system of sinking funds is immense since it will place at the disposal of the government a capital of 100 millions, which might be utilized in case of hostilities. Parliament will then be provided with a strong and powerful lever. Perhaps, Vansittart had added, it will be objected that this immense sum may make possible an "arrogant or ambitious conduct of our Government" and that it might be "used for the purposes of ambition, rapine, and desolation." To this sensible objection, Ricardo observes, Vansittart replies with specious phrases: if such a policy were followed, the responsibility would fall upon the ministers guilty of a misuse of their powers, and not upon those who in good faith provided them with "the means of preserving the greatness and glory of the country."

After citing these passages of Vansittart, Ricardo counters: "These are very natural observations from the mouth of a minister; but we are of opinion that such a treasure would be more safe in the custody of the people, and that Parliament have something more to do than to furnish ministers with the means of preserving the greatness and glory of the country. It is their duty to take every security that the resources of the country are not misapplied 'by the arrogant and ambitious conduct of our Government,' or 'used for the purposes of ambition, rapine, and desolation.' "[20]

This attitude of Ricardo is a logical consequence of his distrust of the State, which is only too frequently inclined to follow a bellicose policy. "There cannot be a greater

[20] *Ibid.*, p. 547.

security for the continuance of peace, than the imposing on ministers the necessity of applying to the people for taxes to support a war."[21]

Giving up war loans, financing a war by taxation (income taxes and, if necessary, capital levies), carrying the entire load during the shortest possible time, that is, while the war is on or, at the most, within a few years after it, these are, according to Ricardo, the best means of financing a war—and at the same time of avoiding military conflicts. Distrusting the political capacity of governments and convinced of their all too frequent badness, and their proneness to start wars in order to defend private interests, the great economist is desirous of making this difficult by raising an obstacle which, though perhaps not insurmountable, is none the less very serious. If such a system were adopted, both government and citizens, feeling the whole burden of armed conflicts, would reflect long before rushing into war.

Nevertheless, while trying to prove the feasibility of financing a war without loans, Ricardo seems to underestimate the economic and political difficulties, however temporary, which might result for the State, particularly in the case of long and very expensive wars. It would seem impossible to define in an absolute manner the best way of financing a war; for it cannot be laid down on the basis of a general and universal principle but only by taking into account the peculiar conditions of each country and of each war.

Ricardo's manner of sizing up the difficulties of financing a war exclusively by taxation brings out clearly his own pacifist convictions. He lists these obstacles with a certain satisfaction because he thinks them susceptible of preventing wars. And it should not be forgotten that, in his opinion, "the preservation of the peace of Europe is a great object."[22]

How can this goal be attained? Ricardo does not examine

21 *Ibid.,* p. 546.
22 *Letters of D. Ricardo to H. Trower 1811-1823,* p. 213.

this problem. Might the triumph of free trade, which he anticipates, bring about, automatically, the establishment of permanent peace? Or would it merely tend to do away with economic antagonisms which often lead nations to war? Ricardo also leaves these questions open. It is worth noting, however, that, unlike many free traders, he does not expressly state that freedom of trade among nations will inevitably produce international peace.

Is universal peace possible and to be hoped for? His work contains no answer to this question, which, besides, he does not pose. One may try, however, to draw the answer from his writings. He asserts, indeed, that "wars are entered into for the sake of private advantage, and the nation is borne down with great and unnecessary expenses."[23] On the other hand he claims that the well considered interests of nations do not clash. He also declares that "good government" "can never be prejudicial to the general happiness."[24] From this we may infer that, if nations had good governments, there would be no wars. Peace would be maintained without the intervention of any international organization. The good will and the well considered interest of governments would be sufficient guarantees.

To examine Ricardo's views on how to obtain a good government would transcend the scope of this study. Suffice it to say that he favors a representative system that would exclude from the government all those who have "interests separate and distinct from the general interest."[25]

[23] Ricardo, *Observations on Parliamentary Reform*, p. 553.
[24] *Ibid.*
[25] *Ibid.*

III. JAMES MILL

IT is mainly in a piece of polemics against Thomas Spence (1750-1814) and William Cobbett (1763-1835) that James Mill[1] studies the problem of war. In 1807 James Mill published a treatise under the rather long title of *Commerce Defended. An Answer to the Arguments by which Mr. Spence, Mr. Cobbett and Others, Have Attempted to Prove that Commerce Is Not a Source of National Wealth.* It is chiefly in this piece of polemics, a true apology of trade, that he studies the problem of war. A critical analysis of the ideas of his opponents offers him the opportunity to express his own views on foreign trade and on armed conflict.

In his subsequent publications Mill pays very little attention to war in its relation to economics. A passage in his *Elements of Political Economy* (1821) explains this lack of interest, as we shall see presently.

In the matter of international relations, two articles by James Mill, published in the supplement to the *Encyclopaedia Britannica* (1824), deserve mention: one on colonies, the other on the law of nations.

1. Trade and Armed Conflict

Spence's theory criticized by Mill may be summed up briefly as follows: Men, thinks Spence (*Britain Independent of Commerce*, 1807), are in general too much inclined to saving. To create a large demand, they should restrict the accumulation of capital and spend their income rather in consumer goods and luxuries. Unfortunately, they frequently fail to do so to the extent that would be desirable. Happily the government takes this duty upon itself by

---

1 James Mill (1773-1836), philosopher, historian, and economist. The son of a shoemaker, he struggled, until 1819, with serious material difficulties. A year after the publication of his *History of British India* (1818), which had considerable success, he obtained a lucrative post in the service of the East India Company. He was on terms of friendship with Bentham and Ricardo. On his life cf. A. Bain, 1882.

spending unproductively the money obtained by public loans and taxation. According to Spence the public debt and taxes are therefore highly favorable to the national well-being. He goes so far as to say that the heavier the taxes, the greater is the prosperity of the masses. From this he deduces that in time of war, when taxes are highest, the larger part of the population enjoys greater prosperity than in any other period.

Mill combats this theory. Since its premises, he says, are erroneous, one might reject *a limine* Spence's conclusion. He thinks it however useful to examine more closely a thesis as shaky as it is cruel, being bound, so far as it may influence minds, to prolong a national calamity such as war. Basing himself upon the statistical data then available, he rapidly sketches a picture of the wretched condition of England's lower classes. The allowances distributed among the indigent under the "poor laws," more than doubled between 1793 and 1803. One sixth of the population was living on public relief. The real wages fell. Such are the facts he quotes. Since, he concludes, national prosperity is measured by the degree of well-being enjoyed by the working classes, it is impossible not to recognize the disastrous effects of war.

The consequences of armed conflicts are so ruinous that it is of importance to know their causes. Though Mill does not go into this subject as a whole, he at least examines one important angle. He asks himself whether, as William Cobbett[2] asserted, war is in most cases provoked by trade. If some minister overrates the importance of trade, if he spreads false ideas on its value and in this connection introduces absurd ordinances, one cannot, like Cobbett, fairly hold trade itself responsible for this but must fix the blame on the guilty minister alone. Cobbett's arguments against trade recall those of infidels against religion: because governments have often used it as a cloak to justify the most abominable crimes, certain atheists conclude that it should be abolished.

[2] *Cobbett's Weekly Political Register*, vol. XII (London, 1807), p. 822.

How many wars have been provoked by trade! How much bloodshed has it caused! What chains has it forged for mankind! These are the main grievances of its adversaries. James Mill does not deny the wrongs resulting from an erroneous conception of foreign trade. The harm inflicted in the name of religion has been no less infinite and abominable. None the less, he observes, the effects of religion, like those of trade, are beneficent. Even if religion and trade were eliminated, ignorant ministers would still go on to misconceive their duty, and venal governments would still find pretexts in order to delude the people. Past experience leaves no doubt on the subject.

In reality, there is only one guarantee against deception: sufficient knowledge to discover the fraud. So long as the people are ignorant enough to be taken in by lies, it is impossible to protect them effectively. A contrary assumption would be absurd. Wherever the people, by their ignorance, have allowed their leaders to mislead them, by means of a false glorification of trade, wherever their scanty knowledge did not permit them to oppose imprudent policies, it would have been easy to find other specious reasons to deceive them, had commerce not existed. The disappearance of trade therefore would not really eliminate any source of war and, contrary to the view of some, would have no salutary effects whatever. Can one seriously believe that without trade men would be sufficiently enlightened to be safe from any other form of delusion? Or is it likely that the means of deception are so few in number as to be summed up in one word, Trade?

It is thus illusory to believe that foreign trade as such is necessarily a source—the chief source—of wars. It is harmful to work for its disappearance which, without reducing the chances of armed conflicts, would mean the loss of the economic advantages it offers to a nation. For it permits buying and selling abroad at more advantageous prices than in the country itself. It is therefore useful. It is an important auxiliary to agriculture and industry, the two main springs of national wealth and prosperity. Far from vouchsafing peace, its suppression would certainly lead to the impoverishment of nations.[3]

Though Mill does not examine what is now called by some the economic causes of war, he at least indicates what, in his view, is *not* at the bottom of international conflicts. In contrast to those who confuse the phenomenon itself with the notion man forms of it, he thinks that trade cannot constitute a true source for wars. At the most it frequently is a specious pretext for war. The government often has recourse to this clever subterfuge by which it easily deceives public opinion. None the less, the responsibility for this deceit falls less upon trade than upon the credulity or, if one prefers, the ignorance of the public.

2. *The Noxiousness of War*

Though man's desire to satisfy his immediate wants is very strong, his disposition to accumulate seems to Mill to be a still more powerful propensity. Wherever private property is secure, many men try not to consume their entire income but devote part of it to an increase in production. Thanks to this accumulation, nations increase the total produce of their industry from year to year; thanks to it the population grows and nations progress. According to circumstances, the structure of one society may be more favorable to this progress than that of another. But whatever the structure, in every country with a tolerable degree of freedom and security, it cannot prevent the accumulation of capital and the increase of the annual produce.

The well-being of the masses, which depends essentially upon this produce, must be attributed to this admirable tendency of man to accumulate wealth and which itself is based on a natural gift, namely foresight. Nature, which conferred upon man the ability to foresee future wants and to accumulate wealth, has supplied him with the natural propensity for a gradual and assured improvement of his material condition.

None the less, looking at the real situation of mankind,

[3] James Mill, *Commerce Defended*, 2nd ed. (1808), pp. 97-102, 111-116.

one cannot but be struck with grief and sorrow. From the action of a factor as powerful as the accumulation of wealth one should reasonably expect opulence and prosperity everywhere. In reality, however, one finds only poverty and wretchedness. How are we to explain this strange contradiction? Who devours this wealth which men as individuals have so strong an inclination to increase?

The wastefulness of governments, however harmful, is not sufficient to explain this misery. A spendthrift government is a curse, for each farthing wasted reduces wealth and the happiness of the nation. Nevertheless, if the latter is large and its industry advanced, even prodigal government expenditures are not very high when compared with the whole of the annual produce. Private savings almost invariably surpass the ordinary expenses of the State. In spite of these and in spite even of government waste, the nation might be prosperous and happy; it might progress, though less rapidly than under a thrifty government.

"To what baneful quarter, then, are we to look for the cause of the stagnation and misery which appear so general in human affairs? War! is the answer. There is no other cause. This is the pestilential wind which blasts the prosperity of nations. This is the devouring fiend which eats up the precious treasure of national economy, the foundation of national improvement, and of national happiness. Though the consumption even of a wasteful government cannot keep pace with the accumulation of individuals, the consumption of war can easily outstrip it. The savings of individuals, and more than the savings of individuals, are swallowed up by it. Not only is the progression of the country stopped, and all the miseries of the stationary condition are experienced, but inroads are almost always made upon that part of the annual produce which had been previously devoted to reproduction. The condition of the country therefore goes backwards; and in general it is only after the country is so exhausted that the expence of the war can hardly by any means be found, that it is ever put an end to. When the blessing of peace is restored, the country slowly recovers itself. But hardly has it gained its former prosperity when it is generally re-struck by the calamity of war, and compelled to measure back its steps. In this alternation between misery and the mere beginnings of prosperity, are nations for the most part, condemned to remain; the energies of human nature are exerted to no purpose; its beneficent laws are counteracted; and the happiness of society, which seems to be secured by such powerful provisions, like the water of Tantalus, is only allowed to approach the lip, that it may be immediately dashed away from it."[4]

In support of his thesis, Mill quotes a passage from Vauban, who says in effect that, if France is suffering, "this is due neither to the intemperateness of the weather nor to her inhabitants, nor even to the sterility of her soil, since her climate is excellent, while her people are hardworking, skilful, ingenious, and very numerous; but it is due to the wars which have disturbed her for a long time and to a want of economy, the importance of which we [i.e. the French] do not sufficiently understand."[5]

Mill then continues: "In every country, therefore, where industry is free, and where men are secure in the enjoyment of what they acquire, the greatest improvement which the government can possibly receive is a steady and enlightened aversion to war. While such a nation remains at peace, the faults of the government can hardly ever be so great, that the merits of the nation will not more than compensate them, and that society from its own beneficent tendency will not improve. Nothing however can compensate the destruction of war. The creative efforts of individuals can never equal its gigantic consumption, and the seeds of prosperity are eaten up."[6]

4 *Ibid.*, pp. 119-120. Cf. also pp. 117-118.
5 Vauban, *Projet d'une dixme royale* (1707), ed. 1843, p. 50: "ce n'est ni à l'intempérie de l'air, ni à la faute des peuples, ni à la stérilité des terres, qu'il en faut attribuer la cause, puisque l'air y est excellent, les habitants laborieux, adroits, pleins d'industrie et très-nombreux, mais aux guerres qui l'ont agitée depuis longtemps, et au défaut d'économie que nous n'entendons pas assez."
6 *Commerce Defended*, pp. 120-121.

By such truths clearly and strikingly formulated, one may hope to exert a far-reaching influence on the government and the nation which, too, is responsible for this state of permanent warfare. History teaches in fact that the blindness of peoples is no less than that of their leaders. The people are no less to blame than their governments. An analysis of the causes of all known wars proves, according to Mill, that to avoid international conflicts is not as difficult as is generally supposed. In the overwhelming majority of cases both belligerent parties have been at fault, and "a little more wisdom" on both sides would have sufficed to prevent the calamity.[7]

3. Colonies as a Source of Armed Conflict

Among the multiple causes of war Mill examines only one, viz., colonies. He follows, largely, the reasoning of his illustrious master, Jeremy Bentham, who built his project of permanent peace on the principle of the emancipation of all colonies by their mother countries.[8] Without going quite as far as Bentham (whom he liked to call his "spiritual father") that is, without demanding explicitly the emancipation of colonies, Mill admits their uselessness, nay, their noxiousness, for the mother country. All hopes of extracting from them large tribute extending over a long period of time, are vain. History has amply shown that their upkeep costs more than the amount of taxes they pay. As for the wasting of public money, it is even greater in colonies than in the mother country because it is more difficult to control.

On the other hand, the so-called commercial advantages derived by the mother country from the colonies really amount to nothing. Such advantages can accrue only from a monopolized colonial trade. However, in that case it is not the nation as a whole but a privileged company which

[7] *Ibid.*, p. 121.

[8] Cf. Silberner (1939), pp. 257 f. Bentham's ideas on colonies were forcefully reaffirmed by the Italian liberal economist Romagnosi (1835), pp. 543 f.

reaps the profits. The mother country would be better off trading freely with emancipated former colonies. The maintenance of colonies with an eye on commercial profits is therefore a poor policy.

Finally, in order to have a strong navy able to defend the country, the possession of colonies is not necessary either. Those in favor of colonial expansion claim the opposite; but their argument is only a fallacious pretext. In general, the fear of the English of seeing their country invaded has induced them to adopt an infinite number of precautions tending rather to attract an enemy than to keep him at a distance. Nowhere, perhaps, has fear produced as much harm as in the domain of national security. Bad governments easily persuade their frightened peoples that they can never enjoy enough security; hence the large standing armies, the excessive growth of military institutions, and all the sufferings necessarily resulting from this policy. Such are the effects of an exaggerated security from the enemy.

If colonies procure no advantage to nations, how are we to explain that States, particularly those of modern Europe, attach so much importance to them? Is this due to erroneous ideas on the usefulness of colonies, or is it explainable, at least in part, by other considerations? The explanation is as easy as it is simple. In every country there are "the ruling few" and "the subject many." In all countries whose government is not very good, the interest of the former prevails. Now the State maintains colonies for the exclusive advantage of this minority.

Colonies provide the ruling class with well-paid posts in the colonial administration. They also assure it the monopoly of a number of lucrative trades. Furthermore, since colonies are an important source of innumerable wars, they furnish it with an opportunity of enlarging its power in the interior of the country and of increasing the military power of the State.

War offers to the State a means of enlarging its financial base. As a matter of fact, nothing increases more than war the volume of that part of the national wealth which is subject to the authority of the State. This is a sufficient reason to prompt the ruling minority to conquer colonies and to perpetuate their possession even to the disadvantage of the nation as a whole.[9]

James Mill takes a firm stand against the privileges of this minority. He shows the harmfulness of colonies for the mother country and suggests indirectly that they be given up.

His thesis is tenable in a world ruled by liberal principles. In a free-trade world, that is, in a world where each nation would have free access to all markets, the political domination over any territory would indeed be of no particular economic advantage. The few advantages which accrue from the fact that a colony, because of its cultural and administrative ties with the mother country, prefers to trade with the latter, are more than offset by the expenses of the colonial administration.

The situation is, however, different in a protectionist world, where a State, even if guided by liberal policies, may find itself excluded from the colonial market of foreign powers. Hence it is of advantage to have colonies.

We disregard the political interest a State may have in possessing colonies. Even if it were willing to give them their freedom, it might refrain from doing so from fear lest other powers seize them. By giving them up it might lose not only a market but also territories of great value for the defense of the mother country.

This complex of ideas is not discussed by Mill. He probably thought British naval power so strong that it might dispense with colonial possessions, without having to fear for its national defense. The eventual loss of colonial markets does not seem to worry him either.

[9] Mill, art., *Colony* (1824), pp. 263-264, 268, 270; "Of the proposition, that colonies are a great source of wars, and of additional expence in wars; that expence, by which the ruling few always profit at the cost of the subject many; it is not probable that much of proof will be required." *Ibid.*, p. 272.

4. *Economic Policy and National Defense*

In his chief work, *Elements of Political Economy* (1821) Mill virtually does not deal at all with war. It is only incidentally in discussing paper money, that he is led to introduce certain observations on the subject. After enumerating the advantages derived from the use of paper money, he replies to the various objections which had been formulated against this system. Some recognize these advantages but claim that the inconveniences incidental to the use of paper money in times of civil war or foreign invasion by far outnumber its usefulness in time of peace. Mill admits, on the contrary, that, if the paper money were issued by a government worthy of popular confidence, a foreign invasion concentrating the affections of the people toward the government, would not destroy the credit of its notes. In this connection he makes an important general statement:

"Civil war, and foreign invasion, are words which raise up vague conceptions of danger; and vague conceptions of danger are too apt to exert a mischievous influence on the understanding.

"In the first place, there is, in the present advanced stage of the civilized world, in any country having a good government and a considerable population, so little chance of civil war or foreign invasion, that, in contriving the means of national felicity, but little allowance can be rationally required for it. To adopt a course of action, disadvantageous at all times, except those of civil war and foreign invasion, only because it were good on those occasions, would be as absurd, as it would be, in medicine, to confine all men continually to that species of regimen which suits a violent disease. If the advantages which arise from the use of paper money, are enjoyed, without any considerable abatement, at all times, excepting those of civil war and foreign invasion, the utility of paper money is sufficiently proved."[10]

Disregarding the problems of paper money and civil war,

[10] *Elements*, chap. iii, sect. 12, pp. 151-152.

subjects not included in the scope of this study, we think it important, on the other hand, to stress the general principle which may be deduced from this text. A foreign invasion or, in more general terms, war, being an exceptional event, must not constitute the decisive factor of economic policy in time of peace. It would be erroneous to erect a system of economic policy on such a transient phenomenon as war. One must not, in Mill's view, give permanency to temporary measures useful only in times of emergency. By making them permanent one would deprive economic policy of all its usefulness. Applying, in time of peace, measures useful only in time of war does not lessen the danger of war but simply adds to its serious consequences. The possibility of a foreign conflict would therefore not justify an essential modification of economic policy in time of peace.

Nor does war warrant protectionist measures. Agricultural protectionism is no less harmful to the nation than is industrial protection. The defenders of agricultural protection are wrong when they think that a nation which does not grow on its own soil the wheat it consumes may be deprived of it by the hostility of foreign powers and thus find itself reduced to the greatest distress. History as a whole, Mill asserts categorically, invalidates this argument which to him does not seem to have a sound basis.[11]

In the text quoted above James Mill touches the basic problem of economic policy, namely, to what extent must this policy be determined by the factor of war? In this text he makes no mention of wars of aggression. A "good" government does not attack; consequently, it would be superfluous to examine whether economic policy should be adapted to the requirements of aggression. Nor is there any necessity for an adaptation of this policy to the requirements of national defense; for, according to Mill, in the advanced stage of modern civilization a well peopled and well governed country runs no great risk of being invaded.

It seems that Mill is somewhat hasty when he asserts that

11 *Ibid.*, chap. iii, sect. 17, p. 197.

for any country enjoying a good government and a considerable population the risk of a foreign invasion is negligible. In the first place, how are we to determine what is a "good government" and a "considerable population"? And even if this could be done with a fair degree of accuracy, is it safe to assert categorically that national defense requires no economic intervention by the State in time of peace? If there is danger of invasion—and history clearly shows that there is such danger—a State cannot afford to follow Mill's recommendation and disregard it. A nation may feel obliged, even against its own will, to consider this factor in its economic policy.

Mill often thinks in insular terms. This attitude is clearly seen when, for example, he declares that "foreign invasion" is one of those words "which raise up vague conceptions of danger; and vague conceptions of danger are too apt to exert a mischievous influence on the understanding." Undoubtedly, this word may exert a mischievous influence, as do many other misapplied terms. But for the countries of the continent foreign invasion is more than a vague and indefinite danger: on the contrary, it expresses a real and permanent peril.

5. International Arbitration

As we have seen, James Mill draws up a severe indictment against war, which he considers the true and only cause of social stagnation and misery. If society does not develop rapidly enough, or remains in a stationary condition, or even retrogresses, war, and war alone, is to blame.

One might obviously reply that society does progress, in spite of war. But then Mill, who is an implacable logician, would not fail to retort that this objection does not change his thesis. If society advances in spite of continual wars, the pace of human progress would be infinitely more accelerated if war did not put enormous obstacles in the way of the accumulation of capital and the growth of social wealth.

Human perfectibility constitutes the basic postulate of

James Mill's social philosophy. Now this perfectibility, which is a distinctive characteristic and a valuable attribute of human nature, is nothing but "the power of advancing continually from one degree of knowledge, one degree of command over the means of happiness, to another."[12] A partisan of utilitarianism, Mill wishes to promote this perfectibility and regards utility as the true criterion of the improvement of society: "Exactly in proportion as *Utility* is the object of every pursuit, may we regard a nation as civilized."[13]

The true objective of the State is to provide, as far as circumstances permit, the greatest happiness to the greatest possible number. But what does the famous formula "the greatest happiness of the greatest number" mean to Mill? According to him the highest degree of social happiness is attained by insuring to every man the greatest quantity possible of the produce of his labor.[14]

Among all the checks to the advancement of civilization and happiness so conceived it is difficult to imagine a greater obstacle than war. Thus it is easy to understand why James Mill is so grimly opposed to bellicism.

In his view, war is more dangerous because of its permanent tendency to hamper economic progress than because of its immediate effects. Having pleaded, in his *Commerce Defended*, the cause of peace, Mill could not but ask himself whether an international organization is indispensable for the prevention of war. In an article on the law of nations he comes to the conclusion that an international court of arbitration, for which he outlines a project, would suffice to attain this goal.

In this scheme he is very much under the influence of Bentham. True enough, Bentham's project of international peace was published (1843) after Mill's article (1824). It is to be noted, however, that Bentham drew up his plan between 1786 and 1789. In view of the close relations be-

12 *Ibid.*, chap. ii, sect. 2, paragraph 4, p. 64.
13 J. Mill, *The History of British India* (1826), vol. II, p. 134.
14 Mill, art., *Government* (1824), p. 492.

tween the two men, it would seem reasonable to assume that he informed James Mill of his ideas.

In this project, Mill does not examine the political and economic conditions of a durable peace. He is satisfied with analyzing its legal aspect. His whole attention is focused on the necessity of codifying the law of nations and of establishing a court of arbitration whose duty it would be to settle international disputes. Such a court would have at its disposal no coercive force; but, a great school of morality, it would create in the long run (thanks largely to the publicity of its work) the spiritual conditions favorable to the maintenance of peace among nations.[15]

Mill does not believe it necessary to go further into the international organization of peace. He admits implicitly the idea that free play of economic forces favors international solidarity. By appeasing temporary conflicts among peoples, the legal institution he suggests would further consolidate the spirit of international concord. It would thus strengthen the pacific trend in a free-trade world.

[15] James Mill, art., *Law of Nations.*

IV. MacCULLOCH
AND JOHN STUART MILL

JOHN Ramsay MacCulloch, known above all as the popularizer of Ricardo's work, devotes much space to the problem of war. He examines it in his *Discourse on the Rise, Progress, Peculiar Objects and Importance of Political Economy* (1824) and in his *Principles of Political Economy* (1825), a manual widely used prior to that of John Stuart Mill. His analysis faithfully expresses the liberal point of view and for this reason deserves being noted even today.

John Stuart Mill's observations on the problem of war are interesting but small in number. They are found scattered in several of his writings: *Principles of Political Economy* (1848), *A Few Words on Non-Intervention* (1859), *Considerations on Representative Government* (1861), *Autobiography* (1873), and his unedited correspondence with Gustave d'Eichthal. It is sufficient to glance over all these writings to gain a conviction that the illustrious English philosopher voices his views on international armed conflicts only very fragmentarily.

The end of this chapter is devoted to the two last representatives of the classical school of the nineteenth century: John Elliot Cairnes and Henry Fawcett. The former expresses himself on militarism in an article published in 1871, entitled *Our Defences: A National or Standing Army?* The latter deals with war in two of his works: *Manual of Political Economy* (1863) and *Free Trade and Protection* (1878), both of which went through a large number of editions.

Some readers may be astonished not to find in this chapter at least a mention of Alfred Marshall (1842-1924), linked by several ties to the classical school. The truth is that we have not discovered in his writings a general view on the relationship of the economic and war. In his *Industry and Trade* (1923, p. 2) he notes however that the relations between the contemporary States are such that a certain form of militarism seems necessary.

1. MacCulloch

(A) HOSTILITY TO AUTARKY

Like many other economists, MacCulloch[1] points out the necessity of possessing an armed force to vouchsafe security and protection to the nation. This necessity, he observes, is too evident to require proof. The best laws become ineffective if they may be violated with impunity. Each State must therefore have at its disposal a force sufficient to execute its orders in the interior of the country and to defend the national territory against foreign aggression.

It goes without saying that the army has in the first place a military function. But this does not exhaust its role. Indirectly it also plays an important economic part: in guaranteeing order and security, it ensures the normal course of the national economy. Its members have thus a useful function and must be considered as eminently productive, to use MacCulloch's expression.

How should an army be recruited to the greater advantage of the country? The investigation of this problem belongs rather to politics proper than to political economy.

"It may, however, be remarked," observes MacCulloch, "that in nothing, perhaps, has the beneficial influence of the division of labour been more perceptible than in the employment of a distinct class of individuals to maintain national tranquillity and security. To be a good soldier, or a good police-officer, a man should be nothing else. It is hardly possible for an individual taken, to serve as a militia-man, from one of the ordinary employments of industry, to which after a short time he is to be restored, to

[1] MacCulloch (1789-1864), for twenty years a collaborator of the *Edinburgh Review*, professor of political economy at the University of London (1828-1832), Comptroller of the Stationary Office (1838-1864).

acquire those habits of discipline, and of prompt and willing obedience, so indispensable in a soldier."[2]

MacCulloch consequently advocates the maintenance of professional armies who to him are superior, from every point of view, to the national militias.

If a nation desires to be powerful, an army alone is not sufficient. The country must have, in addition, a strong economic armature. In this sense, free trade, since it increases national wealth to the highest degree, is the system most calculated to augment the power of a country.

Formerly, erroneous ideas on trade were the cause of a large number of wars and of much bloodshed. "But the folly of the monopoly system, and the ruinous nature of the contents to which it has given rise, have been made obvious. It has been shown, over and over again, that nothing can be more irrational and absurd, than that dread of the progress of others in wealth and civilization that was once so prevalent; and that the true glory and real interest of every people will be more certainly advanced by endeavouring to outstrip their neighbours in the career of science and civilization, than by engaging in schemes of conquest and aggression."[3]

Mercantilist ideas on precious metals have often given rise to trade restrictions. Likewise the desire to favor the interests of national producers has frequently been at the root of trade barriers. Yet a considerable number of these obstacles owe their existence to ideas which, however patriotic, are hardly less erroneous—to the desire to be independent of foreign supplies, to avenge the prohibitions of foreign States by retaliatory measures, and to provide for public security.

It is easy to show the direct influence exerted by foreign commerce on the growth of the productive power of labor and of national wealth. It is evident that the English, in limiting themselves to the manufacture of cloth and to ex-

[2] MacCulloch, *Principles*, pt. II, chap. x, p. 266. Cf. also *ibid.*, pt. IV, p. 591.
[3] *Ibid.*, pt. I, chap. v, p. 145.

changing it for wine, would obtain a much larger quantity of the latter than if they tried to cultivate the grapevine in their own country. On the other hand, the Portuguese, in exchanging their wines for English cloth, would obtain much more than if they displaced a part of their capital and labor devoted to vine-growing, a field in which they have a vast superiority, to apply them to the manufacture of cloth, an industry in which other countries enjoy an indisputable superiority.

The idea of economic independence is none the less very seductive, and it is not surprising that a system promising to place a nation in this position, which at first blush seems highly enviable, should enjoy considerable popularity. Nevertheless, "national independence rests on far other foundations than the miserable machinery of custom-house regulations."[4] The independence of individuals is obtained in two ways which, however different, are equivalent from the economic point of view. A man may provide directly for his own needs by the produce of his own labor, without resorting to exchange. But he may obtain the same result if he is able to furnish an equivalent in exchange for the goods he wishes to acquire. Those who devote themselves to callings for which they have a natural or acquired aptitude obtain these goods more easily by means of exchange with other individuals. In other words, they will be "more opulent, and, consequently, more independent,"[5] than if they themselves produced the goods in question. "The same is the case with nations," concludes MacCulloch.[6]

The dependence of two men who exchange their products is mutual: it is then no true dependence. If by independence we mean the faculty to provide for one's necessities without any obligation to others, those who exchange their goods or services with foreigners remain completely independent of them. Foreign no less than domestic commerce is based on reciprocal agreements: one gives and receives equivalents, one satisfies mutual needs, and one grants mutual advantages.

[4] *Ibid.*, p. 159.   [5] *Ibid.*   [6] *Ibid.*

"To wish to be wholly unconnected with foreigners, and at the same time to continue as rich and prosperous as ever, is to wish what is contradictory and inconsistent with the nature of things."[7] No doubt, a nation may do without international trade; but in that case it must also resign itself to doing without the wealth and the power to which such commerce would have raised it.

"The individual who prefers swimming across the river, is, of course, independent of the bridges, in the same way that the nation, who should prefer poverty and barbarism to wealth and refinement, would be independent of foreign commerce. But this is the independence of the savage. To be truly independent in the enlarged, and, if we may so speak, civilized sense of the term, that is, to have the greatest command of necessaries and conveniencies, a nation must avail itself of the productive energies of every other people, and deal with all the world on fair and liberal principles."[8]

The comparison of autarky and barbarism is not lacking in either interest or beauty. It illustrates very well, besides, the thought of all liberals. MacCulloch's reasoning seems logical so long as we stick closely to his terms. In fact, a people desiring to live as economically as possible, that is, to acquire a maximum of goods with a minimum of effort, must trade with the entire world according to "fair and liberal principles." But let us suppose that such a State runs up against others unwilling to live according to this principle, following an aggressive policy, and preferring war to peace: what happens in that case to MacCulloch's precept? Can, in such an event an "economic" people utilize the productive forces of its potential enemies and trade with them according to fair and liberal principles? Or would not rather the enemy oblige it to renounce this liberal aspiration for the simple reason that economic or political peace is not a unilateral act but a relation between two or more powers?

MacCulloch does not go into these problems. He thinks

7 *Ibid.*, p. 160.   8 *Ibid.*

he has said all there is to be said when stating that economic dependence is reciprocal and that for this reason it no longer is a true dependence. Though it cannot be denied that economic dependence is reciprocal, it is equally true that there are several degrees of interdependence and that, consequently, the less dependent nation, in the course of a war, is in a more advantageous position than the more dependent one. Now this fact can hardly be disregarded in the economic policy of a State even in time of peace.

(b) FREEDOM OF TRADE AND NATIONAL POWER

MacCulloch does not underestimate the importance of measures adopted by a State to strengthen its national security or to cause damage to some hostile power. He believes, however, that their effect has been greatly exaggerated. If a single nation had the monopoly of an article necessary for its defense and for that of other countries, it might, by prohibiting its exportation, provide for its own security and at the same time cause a serious injury to its enemies. But no article of this type is known, and it is doubtful that it will ever be found. Restrictions cannot therefore constitute a sound basis for international policy.

The dangers resulting for a State from a refusal of foreign countries to trade with it are imaginary. There are too many commercial States and their interests are too divergent to imagine a case where a wealthy nation might be unable to buy the goods it needs. If trade is intercepted by one route, it will force a passage for itself in some other part of the world. If a given country refuses to trade with a certain State, the latter need not worry about it: some other nation will be delighted to have an opportunity of supplying it with the commodities needed. "Nothing, indeed, can be a greater error than to imagine that, in the present state of the world, the security of any particular country, or her means of defence or aggression, can be materially increased by prohibitory regulations."[9]

Modern conflicts involve huge expenditures. It is certain

[9] *Ibid.*, pp. 164-165.

that money is the sinews of war and that the wealthiest nation, all other things being equal, is also the most powerful. Peoples possessed of sufficient wealth will never want either soldiers or arms. Wealth enables them to cover the land with armies and the ocean with fleets against whose power the purest patriotism and the most inflexible courage will fight with difficulty.

"But when such is the case, when it is admitted on all hands that wealth is the main source of power and influence, and when it admits of demonstration, that a free and extended commerce is the most prolific source of wealth, can anything be more contradictory than to attempt to increase the defence or security of a country by enacting measures that must necessarily fetter and narrow its commerce? The possession of wealth is the best security; and as the freedom of commerce is, of all others, the most efficacious means of increasing wealth, it follows that those who are exerting themselves to give every facility to commerce, are, at the same time, exerting themselves in the most effectual manner to add to the power and independence of the country; and it also follows, that the apologists and defenders of restrictions and prohibitions are, though without knowing it, labouring to sap the foundations of our power, and to cast us down from our high place amongst the nations of the earth."[10]

MacCulloch's thought may be summed up as follows: Since it is true that the wealthiest is at the same time the most powerful, it is equally true that the nation enjoying the greatest freedom of trade is the most powerful, too, for nothing favors national wealth as much as does free trade.

Now it would seem that MacCulloch reasons in terms too vague. He should at least have given a definition of national power. It is by no means certain that the wealthiest State is at the same time the most powerful if by "power" we mean the comparative strength of two States at any given moment. It is possible that, all other things being equal, two States enjoy the same amount of wealth but are

[10] *Ibid.*, p. 165.

none the less not equal in strength. All depends upon the composition of their wealth, the main point being the adaptability of the latter to the exigencies of war. If the wealth of a country is composed in such a manner as to allow a better utilization for war, this country can beat an enemy having at his disposal the same amount of wealth but of a composition less advantageous from the military point of view. Thus even a poorer country can overcome a wealthier one. Now if the comparative strength of international forces depends upon the composition of the wealth of each nation, it is equally certain that economic policy may influence this composition. If a State wishes to prepare for war, it must adopt an economic policy susceptible of affecting accordingly both the formation of the national wealth and its composition, thus assuring to the nation a maximum of war potential. The economic policy chosen will depend upon the concrete conditions at a given moment. Generally, the State will resort to a protectionist policy, and it will not be possible to say that the means adopted does not lead to the end in view.

(C) ECONOMIC SCIENCE AND PEACE.
SOME CONTEMPORARIES OF MAC CULLOCH. COBDEN

Like many other liberals, MacCulloch considers political economy as an eminently pacifist science. He is convinced that wars of aggression, so far as they are provoked by economic motives, are always based on an erroneous premise. He assigns to political economy the task of extirpating the ignorance which makes possible wars waged for so-called trade advantages. Economic science should persuade men that it is wholly in their interest to avoid war and to live in conformity with the principles of liberalism.

In his *Discourse on the . . . Importance of Political Economy*, MacCulloch expresses his point of view in the following terms:

". . . the American war, and the greater part of the wars of the last century, with the exception of those that grew out of the French Revolution, were waged for the purpose of preserving or acquiring some exclusive commercial advantage. But does any one suppose that these contests could have been carried on, at such an infinite expence of blood and treasure, had the mass of the people known that their object was utterly unattainable?—had they known that it is impossible for any one country to monopolize wealth and riches; and that every such attempt must ultimately prove ruinous to itself, as well as injurious to others? It is to Political Economy that we owe an incontrovertible demonstration of these truths;—truths that are destined to exercise the most salutary influence on humanity—to convince mankind that it is for their interest to live in peace, to deal with each other on fair and liberal principles, and not to become the dupes of their own short-sighted avarice, or the willing instruments of the blind ambition, or petty animosities, of their rulers."[11]

Ideas resembling those of MacCulloch are found in several of his contemporaries. Let us mention, in the first place, Senior. Mercantilism, in his view, is a theory which has been, and still is, responsible for more vice, misery, and wars than all other errors taken together. An attempt by a nation at economic independence must increase infinitely the chances of war by reducing the incentives of other countries to remain at peace with it. Besides, by impoverishing it, autarky is certain to make it less able to wage successfully the wars to which such a policy inevitably leads. To mercantilism, in addition to the follies peculiar to it, one may in general attribute the greatest of all human follies, the waging of wars between civilized countries.[12]

Torrens points out the influence of free trade, especially in grain, on national power. Chalmers observes that, if the

[11] MacCulloch, *A Discourse* (1824), pp. 85-86.
[12] Senior (1828), pp. 35, 51. Let us note in passing that the pacifist spirit of several economists comes out in their severe criticism of mercantilist bellicism. Cf. Sartorius (1806), p. 129; Hufeland (1815), pp. vi, xxv; Storch (1823), vol. I, pp. 102-103 (cf. also vol. III, p. 424); Cooper (1831), pp. 197 f.; Kautz (1860), p. 297.

essence of foreign trade had been better understood, innumerable wars waged for the preservation of some monopoly would not have been undertaken. A sense of national honor may still divide peoples, but not a sense of national interest. Whately asserts that just notions of political economy tend to prevent wars. The American Wayland maintains that the most economic means of national defense is the exercise of justice and benevolence. According to his compatriot Bolles, protectionism weakens the spirit of international concord and encourages war, the greatest scourge of mankind.[13]

Of all the contemporaries of MacCulloch, Richard Cobden[14] was the most assiduous in propagating the idea that correct notions of economic science tend to prevent international conflicts. War is, to use his expression, "an expensive luxury,"[15] or, in other words, a money-losing business for the nation. No class derives, and can ever derive, any substantial or permanent profit from it. Trade, whose true arm is cheapness, does not require the support of armies and navies. Nor does the colonial system, which is also sharply criticized by Cobden, deserve protection by arms. Colonies should be got rid of, if possible, or at least be granted self-government.[16]

Free trade is for Cobden, as goes without saying, the best instrument for increasing the material well-being of peoples. It is however more than a factor of economic welfare: it is the only way of bringing about permanent peace. Linking as it does all peoples through the medium of mutual exchanges, it is synonymous with universal concord. To establish it means making war between two nations as

13 Torrens (1815), pp. 330-336; Chalmers (1832), p. 192; Whately (1847), pp. 159-161; Wayland (1837), p. 462; Bolles (1874), p. 198.

14 Cobden (1804-1865), British industrialist, writer, and statesman. He was the head and the hero of the famous Anti-Corn Law League and negotiated the Anglo-French commercial treaty of 1860. Among the economists profoundly influenced by him are Frédéric Bastiat and Thorold Rogers. On his eventful life cf. Morley (1881).

15 *Congress 1849*, p. 42.

16 Cobden, *Political Writings*, vol. I, pp. 290, 322-324, 30-31; cf. also Dawson (1926), chap. ix.

impossible as it is between two counties of Great Britain. Under a system of free trade each trading station, each store, each factory will become the center of a diplomatic system bent on peace, in spite of all the arts of statesmen to produce war.[17]

"I see," says Cobden, "in the Free-Trade principle that which shall act on the moral world as the principle of gravitation in the universe,—drawing men together, thrusting aside antagonism of race, and creed, and language, and uniting us in the bonds of eternal peace."[18]

Considering excessive armaments a procedure as costly as it is ineffective, he suggests a reduction of military and naval forces. Great armaments are harmful since they tend to excite dangerous animosities among peoples, to perpetuate fear, hate, and suspicion, that is, passions which are bound, sooner or later, instinctively to seek an outlet in war. A reduction of armaments would have a contrary effect: it would lessen international tension. Without endangering national security, it would diminish military expenses and taxes. It would thus be conducive to an increase of the material well-being of peoples.[19]

Arbitration is a more rational, fair, and humane means than recourse to arms. Consequently, Cobden never tires of recommending it most fervently. He regards it as sufficient to guarantee international peace. Opposed to a limitation of the sovereign rights of the State, he is evidently adverse to the establishment of a supernational peace organization: "I am," he notes, "no party to the plan which some advocate—no doubt with the best intentions—of having a Congress of nations, with a code of laws—a supreme court of appeal, with an army to support its decisions. I am no

[17] Cf. Morley (1881), vol. I, p. 230; Bastiat, *Cobden et la Ligue*, pp. 86-87.

[18] Cobden, *Speeches*, vol. I, pp. 362-363. John Prince-Smith (1843, p. 147, 1848, 1860, pp. 132-133) develops an economic philosophy resembling Cobden's. Toward the end of his life Prince-Smith (1873, pp. 166-167) seems however to have lost his pacifist enthusiasm.

[19] Cobden in *Congress 1849*, pp. 27-28.

party to any such plan. I believe it might lead to more armed interference than takes place at present."[20]

Cobden's pacifist program contains four main points: arbitration in lieu of war; simultaneous reduction of armaments; nonintervention of any nation in the internal affairs of another; and refusal to grant loans to bellicose governments.[21]

In a speech pronounced at the Congress of the Friends of Universal Peace, held in Paris in 1849, Cobden proposes to condemn any loan raised for purposes of wars of ambition or conquest. He desires to bring about peace by cutting the sinews of war: "Warlike governments," he says, "can find resources [for war] only in the savings of merchants, manufacturers, farmers, and rentiers, and we appeal to them, in the name of humanity and their own interest, to refuse to lend their aid to a barbarous system which paralyses trade, ruins industry, destroys capital, stops work, and waxes fat through the blood and the arms of their brothers."[22]

2. *John Stuart Mill and the Last Classics*

(A) JOHN STUART MILL

Our review of the work of John Stuart Mill[23] will be short. The great English economist is in fact brief on the subject of war. He seems to admit that virtually everything that can be said on this theme had already been brought out before him.

(1) The Navigation Acts. Mill's attitude toward industrial protectionism recalls that of Adam Smith. The latter, as is well known, favored the protection of certain indus-

---

[20] Cobden, *Speeches*, vol. II, p. 174. Cf. also pp. 170, 176.

[21] Cobden, *Speeches on Peace . . . Delivered during 1849*, p. 163.

[22] *Congress 1849*, pp. 41-42. For more details on Cobden's ideas cf. the works of Rogers (1873), Hirst (1903), and Dawson (1926).

[23] A son of James Mill, who subjected him to an education as strange as it was severe, John Stuart Mill (1806-1873) at the early age of sixteen started on his career as a writer. He held a post in the administration of the East India Company (1822-1858) and was a member of Parliament (1865-1868). Cf. his *Autobiography*.

tries indispensable to national defense, and particularly the Navigation Acts. These acts were promulgated to encourage the merchant marine, a "nursery of sailors" for the navy.

Like Smith, John Stuart Mill recognizes the usefulness and legitimacy of the Navigation Acts. He asserts that "a country exposed to invasion by sea, if it cannot otherwise have sufficient ships and sailors of its own to secure the means of manning on an emergency an adequate fleet, is quite right in obtaining those means, even at an economical sacrifice in point of cheapness of transport."[24]

When the English Navigation Acts were promulgated, the Dutch, thanks to their maritime skill and their low rate of profit at home, were able to carry for other nations, England included, at cheaper rates than those nations could do for themselves. All other nations were consequently placed at a great comparative disadvantage in obtaining experienced seamen for their warships. "The Navigation Laws, by which this deficiency was remedied, and at the same time a blow struck against the maritime power of a nation with which England was then frequently engaged in hostilities, were probably, though economically disadvantageous, politically expedient."[25]

At the present time (1848) they have long since been unnecessary, because the objective aimed at by them had already been attained. As a matter of fact, British ships and sailors may engage in the carrying trade at as low cost as those of any other nation and meet the competition of all countries under at least equal conditions: "The ends which may once have justified Navigation Laws require them no longer, and afforded no reason for maintaining this invidious exception to the general rule of free trade."[26]

In his discussion of the Navigation Acts, Mill does not express himself in general terms on industrial protection for the purpose of national defense. None the less, the arguments put forward by him in favor of these Acts are susceptible of justifying, generally, all protectionism of a

[24] John Stuart Mill, *Principles*, bk. v, chap. x, sect. 1, p. 920.
[25] *Ibid.*   [26] *Ibid.*

military character. These arguments recognize implicitly the impossibility for a State not to take into account, in its economic policies, certain military factors. Mill's attitude is interesting because it shows that even a liberal such as he cannot close his eyes to the grave difficulties which would be encountered by States that, without enjoying military superiority, might wish to pursue a free trade policy in a bellicose world.

While not altogether hostile to industrial protectionism, John Stuart Mill is decidedly so to agricultural protection. "It is ridiculous," he says, "to found a general system of policy on so improbable a danger as that of being at war with all the nations of the world at once; or to suppose that, even if inferior at sea, a whole country could be blockaded like a town, or that the growers of food in other countries would not be as anxious not to lose an advantageous market, as we should be not to be deprived of their corn."[27] He thus adopts a point of view similar to that of Ricardo and of James Mill.

(2) Observations on War. In Mill's view, the losses entailed by war do not seem to have too serious consequences for economic life. Capital maintains itself, not by its conservation, but by a perpetual reproduction. Now this reconstitution of capital is astonishingly rapid, which explains why countries recover quickly from a state of devastation.[28]

The possibility of a prompt reparation of damages caused by war depends chiefly upon the population surviving the ravages. If this population is not extirpated, if it does not perish from hunger and misery, then its skill and knowledge, its lands, which have lost nothing of their fertility, its buildings which have remained intact, or been destroyed only partially, make up virtually everything required to

---

[27] *Ibid.,* pp. 920-921.

[28] *Ibid.,* bk. i, chap. v, sects. 6-7. This assertion of Mill's is considered wholly erroneous by Leroy-Beaulieu: "Si le capital paraît très rapidement se reconstituer dans une société éprouvée par une guerre, c'est que la déperdition du capital, dans la plupart des guerres modernes, est, en réalité, beaucoup moindre qu'en apparence." *Traité* (1896), vol. i, p. 258. Cf. also vol. ii, pp. 163-164.

repair its losses without delay. If only it has food sufficient to keep it physically fit to work, it will in a short time repair its losses and acquire as much wealth as it had before.[29]

Whatever the economic consequences of war, Mill is fiercely opposed to bellicism. The army and navy, according to him unproductive bodies, must not be used as instruments of aggression. Their work must be limited to the defense of the country, preserving it from being conquered, injured, or insulted.[30]

A discussion of the immorality of wars of aggression would in Mill's opinion be an affront to the reader. Forcible annexation of a civilized country is immoral. All wars of aggression, excepting those necessary to remove a national danger, are iniquitous.[31]

Like his father, John Stuart Mill is a partisan of international arbitration. His *Considerations on Representative Government* contain a chapter devoted to federal States, in which he examines, among other things, the role of the United States Supreme Court. This Court, he says, "dispenses international law, and is the first great example of what is now one of the most prominent wants of civilized society, a real International Tribunal."[32]

Mill sees in international trade the chief factor of peace. The spirit of trade was, during a certain period of European history, the chief cause of international conflicts. At the present time it has become one of the greatest deterrents of war.[33]

The economic advantages of international trade, how-

[29] Mill, *Principles*, bk. I, chap. v, sect. 7. Mill is opposed in principle to the financing of war by loans. By reducing the national capital, loans diminish also that part of it which is paid annually to the workers in the form of wages. Unless loans are limited to the surplus capital of a nation, they thus have a tendency to lower the standard of living of the working classes. *Ibid.*, bk. v, chap. vii, sect. 1. Cf. also bk. I, chap. v, sect. 8.
[30] *Ibid.*, bk. I, chap. iii, sect. 2, p. 46.
[31] John Stuart Mill, *A Few Words*, p. 171. Cf. also the same author's *Autobiography*, p. 261; *Correspondance inédite*, p. 213.
[32] John Stuart Mill, *Considerations* (1861), p. 306.
[33] John Stuart Mill, *Principles*, bk. III, chap. xxv, sect. 1, p. 678.

ever great, are surpassed by its moral and intellectual effects. Contact with foreigners whose modes of thought and action are different from ours, is invaluable. Trade offers now, as did war in the past, the chief opportunity for this contact. It is, in modern times, the purpose of most relations between the inhabitants of the civilized countries. These relations have always been, and are particularly in our age, one of the most important sources of progress. There is no nation which is not under a necessity of borrowing from others not merely technical procedures but also moral qualities which it does not possess to a sufficiently high degree.

"Finally," says Mill, "commerce first taught nations to see with good will the wealth and prosperity of one another. Before, the patriot, unless sufficiently advanced in culture to feel the world his country, wished all countries weak, poor, and ill-governed, but his own; he now sees in their wealth and progress a direct source of wealth and progress to his own country. It is commerce which is rapidly rendering war obsolete, by strengthening and multiplying the personal interests which are in natural opposition to it. And it may be said without exaggeration that the great extent and rapid increase of international trade, in being the principal guarantee of the peace of the world, is the great permanent security for the uninterrupted progress of the ideas, the institutions, and the character of the human race."[34]

Unfortunately, events have taken a different turn, and Mill evidently did not fail to note it. The Franco-Prussian War of 1870-1871 afflicted him particularly. In a letter to his friend Gustave d'Eichthal, dated August 27, 1870, he writes: "A long time ago I arrived at the sad conviction that, in spite of the incontestable reality of modern progress, we are not yet safe from the great misfortunes and the great crimes which our century was flattering itself of hav-

34 *Ibid.*, bk. III, chap. xvii, sect. 5, p. 582.

ing succeeded in banishing from the earth."[35] And he goes on to refer to the war.

(B) CAIRNES AND FAWCETT

The two last representatives of the classical school, John Elliot Cairnes and Henry Fawcett,[36] disciples of John Stuart Mill, share this "sad conviction" of their master.

Cairnes does not underrate the losses in production caused by military conflicts.[37] Still, in his opinion, contemporary relations between States are such as to require a certain form of militarism. Though it is useless to throw up cries of horror against what is inevitable, it is intelligent to reduce the necessary evil so far as possible. With this end in view Cairnes recommends to England a national army organized on the pattern of the Swiss militias. This system has certain economic, political, and social advantages. Its strength lies in its power of resistance. Unfit for wars of aggression, such militias are the best form of national defense. Consequently, if the civilized nations were to adopt this system generally, aggressive wars would end in failure.[38]

Henry Fawcett points out the immense losses inflicted on mankind by militarism. Even in time of peace it diminishes national welfare and aggravates trade depressions.[39] The damage caused by armed conflicts is naturally even more considerable. The greatest injury resulting from wars does not lie in the simple destruction of wealth but in the annihilation of capital. If the war destroys only consumer goods, the nations recover rather quickly, regaining soon, as is shown by history, their usual prosperity and often

[35] John Stuart Mill, *Correspondance inédite*, p. 228.
[36] Cairnes (1823-1875), professor of political economy at the University of Dublin (1857), at the Queen's College at Galway (1859), and at the University College of London (1866). Fawcett (1833-1884), professor of political economy at the University of Cambridge (1863-1884), member of Parliament (1865-1884), postmaster general (1880-1884).
[37] *Some Leading Principles of Political Economy* (1874), pt. III, chap. iii, sect. 7, pp. 364-365.
[38] Cairnes, *Our Defences* (1871), pp. 207, 247, 251, and 255.
[39] Fawcett, *Free Trade and Protection*, 4th ed. (1881), pp. 169-171.

even surpassing it. Conversely, the sufferings are infinitely more protracted when the invader destroys the industrial equipment of a country. The richer a country is, the greater are the losses it suffers from war if the enemy destroys a considerable part of the national wealth in the form of fixed capital.

"Of late years," says Fawcett, "a feeling of false humanity has attempted to make the rights of private property respected in war. Life may be sacrificed with as much prodigality as ever. The foremost mechanical genius of this mechanical age is devoted to the production of weapons of death; but civilization, it is said, demands that there should be no wanton destruction of property."[40]

Fawcett does not share this view. "No such attempt to palliate the material disasters of war ought to be encouraged; war will be rendered less frequent, if a whole nation is made to feel its terrible consequences, instead of concentrating all the horrors in the sacrifice of thousands of helpless victims who may be marshalled at the caprice of a despot."[41]

So far as his own country is concerned, Fawcett arrives at the following conclusion: "If any nation should ever threaten England with invasion, England ought to speak in unmistakable language that her vengeance should not be confined to a retributive slaughter of soldiers, but that she would destroy all the public works upon which the wealth of the nation mainly depended. This would give a practical check to vaunting ambition, and might rouse a nation to restrain the military designs of the most despotic ruler."[42]

This is a threat to warmongers, but at the same time it announces the coming of "total" economic war.

[40] Fawcett, *Manual of Political Economy*, 7th ed. (1888), bk. I, chap. iv, p. 32.
[41] *Ibid.*
[42] *Ibid.*

Part Two. The French Liberals

V. JEAN-BAPTISTE SAY

IN his ideas on war, Jean-Baptiste Say[1] shows a good deal of originality. He deduces a pacific doctrine from the system he calls *industrialist*. In his theory of markets (*loi des débouchés*) he believes he has found more than a remedy for commercial crises: the basis of a new conception of international relations.

He systematically develops his views on war in two works: the *Traité d'économie politique* (1803) and the *Cours complet d'économie politique pratique* (1828-1829). The latter is only an amplification of the former. The *Traité* contains a section on the expenditure connected with the army and the *Cours*, some special chapters on the aggressive and defensive systems, on the defense of the State by militias, and on the navy.

The *Traité* had a great success: five editions appeared during the author's life. The sixth, the manuscript of which was revised by the author, is posthumous.

From the first edition of the *Traité* Say reveals himself as an opponent of bellicism. He paints a picture of the ravages of war and its economic effects, and arrives at the conclusion that, "unless imposed by the urgent necessity of defending oneself, it must be regarded as the most execrable of crimes" (vol. II, p. 427). Though already in this edition he sketches his theory of markets, he does not yet draw from it conclusions as to war.

The fate of the *Traité* is well known. The work having

---

[1] Jean-Baptiste Say (1767-1832) was store clerk, journalist, then industrialist. Having by chance read Adam Smith's *Wealth of Nations*, he became enthusiastically interested in the study of political economy. Elected a member of the Tribunate, in 1799, he was dismissed from it in 1804. In 1816 he opened, at the Athénée, a public course of lectures on political economy. In 1819 he was appointed professor of "industrial" economy at the Conservatoire des Arts et Métiers. From 1830 to 1832 he filled the chair of political economy at the Collège de France. Cf. Teilhac, 1927.

caused a sensation, Bonaparte, then First Consul, tried to make use of the famous economist for his own ends. He attempted to persuade him to prepare a new edition and to make of it a book written for the occasion, favoring the policies of the man who was shortly to be an all-powerful emperor. Say refused and was before long dismissed from the Tribunate. For several years, furthermore, he was prevented from publishing the second edition of his *Traité*, which did not appear until 1814, after Napoleon's fall. In it he insists on the economic effects of war and for the first time draws pacifist conclusions from his theory of markets.

The study of Jean-Baptiste Say's doctrines is interesting in itself, but gains added importance by his influence on his successors. He has indeed left his mark on French political economy. His ascendency is, besides, not limited to the liberals. By his influence on Saint-Simon (cf. chap. xii, sect. 1) he has also affected, indirectly, modern socialism.

1. Causes and Effects of Armed Conflict

Peace being, in Say's opinion, essential for the development of nations, it is always in their interest to avoid war. One cannot reasonably consider the army and military expenditures anything except an unfortunate but necessary means to live in security. None the less, bad ministers, to render themselves indispensable, frequently make wars inevitable. Such was, for example, the policy of Louvois. It also happens that a government, not wishing to accede to the just demands of the people, may instigate a war to impose silence on the opposition and to turn public attention in another direction.

The military are frequently responsible for armed conflicts between nations. Unskilled in the arts of peace and considering war as the only opportunity for advancement and fortune, they naturally crave it, and one always finds pretexts to promote what one desires.

An erroneous conception of wealth often gives rise to war. True enough, for the last two centuries nations have no longer been fighting for the sake of pillage or destruction. They continue, however, to fight for the exclusive possession of their neighbor's sources of wealth. All armed conflicts which have not grown out of puerile vanity, have had for their objects the snatching from one another of some colony or some branch of trade. As for naval conflicts, they have no other origin than land wars. Both result from ill-considered national interests. A time will come when people will be greatly astonished that much trouble had to be taken to prove the "foolishness" of a system as hollow as mercantilism and for the sake of which so many battles were fought.[2] "If nations had not been, nor were even now, obsessed with trade balances and with the opinion that a nation cannot prosper except to the detriment of another, one would have avoided fifty years of war in the course of the last two centuries."[3]

Technical progress has made war much more costly than formerly. Military expenditures in peace and in war swallow up an ever increasing part of the national income and capital. "The more industrious a State is, the more destructive and ruinous war is for it. When it attains a country rich in agricultural, manufacturing, and commercial establishments, it resembles a fire which reaches places filled with combustibles; its fury increases, and the devastation is enormous."[4]

To these material losses must be added those in human life. A great loss in full-grown men is at the same time a great loss in wealth; indeed, each represents a capital equivalent to the sum total of the expenditure incurred during several years for his maintenance and education. Now, war takes a large number of victims on the battlefield as well as among the civilian population, whose death rate increases in consequence of hostilities.[5]

[2] *Traité*, 6th ed., bk. II, chap. vii, sect. 5, p. 382; bk. I, chap. xiv, p. 136, chap. xvii, sect. 1, p. 173. Cf. also *Cours*, 6th ed., pt. VII, chap. xviii, p. 441.
[3] *Cours*, 6th ed., p. 10 (*Considérations générales*).
[4] *Traité*, 6th ed., bk. III, chap. vii, sect. 2, p. 485.
[5] *Ibid.*, bk. II, chap. xi, sect. 1, pp. 425-426.

To estimate correctly all the losses caused by war, it is not sufficient to consider the positive losses it gives rise to. "War," Say reminds us, "costs more than its expense; it costs what it prevents from being earned."[6]

From the financial point of view modern wars end by increasing the national debt of both victors and vanquished. The system of State loans favors militarism. The possibility of borrowing, and of obtaining from the taxpayers only the interest due on the sums swallowed up by war, instead of levying on them the sums themselves, multiplies and prolongs armed conflict. Thanks to the loans, the transient calamity of wars is transformed into a lasting misfortune. Like Ricardo, Say prefers taxes to loans. It is better, he thinks, to finance war by means of extraordinary taxes imposed while the war is going on and discontinued at the conclusion of peace, than by means of ordinary taxes which are lighter, to be sure, but lasting and progressive, destined to pay only the annual interest charges on the loans.[7]

"Under the present political system every war is followed by tributes imposed by the victor upon the vanquished, and by tributes imposed on the victors by those who rule them. For what else but a tribute is the interest on the loans contracted by them? Is it possible, in modern times, to cite a single nation which, after the most fortunate war, had had to pay fewer taxes than before it started it?"[8]

From these baneful consequences of war it follows that the domination of foreign territories is carried out only for the profit of those who govern and not at all for the benefit of those they rule, who have only an interest in living at peace and in maintaining free intercourse among each other. For the great mass of the nation armed conflicts are never advantageous. Say's conclusion is clear. "The

6 *Ibid.*, bk. III, chap. vii, sect. 2, p. 485.
7 *Cours*, pt. VIII, chap. xvi, pp. 523-525.
8 *Traité*, 6th ed., bk. III, chap. vii, sect. 2, p. 485. *

most fortunate war," he observes, "is a very great misfortune."[9]

"Governments more ambitious than just have often tried to justify wars in their own eyes and in those of their subjects by vaunting the power and profit they attributed to conquests. With a little calm, and by putting sober calculation in the place of passions, one will find that a conquest is never worth its cost."[10]

Say thus condemns policies of aggression in severe terms: "Aggressive and political wars," he remarks, "are on the part of the governments ordering them or rendering them inevitable true crimes against the peoples. Whatever the outcome of these conflicts, the leaders provoking them, or helping to bring them about, would reap but a harvest of shame if peoples were enlightened. Glory would be reserved for legitimate defense, and under legitimate defense I include the efforts made to free oneself from a yoke imposed by force such as the one which weighed upon the helots of Lacedaemon. Whoever oppresses men puts himself in a state of war with them."[11]

In commenting upon Say's treatise *De l'Angleterre et des Anglais*, Ferrara, an Italian liberal economist, observes that it is difficult to make out whether its author admits the possible usefulness of war, or whether he believes in the inexorable necessity of peace at any price.[12] However, the passage just quoted from another of Say's works clearly indicates his view, which is fundamentally in accord, besides, with Ferrara's.[13]

[9] *Cours*, chap. xvi, p. 523. Benjamin Constant develops the same idea in his admirable essay *De l'esprit de conquête* (1813).

[10] *Traité*, 2nd ed., vol. ii, pp. 262-263. "L'esprit de conquête et l'esprit de commerce sont deux ennemis irréconciliables." Ganilh (1815), vol. ii, p. 465.

[11] *Cours*, pt. vii, chap. xviii, p. 441.

[12] Ferrara (1855), p. xxxiii. Cf. also Ferrara (1938), p. 66.

[13] "Tutta dunque la filosofia economica della guerra sta nella giustizia, cioè nella reale utilità del suo scopo." Ferrara (1855), p. xxxiv.

2. *The Aggressive and the Defensive Systems*

War being a money-losing business for a nation, what military system could political economy recommend to the State?

To safeguard their independence, nations must be prepared to defend it. But a nation which, under pretense of defense, should organize armies fit for a war of aggression, would have a very costly military organism and one rather unsuited to protect it effectively. It would be costly, for standing armies involve very great expenditures. The cost of the military expeditions in which they partake are the higher the more remote the scene of operations happens to be. Naval wars are particularly burdensome. The navy entails an enormous expense, which is all the more regrettable because the active usefulness of warships does not exceed from fifteen to twenty years, even if they have met with no accident. "It would none the less be necessary to accept such great expenditures if there were no other means to preserve national independence; but, far from protecting it, a great military apparatus is perhaps what most jeopardizes it."[14]

By reason of a weakness common to all men, ministers affect toward foreign States a language which is particularly presumptuous when they have at their disposal powerful forces ready for action. Even more dangerous is their influence upon their own nation, to which they communicate this arrogant type of pride. If they were not at the head of fine armies and big navies, excessively ambitious sovereigns would suppress their insatiable desire to have other people, who owe them nothing, bow to their will.

Powerful armies never preserve a country from war. The more redoubtable they are, the more certainly they are bound to bring it on. None of them has ever protected its country from invasion. The old proverb *Si vis pacem, para bellum* is, among modern nations, no longer an expression of the truth.

[14] *Cours*, pt. VII, chap. XIX, p. 443.

"Whenever," notes Say, "a nation oppresses other peoples, whenever it pursues a military, commercial, or diplomatic policy hard on another nation, it instantly puts the latter in a state of hostility, concealed when it is not yet in a position to defend itself, open if it is strong enough. This concealed hostility breaks out in the open on the first favorable occasion. Owing to a vague apprehension of the danger threatening it, the oppressor nation maintains a considerable military apparatus, and thus injustice is expensive."[15]

The risks run by a nation of being attacked by a foreign State almost always arise only from the mistakes or the passions of its own government. Say does not recoil from saying: "In vain do I run through modern history, I do not find any nation of some importance which was attacked except by the fault of its leaders."[16]

People do not yet sufficiently realize how few troops would be required by a State that has no claims on others, a State which would never try to dominate them, and which, by demonstrating a strength derived from its good administration and internal well-being, would hold out, simultaneously, the advantage of free trade to peace-loving nations and the prospect of destruction to those who should dare attack it. The resistance which such a State would offer to aggression would be the more vigorous the more perfect its internal regime happened to be. If the nation is merely a pack of slaves exploited for the benefit of the privileged classes, if the progress of its industry is hampered by artificial obstacles, and if justice is partial, the citizens will display little zeal in defending a social order wherein they bear the whole burden and wherein all the advantages are enjoyed by others. On the other hand, in an "economic and protecting" State in which the citizens identify themselves with their fatherland because society there is organized in their interest, they will courageously defend their country. A foreign aggression on such a nation can become really dangerous solely when there is a coalition of several

15 *Ibid.*   16 *Ibid.*

enemies. But such a coalition, Say thinks, is formed only against a State which oppresses others. Coalitions are not formed, he adds, against a nation which always shows good will to its neighbors and perfect willingness to trade with them. On the contrary, every one has an interest in defending such a nation. "When States are too small for a *levée en masse* to suffice for their defense, they should join others in a federal pact, and once more one must find in political organization bonds which are so strong that the States which are threatened least may not refuse their aid to those which are in greater danger."[17]

Though it is painful to admit it, it is none the less true that military life does not perfect qualities useful in civilian life. It accustoms to idleness and servility, which are not only moral vices but very serious shortcomings in economic activity. "To be a good soldier," writes Say, "one must know how to waste one's own time and never to resist an order, even if it is cruel and unjust."[18]

This waste of time is a military necessity but never an economic virtue. War requires passive obedience, but in civilian life the essential goal of every society—the greatest good of the greatest number—is attained only by the development of individual thought and individual effort. It is therefore useful to society that the forms necessary in military life be, so far as possible, imposed upon the smallest number of men and for as short a time as circumstances permit.

Large standing armies mean a crushing load for the population which is working hard to maintain them. To induce the peoples to take this painful labor upon them-

[17] *Ibid.*, p. 444.

[18] *Ibid.*, p. 445. Still another characterization of the soldier is found in Say: "Smith calls the soldier an unproductive worker. Would to heaven that he were nothing worse! But he is rather a destructive worker; for not only does he *not* enrich society with any product, not only does he consume the products necessary for his maintenance, but only too often he is called upon to destroy, without any personal advantage to himself, the fruit of others' hard labor." *Traité*, 6th ed., bk. iii, chap. vii, sect. 2, p. 485. For the same view cf. Flórez Estrada, 1840, vol. ii, p. 323. For the opposite view cf. Gioja, 1815, vol. i, p. 280.

selves, national vanity is stimulated. "They are fed with ideas of power and military vainglory; they are made to consider a great display of force the only solid basis of their security; their eyes are feasted on parades of infantry and cavalry corps; they are intoxicated, in time of peace, with the sounds of military music, the beating of drums, and the thunder of cannon; but all this costs vast sums; it is a luxury which is no less ruinous than any other. Even so, happy is the nation when from the vanity of having fine armies it does not proceed to the vanity of making use of them. Without speaking of the horror of killing one's fellows, every war, when its object is not to gather the fruits of peace, is only a fraud."[19]

Militarism is immensely costly. Say quotes an example of his own time: Bonaparte, according to him, cost mankind the sum of ten billion francs, not taking into account the massacres and the decay of French institutions. If these ten billions had been used for the benefit of France and the other States of Europe, they would have produced an incalculable amount of good. Diplomats usually see in an acquisition of territory an indemnity for the damages and expenses caused by war. Nothing is wider of the mark according to the French economist, for nothing is gained by the conquest of foreign countries.[20]

Colonies, too, cost more than any monopoly is worth. Their possession is of no advantage to the mother country, whose citizens pay for the exorbitant profits realized by a few monopolists. Colonial conquests, to which the military are so attached, constitute a real loss for the nation.[21]

Is it possible, after this review of the economic consequences of militarism, to hesitate in the choice between the "aggressive system" and the "defensive system?" Say decides in favor of the latter. "Powerful interests, I am well aware, are opposed to the defensive system, but I know one

---

[19] Say, *Cours*, p. 445.
[20] *Ibid.*
[21] *Traité*, 6th ed., bk. I, chap. xix; *Cours*, pt. IV, chaps. xxii-xxiii.

more powerful still which makes it preferable: the interest of the peoples."[22]

As for the military organization most suitable for the
defense of the State, he declares himself a partisan of militias. They suffice to defend the independence of well-gov-
erned nations which have no ambitions to conquer. Peoples
willing to adopt a purely defensive system would enjoy
much greater security at less cost. While standing armies
attract war, militias are an institution calculated to favor
peaceful relations among nations.[23]

3. *Theory of Markets*

The future of international economic relations continually preoccupies Say's mind. The idea he has formed on this
subject flows from his basic view on exchanges summed up
in what he calls the *theory of markets*.

In a society in which the division of labor is far advanced, the producers cannot consume more than a small
portion of their products. For the excess of their production over their consumption they are obliged to look for
buyers. They must find the means of effecting the exchange
of the products of their labor for those which they are in
need of; or, to use a commercial term, they require markets. In this exchange, money is only an intermediary which
facilitates the transaction. It is acquired only to be got rid
of at once and to be exchanged for another product. (Say
rather disregards the cases where one sells without buying
immediately after, and hoarding.) In the last analysis, he
notes, it is with products that we buy goods created by
other producers. "At the completion of exchanges it is
found that products were paid with products."[24] This is
the shortest formula of the famous *theory of markets*.

If products are acquired with products, each article will
find the more buyers the more other articles are multiplied.

[22] *Cours*, pt. VII, chap. xix, p. 446. Dutens (1835, vol. II, pp. 223-226),
too, advocates the "purely defensive system" and militias.

[23] Say, *Cours*, pt. VII, chap. xx; *Petit volume*, p. 691.

[24] *Traité*, 1st ed., vol. I, p. 154.

It is therefore not so much "the abundance of money which makes for easy outlets, as the abundance of other goods in general. This is one of the most important truths of political economy."[25]

From this theory Say concludes that the larger the number of producers, and the more varied the produce, the easier, vaster, and more diversified are the markets. Every one is therefore interested in the prosperity of all, and the prosperity of one branch of industry is favorable to that of all the others. This is the conclusion of the economist. It has, however, also a political side.

"A neighboring nation is in the same case as a province in relation to another province and a town with reference to the flat country: it has an interest in seeing them prosper; it is certain to benefit from their opulence; for one cannot trade profitably with a people which has nothing to pay with. Hence well-advised countries favor as much as they can the progress of their neighbors."[26]

"Prior to the most recent progress of political economy, these important truths were unknown not only to the man in the street but even to the most judicious and enlightened minds. One reads in Voltaire (*Dictionnaire philosophique*, s.v. *Patrie*): 'Such is the condition of mankind that, wishing the greatness of one's own country means wishing evil to one's neighbors. . . . It is clear that one country cannot gain without another's losing.' He adds that, to be a citizen of the world, one must not wish one's country to be larger or smaller, richer or poorer; this is a consequence of the same error. The true cosmopolitan does not desire his country to extend its dominion because in so doing it imperils its own happiness; but he does desire it to become richer, for the prosperity of his country is favorable to all others."[27]

[25] *Ibid.*, p. 153.
[26] *Cours*, pt. III, chap. ii, p. 161. Wolowski (1848, pp. 240 f.) and Villiaumé (1864, vol. I, p. 186) express similar views. Villiaumé (1861, pp. 35-37) favors a "European Congress or Tribunal"; cf. also *ibid.*, pp. v-vi.
[27] *Traité*, 6th ed., bk. I, chap. xv, p. 145.

According to Say, the theory of markets, which he classes among the most important discoveries of the human mind, "will change world politics."[28] By what means will such a profound upheaval come about? By the realization of projects such as that of the Abbé de Saint-Pierre? Certainly not, for this plan is only a philanthropic dream without any practical bearing. Even if it were established, an International Court would have no means of enforcing its judgments. And if it should for this purpose call on the armies of the associated powers, they would intervene only in the interest of their own policies. Victory would again fall to the strongest and not to justice.[29]

The revolution in the relations between individual nations will occur as a result of the advancement of economic science, which will gradually lessen national rivalries. However slow, the advance of knowledge is inevitable: it will transform international relations. To benefit from the very happy effects of enlightenment, it is not even necessary that it be generally and completely diffused. The advantage derived from it by the peoples is proportionate to its extension. It is not important that all branches of knowledge be thoroughly studied by all minds; what does matter is that each has correct ideas on the things with which he is called upon to deal.[30] Now it seems to Say that social evolution is running in this direction. "Ultimately one will come to understand that fighting is not in the interest of nations, that all the miseries of a lost war fall on them, and that the profits they reap from successful wars are absolutely *nil.*"[31]

A knowledge of economic laws will lead to international solidarity and to the peaceful cohabitation of nations.

"All nations are friends in the nature of things, and two governments which go to war with one another are no less hostile to their own subjects than to their adversaries. If

28 *Ibid., Discours préliminaire*, p. 51.
29 *Cours*, pt. vii, chap. xix, p. 442.
30 *Ibid.*, and *Traité*, 6th ed., bk. 1, chap. xvii, sect. 1, p. 181.
31 *Traité*, 6th ed., bk. iii, chap. vii, sect. 2, p. 485.

on either side the subjects take up quarrels of vanity and ambition, which are equally harmful to them, to what is one to compare their stupidity? I am ashamed to say it: to the stupidity of beasts which are goaded into fury and which tear each other to pieces for the pleasure of their masters.

"Though public reason has already made some progress, it will make even more in the future. Just because war has become much more costly now than it was formerly, it is impossible for governments to wage it without the consent of the public openly expressed or tacitly understood. This consent will be obtained with more and more difficulty as the masses among nations gain a better understanding of their true interests. From then on the military apparatus of nations will be reduced to what is necessary to repel invasion."[32]

Say does not hesitate for a moment to believe that the progress achieved by political economy will continue to enlighten public opinion. The latter will make wars more and more difficult. Its influence will become particularly powerful when "representative governments will have been established everywhere."[33]

"The advance of knowledge must consequently turn public opinion toward peace, and the progress of the representative system must bring on the sway of this opinion. A military government which should venture to count only on material force would probably not obtain lasting successes in this century and would be branded in those to come."[34]

The changes which take place in modern society strengthen the tendencies toward peace. The modern age is characterized by a rapid industrialization resulting in a continual increase of the number of those whom Say christens *les industrieux*[35] (a social group composed of all the

[32] *Ibid.*, p. 486.   [33] *Cours*, p. 442.
[34] *Ibid.*

[35] TRANSLATOR'S NOTE: To avoid confusion with the restricted English meaning of "industrial classes"—which usually suggests only those who

scholars, farmers, manufacturers, merchants, and workers of a nation),[36] whose peaceful attitude is the very opposite of the warlike or spoliatory spirit which animates the military. The military system is to the liking only of "people who misuse their power and their adroitness to enrich themselves. They do not produce: they ravish the products of others."[37] Now, as the numerical and political importance of the industrious classes continues to grow, the spirit of peace, according to Say, is becoming predominant.

It is evident that these classes consider the growth of wealth as the chief aim of their activity. Their task is never ending, for production may increase indefinitely. It is interesting to recall, in this connection, that, according to Say, the productive power of human labor is not limited by nature but only by the ignorance and the bad administration of the State.[38]

He remains convinced that the State will fall more and more under the dominance of the industrious classes. The latter, or, more exactly, those among them who will be in charge of public affairs, definitely freed from all the prejudices of the exclusive system, will pursue a liberal policy inspired by the principle of international solidarity. The defensive system will extend from country to country. The military apparatus will be reduced to some corps of cavalry and artillery, which cannot be formed in a hurry and which require previous training. For the rest, the strength of States will consist of their militias and above all of their good institutions.[39]

Such would be the far-reaching effects of the discovery of the theory of markets. One cannot overestimate the importance which Say attributes to this theory. It is significant that he ends his *Cours complet d'économie politique* with this passage: "By showing that the interests of

work with their hands in manufacturing and kindred occupations—we propose in this work to translate *les industrieux* as "industrious classes," those who work.

36 Say, *Épitome*, pp. 586-587.   37 *Traité*, 2nd ed., vol. I, p. 276.
38 *Ibid.*, p. 34.   39 *Traité*, 6th ed., p. 486.

men and nations are not opposed to one another, the theory of markets will necessarily scatter seeds of concord and peace, which will germinate as time goes on and which will not be one of the least blessings of the truer opinion that will have been formed on the economy of societies."[40]

4. *Economics and Politics*

According to Say, economic science constitutes the basis of the ethics of individuals and nations. "A good treatise of political economy," he writes, "must be the first book of morality."[41] As we saw above, it is a function of economics to transform international relations and to change the moral character of the intercourse of peoples. The advances of political economy will bring about a vast mental revolution: Cosmopolitanism, based on a new economic conception, will take the place of the ancient manner of thinking. A time will come when economic principles will be applied in practice, and this application will result in the disappearance of war, "the natural condition of men so long as they are ignorant of social economy."[42]

Such are the ideas developed by Say on the future of international relations. It is however to be noted that he abstained from deducing a political doctrine from his economic postulates. He is very careful not to confuse political economy and politics pure and simple. "Political economy," he says, "is not politics; it is not concerned with the distribution or the balance of power, but teaches the economy of society; it tells us how nations obtain what they require for their subsistence."[43]

For this attitude he was blamed by Charles Dunoyer (1786-1863), a French economist well known in his time.[44] Dunoyer is astonished that Say fails to draw any political conclusions from his own economic doctrine and does not

---

[40] *Cours*, p. 577.

[41] Say, *Olbie* (an VIII), p. 585.

[42] Say, *Cours*, Index, p. 742.

[43] *Catéchisme d'économie politique*, 3rd ed., 1826, p. 3.

[44] We wish to point out that the studies of M. Allix (cf. our Bibliography) have been most helpful to us.

realize that the latter in itself constitutes a policy. A title of one of his articles, "A Policy Derived from Economic Doctrines," sums up rather well Dunoyer's ideal. To elaborate the concept of such a policy is the objective he proposes to attain, in collaboration with Charles Comte, a French writer and politician, in the *Censeur européen.*

The *Censeur* was founded in 1814 by Charles Comte and Charles Dunoyer, as an organ of the liberal opposition. Suppressed after the Hundred Days, it reappears in 1817 under the title of *Censeur européen* and with a new spirit: it borrows from economics the basic principles of politics. After 1830, Dunoyer's opinions change radically, but his attitude toward the problem of war remains unchanged.

The doctrine developed in the *Censeur européen,* namely, the idea of an opposition between producers and nonproducers, between the "active and industrious" class and the "idle and devouring" class (*la classe oisive et dévorante*), between rulers and ruled, is based upon the concept of production. The "spirit of industry" (*l'esprit d'industrie*) is one of the favorite topics of Dunoyer who, in the field of economics, generally contents himself with commenting upon Say's ideas, as is shown by his article on the *Système de l'équilibre des puissances européennes* (1817) and his *Notice historique sur l'industrialisme* (1827). His study *De la liberté du commerce international* (1847-1848) is essentially a repetition of Say's thought, at least in the part dealing with the economic side of war.

"To set up a restrictive regime," says Dunoyer, "because war is possible, is, once more, on pretext that it is possible, to begin with making it inevitable and thus rendering the evil which one claims to guard against, more imminent, and to add thereto a fresh and considerable evil productive of none of the good expected from it. The restrictive regime provokes war but prepares poorly for it. Free trade, on the contrary, prevents it and, on the other hand, increases the means of waging it to the extent of finally making it impossible, since it would become highly ruinous and murderous."[45]

In his well-known work *De la liberté du travail*, published in 1845, Dunoyer sums up his point of view in the following terms: "As soon as industry acts by itself, and wherever it acts by itself, peace comes about naturally in [international] relations."[46]

5. *Conditions of a Lasting Peace*

One point remains to be examined. What are, according to Say, the conditions of a lasting peace? Will it come about automatically and instantaneously with the adoption of a free-trade policy by the States? Or will it be necessary to create an international body in order to coordinate the pacifist efforts of governments? Say seems convinced that history will follow the former course. We advisedly say "seems," for he does not pronounce himself explicitly on the subject. But everything tends to prove that his critical observations on the projects of Henry IV, of the "virtuous Abbé de Saint-Pierre," and of Jean-Jacques Rousseau implicitly contain this idea that any international peace organization is only a philanthropic dream: either it will have at its disposal no coercive force or, if the powers lend it their military aid, they will do so only in the interest of their own policies.[47]

For Say sees the true international court in public opinion, the efficacious guarantee of peace in the advance of knowledge, and a lasting international concord in the universal diffusion of free-trade policies. As a result, he is not seriously concerned with studying the possibilities of an *organization* for peace. He merely devotes a passage of a few lines to the project of the Abbé de Saint-Pierre. This attitude of Say's is understandable from his point of view. The impossibility of an *organization* for peace matters

45 *De la liberté du commerce international*, p. 434.
46 Vol. I, p. 331. Cf. also p. 330 and vol. II, p. 53.
47 Say, *Cours*, pt. VII, chap. XIX, p. 442.

little, since international peace does not require organization.

At the most, some institutions which trouble good-neighbor relations between peoples will have to be suppressed. "I need not add," Say notes, "that, to avoid wars in general, a regime which removes [*écarte*] the causes of war is not sufficient; it is necessary, furthermore, not to have institutions which provoke and foster them."[48]

Among these institutions Say names two, colonies and diplomacy.

"Already," he says, "we foresee the complete destruction of a source productive of bloody strife in the emancipation of colonies. All countries which still bear this name will to all appearances be independent before the century has run its course, and they will be interested in maintaining free-trade relations with Europe, as Europe with them."[49]

Adolphe Blanqui, who follows Say very closely, is no less optimistic than his master. He, too, is convinced that colonies will disappear quickly. "Soon," he writes, "they and their regime will no longer be dealt with in works of political economy; they will be like those old feudal ruins out of which civilization has grown and of which no one thinks except a few antiquarians."[50]

Say sees another source for quarrels in diplomacy. While he praises consuls, necessary and commendable agents, he is very hostile to the diplomatic corps. Peace is in the permanent interest of all nations but not in that of ambassadors. The purely defensive system is not favorable to diplomats, whose policy is to make themselves indispensable. With this end in view they needlessly complicate international relations.

"The true system of preserving peace is to be just toward foreigners, not to try to impose upon them one's own policy and view-point, and to be ready to rise in a body against any kind of invasion. For this it is not necessary to have

48 *Ibid.*, pt. VII, chap. xxi, p. 449.
49 *Ibid.*
50 Blanqui, *Précis élémentaire d'économie politique* (1842), p. 117.

ambassadors. This is one of the ancient stupidities which time will do away with."[51]

A critical observation is called for. It concerns Say's historical economism. It is not exaggerated to consider him one of the most important precursors of the economic interpretation of history and of Marx, in spite of the aversion shown for him by the author of *Capital*. For the French economist, economy is more than a branch of human activity aiming at the material maintenance of our species. It constitutes the axis around which all social activity revolves. In the last analysis it explains the moving forces of social life.

"Political economy alone enables the historian to follow a known effect up to an unknown cause, or to follow a known cause down to an effect which the annals of the nations have neglected to report."[52]

Say is convinced that economic development leaves its essential mark upon historical events. He is persuaded that it is tending gradually to enlarge the influence of the industrious classes by assuring them of an ever-increasing political power. Now, these classes are profoundly peaceful—for it is only in time of peace that their net income reaches a maximum. As soon as the governments of the most important countries in the world pass into their hands, good relations between nations will quickly be established. Such is the logical sequence of the propositions of Say, who lays less stress on his true starting point, historical economism, than on the conclusions he draws from it.

In spite of the hypothetical character of his reasoning, Say is convinced of its irrefutability. He is not aware of all that is problematic in an excessively categorical assertion of the economic interpretation of history. Only his unshakable faith in this interpretation permits him to harbor an optimism which will appear quite baseless to future generations. No doubt, the economic interpretation—it will

[51] Say, *Cours*, p. 449.　　　　[52] Say, *Erreurs*, p. 350.

later be called "historical materialism"—to the elaboration
of which Say contributed a good deal, has rendered great
service to the science, because of the manifold economico-
historical researches to which it gave rise at a time when
scholars neglected to study the economic side of history.
The very exaggerations of this method have borne fruit
precisely because it was at the root of many studies which,
without it, would not have been undertaken. But as for its
intrinsic value, its bearing is more restricted than its protag-
onists think. It explains only one aspect, though an important one, of social life: it brings out the influence of
the economic upon the social; but it does not succeed in
proving that in the last analysis social evolution is determined by the economic factor.

As for the coming to power of the industrious classes,
Say seems to neglect the fact that in their political conduct
they are not exclusively guided by economic interests. Furthermore, these interests which, it must be added, are not
the same for all groups making up these classes, were not
homogeneous even in Say's time. It is therefore not surprising that events have taken a course opposite to the one foreseen by the French economist. Instead of an ever closer
cooperation between wage earners and employers, the nineteenth and twentieth centuries show a manifest antagonism
between these two classes. Neither have the relations between the intellectuals, or (to use Say's term) the scholars,
and the proletariat become what he imagined. Unlike some
of his contemporaries, Sismondi for example, he did not
see the coming rise of profound class conflicts between
those he harmoniously merged in one group, that of the
industrious classes. And this opposition, harmful to international peace, has necessarily produced results contrary to
those he anticipated.

From the fact that the industrious classes—the producers—create values, while the warriors make it their business
to destroy them, Say too hastily concludes that the spirit
of the former is peaceful. He disregards not only the interests of certain factions of the industrious classes to start

a war, but he admits moreover an automatism nonexistent in reality. No doubt, the concept of *Homo oeconomicus* is necessary and useful in economics. But it is an abstract scientific concept which forbids too hasty conclusions as to the reality of things. The passage from abstract notions to real phenomena can be carried out to advantage only by a continuous reasoning: the omission of a single logical link vitiates the final result. Now, even if it can be shown that the economic interest of certain classes taken as a whole demands peace, it is not justified to conclude without more ado that the spirit of these same classes is peaceful. Other factors may intervene and do intervene. Here historical economism carries Say to a too hasty and hence incomplete reasoning.

In the light of his time, Say's optimistic attitude becomes understandable, in spite of all the disappointments which the wars of the Revolution and the Empire had caused to the exalted enthusiasts of pacifism. The Great Revolution had accomplished national reforms whose moral bearing went far beyond the frontiers of the French Republic. The spirit which animated that period was cosmopolitan. The debates of the Constituent Assembly show the existence of an undeniable sentiment of international solidarity which had been absent until then and which will again be absent from any legislative body. The famous constitutional article voted on May 22, 1790, proclaims—for the first time in history—"that the French nation renounces the undertaking of any war with a view to making conquests, and that it will never use its forces against the liberty of any people."[53]

In an admirable glow of patriotism, France seems to give up forever all policies of aggression. True, the Revolution quickly took another course, but, in spite of this bellicism, the cosmopolitan spirit of the Constituent Assembly continued for a long time to dominate French thought. It was still very much alive when Say published his *Traité*

[53] *Gazette Nationale ou le Moniteur universel*, No. 143 of May 23, 1790 (*Réimpression de l'Ancien Moniteur*, vol. IV [Paris, 1847], p. 432).

(1803). When the second edition appeared (1814), a fresh stimulant strengthened the opposition to militarism in France. Exhausted by an unprecedented effort, France felt an immense need for peace. Long and murderous struggles ending in defeat and invasion had inspired her with a horror of war: the country wanted to be rid of the military regime.

On the other hand, the industrial revolution, which had already made great progress in England and was now starting in France, was opening up new prospects. Technical progress was transforming thoroughly economic life, rapidly increasing production and holding out unlimited possibilities for human industry. Carried away by the progressive movement in the sciences and the arts, Say notes this, not without pride: "We begin a century destined to win a glory which it will share with no other."[54]

A contemporary of these two revolutions, the political and the economic, he is imbued with the ideas of the one and with the possibilities of the other.

Such are the historical events and the general ideas which inspired him. He was influenced also by several of his predecessors. One can trace in his work not only the ascendency of Adam Smith and the physiocrats but also that of the Abbé de Saint-Pierre, of Forbonnais and, above all, we think, of Condorcet. He is acquainted with all these authors. Through his reading of Smith and the physiocrats he was initiated in economic science. In spite of his opposition to the project of the Abbé de Saint-Pierre, an opposition of principle which singularly resembles the attitude of the physiocrats, he accepts his general ideas on the relationship between trade and peace. The cosmopolitanism of Forbonnais, "a citizen of the world," cannot have escaped his attention. But his conception of peace recalls above all—and in their very essence—certain principles which had been developed by Condorcet. The latter had indeed insisted most strongly on the idea that the advance of knowledge will keep abreast of the progress of the free-

[54] *Traité*, 1st ed., vol. I: *Discours préliminaire*, p. xliv.

trade system. The synthesis of intellectual advancement and economic freedom, he asserts, will end in international concord. Say rejects only one of Condorcet's conclusions: the possibility of the establishment of an international court of arbitration. He accepts all others.[55]

Such is the doctrinal origin of Jean-Baptiste Say's thought. He borrows a number of points from his predecessors, but he adds others. By the particular attention he devotes to the problem of war and by the happy solution which he seems to have found for it, he exerts a profound influence upon his successors in France. His originality must be sought not so much in his discovery of the theory of markets—a formula he gave to a phenomenon known to the economists before him and to which he attributed an exaggerated importance—as in his "class conception" of future peace. There is, he thinks, only one means to bring about lasting peace, namely to act in conformity with the laws established by political economy; and there is but one medium through which this can be accomplished: the industrious classes.

[55] On the authors mentioned in this paragraph, cf. Silberner (1939), pt. II, chap. ii, sect. 2; chap. iii, sect. 1; chap. iv, particularly pp. 218-220; chap. v, sect. 5.

VI. BASTIAT

THE initiator and apostle of the free-trade movement in France, Frédéric Bastiat,[1] is the most illustrious representative of the Optimist School. As a theoretician he is certainly not comparable to the great lights of economic science: Quesnay, Smith, or Ricardo. None the less, his work is remarkable. He summed up the wholly optimistic and enthusiastic social dream, of one or two generations of economists. As one of his best biographers notes, his *Harmonies économiques*, "are not so much an original work as a revival of the ancient optimism of the physiocrats, corrected by more recent theories."[2]

This book, which was destined to crown Bastiat's literary career, was to comprise several volumes. However, struck down by a premature death, he was able to draft only the first, which appeared in 1850. Even this volume is not entirely finished, and the chapter on *War* remained incomplete.

Fortunately, several other publications of his permit us to fill this gap. The most important among these are: *Cobden et la Ligue* (1845), *Sophismes économiques* (1845-1848), *Le libre-échange* (1846-1848), *Capital et Rente* (1849), *Ce qu'on voit et ce qu'on ne voit pas* (1850), and above all, *Paix et liberté ou le budget républicain* (1849). His *Correspondance* contains a very interesting letter addressed to the Peace Congress held at Frankfort-on-the-Main, in 1850.

1. The Decline of Spoliation

Bastiat divides, into two categories, all the procedures

[1] Bastiat (1801-1850), the son of a Bayonne merchant, became an orphan at the age of nine. Shortly after leaving college, he made not very successful attempts first in commerce, then in agriculture. Having heard, almost by chance, of the free-trade movement in England, he became at once enthusiastic over Cobden's work. He was secretary general of the "Association du Libre-Échange," a member of the Constituent Assembly (1848), and later of the Legislative Assembly (1849).

[2] Bidet, *Frédéric Bastiat, l'homme, l'économiste*, 1906, p. 273.

adopted by man to procure a means of existence: production and spoliation. The latter is carried out in the interior by violence and trickery, in the exterior by arms. "Spoliation in the exterior is called war, conquests, and colonies."[3]

What is, in Bastiat's opinion, the origin of this spoliation?

"Spoliation by war," he says, "that is, spoliation frank, simple, and crude, has its root in the human heart, in human organization, and in this prime mover of society: the lure for pleasure and the dislike of pain; in a word, in the motive which we all bear within ourselves: which is personal interest."[4]

The desire to despoil the labor of others is therefore at the root of armed conflicts between nations. Spoliation by war is not an accidental and transient fact; it is a general and constant phenomenon, only less permanent than work. However, it was God's will, says Bastiat, that man should engage in a peaceful strife with Nature and reap directly from it the fruit of victory. By diverting the product of another's labor, man misuses his strength.

Are there indications which permit us to believe that this spoliation, of which war is one of the many forms, will disappear in the future?

"Spoliation," replies Bastiat, "having, like production, its root in the human heart, the laws of society would not be harmonious . . . if production were not in the long run to dethrone spoliation."[5]

The unfinished chapter on war ends with this very passage, which is not highly explanatory. It would have been interesting to know how Bastiat imagined this "dethronement" of "Spoliation" by "Production." The text does not say. It is however possible to gather, from the ensemble of his work, the answer he would very probably have given. It is likely that he would have said that since aggression is becoming more and more difficult and costly, while the

[3] Bastiat, *Cobden et la Ligue*, p. 11.
[4] *Harmonies économiques*, chap. xix, pp. 524-525.
[5] *Ibid.*, p. 530.

means of defense are becoming more and more perfect, the spoliation of others' labor—in the form of war—is consequently becoming less and less popular, and is even likely to disappear altogether. Even if this spoliation were still to remain advantageous to some individuals, the masses would not condone it, for they would see in labor, and not in pillage, the best, that is, the most economic, source of wealth. Pursuing its material and selfish interest, rendered clear by economic science, mankind will attain the goal which neither religion nor philosophy was powerful enough to carry into effect: peace. Political economy proves by hard figures that loss exceeds gain in all conquests, whether continental or colonial. The "monopolists" alone profit from war or from its ever-present eventuality.[6]

"Political economy," says Bastiat, "shows that, even if we consider only the victorious people, wars are always waged in the interest of the few and at the expense of the many. It is therefore sufficient that the many realize this truth clearly. The weight of Public Opinion, which is as yet divided, will bear entirely on the scale of peace."[7]

He bases his pacifism on the material interest of nations. This sort of materialism seems to him normal and reconcilable with morality. He anticipates that some will hold this against him but he is not frightened by this prospect.

"I know well," he observes, "that I shall be reproached (it is the fashion of the day) with basing the brotherhood of nations on men's personal interest—vile, prosaic self-interest. One would prefer to find its principle in charity and love, and even in a little self-abnegation, and that, hurting the material well-being of men, it should have the merit of a generous sacrifice.

"When at last shall we have done with these puerile declamations? When shall we banish hypocrisy from science? When shall we cease exhibiting this nauseating contradiction between our writings and our actions? We boo and jeer *personal interest*, that is, the useful and the good (for

<hr />

[6] Bastiat, *Le libre-échange*, pp. 196, 204.
[7] Bastiat, *Sophismes économiques*, p. 134.

saying that all peoples are interested in one thing is to say that the thing is good in itself), as if personal interest were not the necessary, eternal, and indestructible mainspring to which Providence has entrusted human perfectibility."[8]

2. *Immediate Disarmament*

(A) MILITARY DISARMAMENT

The foreign policy advocated by Bastiat flows from his concept of the natural order, a concept he borrows from the physiocratic doctrine. "The general laws of society," he says, "are harmonious; they tend in every sense toward the improvement of mankind."[9] What is of importance for humanity is not to try to change them (an attempt futile in any case) but to know them and to conform to them.[10]

In taking up the foreign policy of his country, Bastiat, to begin with, establishes two propositions, outside of which (as he expresses it) there is no salvation: 1. the development of brute force is superfluous and unfavorable to France; 2. an increase in her military strength is useless and harmful to her external or internal security. From this he concludes, at the risk of being called a traitor by the so-called patriots, that "it is necessary to disarm on land and on the sea, and to do so at the earliest possible time [au plutôt]."[11]

The prosperity of the country cannot be obtained without a reduction of taxes and a restriction of the expenditures of the State to an even greater proportion. To express this financial thought in a political formula, Bastiat observes: "Freedom in the interior, peace abroad. This is the whole program."[12]

Peoples react upon one another through their civilization: through the arts, literature, philosophy, journalism, trade, and above all by example. True enough, sometimes

[8] *Ibid.*, p. 98. A similar view is found in Roux (1801), pp. 166 f., 153 f., and in Ganilh (1809), vol. I, p. 61.

[9] *Harmonies économiques*, chap. xiv, p. 431.

[10] Bastiat, *Gratuité du crédit*, p. 319.

[11] Bastiat, *Paix et liberté ou le budget républicain*, p. 449.

[12] *Ibid.*, p. 419.

they act also by constraint, but it is impossible to admit that this type of influence is calculated to develop principles favorable to the progress of mankind. Now, since France, according to Bastiat, runs no risk of invasion, he suggests that she disarm. He is quite aware that national security is the greatest of blessings,[13] but he sees no threat from abroad dangerous to France.

"For my part," he writes, "I shall not hesitate to vote for disarmament, because I do not believe in invasions. Whence would they come? From Spain? from Italy? from Prussia? from Austria? This is impossible. There remain England and Russia. As for England, she tried it already and a debt of twenty-two billions, the interest of which is still being paid by her workers, is a lesson which can't be lost. As for Russia, this is a chimera. She does not seek, but rather avoids, contact with France. If the emperor Nicholas should venture to send us 200,000 Muscovites, I sincerely believe that the best thing we could do would be to receive them well, to give them a taste of the sweetness of our wines, to show them our streets, our stores, our museums, the happiness of the people, the mildness and equality of our penal laws, after which we should say to them: Return as quickly as possible into your steppes and tell your brothers what you have seen."[14]

This good-natured peroration shows how unreal the prospect of a war appeared to Bastiat.

"I believe," he says, "that the time has come when France should declare resolutely that she sees the solidarity of peoples in the linking of their interests and in the communication of their ideas, and not in the intervention of brute force. And to give this declaration an irresistible weight—for what is a manifesto, however eloquent?—I believe the time has come for her to dissolve this brute force herself."[15]

If in Europe democratic France were to take the initiative in this revolution, the happiest consequences would

---

[13] *Ce qu'on voit et ce qu'on ne voit pas* (1850), p. 340.
[14] *Paix et liberté*, p. 456.   [15] *Ibid.*, p. 453.

flow from it. With one stroke military expenditures would disappear and public finances would be relieved.

"Then," observes Bastiat, "taxes will be lightened; there will be work, confidence, welfare, credit, and consumption within reach of the masses; the [French] Republic will be loved, admired, and consolidated by all the strength which popular sympathy confers on institutions; the threatening specter of bankruptcy will no longer beset the imagination; political disturbances will be relegated to past history, and France will at last be happy and glorious among all nations, radiating the irresistible power of her example."[16]

In short, if he thus advocates disarmament, the reason is that to him armed peace is "an organ without function," to use Martello's words[17] of half a century later.

None the less, military disarmament alone is not sufficient in Bastiat's opinion. Nations should proceed also to economic disarmament.

(B) ECONOMIC DISARMAMENT

French foreign trade requires no military protection. Markets are acquired not by arms but by low prices. Send goods costing five cents less, Bastiat remarks, and you will not need cannon and ships to sell them. (He forgets to add that this assertion is true only in a free-trade world.)

"If then," he continues, "low prices are the true safeguard of trade, what does our government do to bring them into being? First of all, by duties it raises the prices of raw materials, of all tools, and of all consumer goods. Then, by way of compensation, it overwhelms us with taxes on the plea of sending its fleet in quest of markets. This is barbarism, the most barbarous of barbarisms, and the time is not far off when people will say: Those Frenchmen of the nineteenth century had queer commercial systems, but they should at least have abstained from believing that they lived in the *century of enlightenment*."[18]

16 *Ibid.*, p. 454.
17 *L'economia politica antimalthusiana e il socialismo* (1894), p. 45.
18 *Paix et liberté*, p. 457.

Quite true, among the arguments in favor of the restrictive regime national independence is frequently cited. Bastiat thinks this argument specious. What will France do in the case of a war with England if for her iron and coal supply she has become dependent upon that country? ask the French protectionists. On the other hand, the British monopolists cry: What will become of Great Britain, in time of war, if for her foodstuffs she relies on the French? Now the interested parties seem to forget that the dependence resulting from commercial exchange is reciprocal. If a country is economically dependent on foreign countries, the latter depend no less on it. Economic dependence, by reason of its being always mutual, presents no danger to national independence. On the contrary, by reducing the chances of armed conflict between nations, it is favorable to their political autonomy.

"To break off natural relations," says Bastiat, "does not mean putting oneself in a state of independence, but in a state of isolation.

"And note this: nations isolate themselves in anticipation of war, but the very act of isolation is a beginning of war. It renders it more easy, less onerous, and hence less unpopular. Let nations be permanent markets for each other's products. Let their relations be such that they cannot be broken without inflicting upon them the twofold suffering of privation and glut, and they will no longer need those powerful navies which ruin them, those large armies which crush them; world peace will be no longer endangered by the caprice of a Thiers or a Palmerston, and war will disappear, having no nourishment, resources, motives, pretexts, and popular sympathy."[19]

Political economy is thus opposed to the protectionist doctrine, which represents exclusively the interest of the monopolists. The latter need an always imminent eventuality of war. The continuation of their monopolies depends on this condition. This explains the pretended patriot-

19 *Sophismes économiques*, pp. 97-98.

ism they display.[20] Their policy leads straight to international conflicts. "Trade barriers constitute isolation; isolation gives rise to hatred, hatred to war, and war to *invasion*."[21]

The interest of the masses, of the people, demands the establishment of complete freedom of commerce. The proletarians, if they understood their own interest, ought to rise up, with quite particular vehemence, against the spirit of monopoly and war.[22]

Economic freedom alone will guarantee a better future and lasting peace to the world. "We are profoundly convinced," Bastiat asserts, "that free-trade means harmony of interests and peace among nations, and we certainly place this indirect and social effect a thousand times above the direct or purely economic effect.

"For assured peace among nations means disarmament, the discrediting of brute force, the revision, reduction, and just distribution of public taxes; it means, for the peoples, the dawning of a new era."[23]

Several French free traders of the nineteenth century share this point of view; but it would be of no particular usefulness to enumerate all of them here. We shall cite only two, both relatively little known in economic literature: Dupuit and Dameth. Like Bastiat, they emphasize the peaceful aspect of the free-trade system.

Encouraged by the conclusion of the Anglo-French commercial treaty of 1860, Dupuit writes: "One of the greatest advantages of freedom of trade is peace, one may even say universal peace. This is not a Utopian dream, for it is sufficient to examine what is happening to be convinced that it will come into being."[24] Free trade is synonymous with material welfare, with intellectual progress, and with in-

20 Bastiat, *Le libre-échange*, pp. 204-205.
21 Bastiat, *Sophismes économiques*, p. 116.
22 Bastiat, *Capital et rente*, p. 60.
23 *Le libre-échange*, p. 194.
24 Dupuit, *La liberté commerciale* (1861), p. 170.

ternational concord. "Freedom of trade means abundance, civilization, and peace."[25]

For Dameth, too, commercial freedom is susceptible of radically transforming the economic and social world. He expresses himself on free trade in the following terms:

"It means the establishment of a great economic sociability in place of the petty prejudices of national antagonism. It means an era of universal peace, the wish of all great souls, which is drawing near for the world. It means general disarmament, relieving our modern finances of the enormous and crushing military budgets, and restoring to the family, to the country, and to production millions of young and robust arms. It means for this very reason public opinion becoming in effect the first of the powers in every civilized country. It means the policy of interests replacing, under the auspices of human rights, the stupid and bloody force of the cannon."[26]

3. The Pacifist Movement

Like all free traders, Bastiat aspires to a pacifist revolution, to peace in prosperity. No one of them, however, believed this revolution—perhaps the most profound of all—of as easy accomplishment as he did.

To hasten its coming, he actively participated in the pacifist movement which, about the middle of the nineteenth century, sprang into vigorous action. In 1848, the first international congress of the Friends of Peace met at Brussels. The economists were not represented;[27] but they attended in large number the second congress, which was held in Paris the following year. Bastiat, Michel Chevalier, Charles Dunoyer, Horace Say, and Gustave de Molinari were among its participants. The organization committee of the congress had for secretary Joseph Garnier, a well-known pacifist and chief editor of the *Journal des Écono-*

25 *Ibid.*, p. 171.
26 Dameth, *Introduction à l'étude de l'économie politique* (ed. 1878), p. 293.
27 Cf. *Congress 1848.*

mistes.[28] Bastiat, who set forth the viewpoint of the economists, obtained a brilliant success.

Large armaments, he declares, force governments to impose heavy taxes and to have recourse to indirect taxation.
Now taxes are opposed to the principle of proportionality
and increase the misery of the poor. The masses naturally
feel their inequity. For this very reason they augment social discontent and thus strengthen revolutionary tendencies. To equalize the tax loads, it is necessary to reduce
them, and to reduce them, it is imperative to abolish or to
diminish the armed forces. Disarmament would involve no
real danger for the people, and it would not mean political
abdication. In the name of economic science, which more
than any other contributes to international concord, Bastiat
launches the following appeal to the nations: "Live in
peace, for your interests are harmonious, and the apparent
antagonism which often puts arms in your hands, is a gross
error."[29]

A resolution adopted by the congress recommends to the
governments international arbitration and disarmament
and reproves "loans and taxes destined to support wars
of ambition and conquest."[30] It reflects the influence of
the economists, particularly of Bastiat. The pacifist movement of that epoch draws its inspiration from the idea,
which was then in vogue, that "political economy is the
science *par excellence* of peace."[31]

What were the aims which the economists proposed to
attain through their participation in pacifist congresses?
It is once more Bastiat who gives us the best information
on the subject. Detained in Paris by illness, he addresses,
under date of August 17, 1850, a letter to the peace congress, held at Frankfort, in which he defines the role of
pacifist propaganda:

"No doubt," he writes, "there was a time when a peace

[28] Cf. Garnier, *Éléments* (1848), pp. 291, 389; *Note historique* (1849);
Réponse (1851).
[29] *Congress 1849*, p. 26. Cf. also A. Schumacher (1929), pp. 165-169.
[30] *Congress 1849*, p. 63.
[31] According to an expression of Horace Say, *ibid.*, p. 53.

congress would have had no chances of success. When men waged war to conquer booty, lands, or slaves, it would have been difficult to stop them by moral or economic considerations. Even religions failed to accomplish it.

"To-day, however, two circumstances have completely changed the question.

"The first is that wars no longer have [material] interest for their cause or even for their pretext, since they are always opposed to the true interests of the masses.

"The second is that they no longer depend on the caprice of a leader, but on public opinion.

"From the combination of these two circumstances it follows that wars are bound to become less and less frequent and, owing to the force of events, finally to disappear independently of any intervention by the congress, for anything harmful to the public and yet dependent on the public must necessarily cease.

"What is then the role of the congress? It is to hasten this outcome, inevitable in any case, by showing to those who do not yet see it where and how wars and armaments are harmful to the general interest."[32]

What is utopian in such a program? The masses have an evident interest in peace and should at last understand it. To this end it is, however, necessary to speak to them clearly and comprehensibly. This is what Bastiat proposes to tell them:

"Consult not only your interests in the other world but also those of this world. Examine the effects of war. See whether they are not tragic for you. Observe whether wars and heavy armaments do not lead to interruptions of work, to industrial crises, to loss of strength, to crushing debts, to grinding taxes, to financial impossibilities, to discontent and revolutions, to say nothing of deplorable moral habits and culpable violations of the religious law?

"Is it not permitted to hope that this language will be understood? Take courage, then, men of faith and devotion, have courage and confidence! Those who to-day can-

[32] Bastiat, *Correspondance*, p. 198.

not join your ranks follow you with their eyes and with their hearts."[33]

Among French economists Bastiat was not the only one who participated actively in the pacifist movement. His faith was doubtless more ardent and more unshakable than that of the others. But many of them have collaborated with pacifist organizations. Thus we find[34] among the founders of the Ligue Internationale et Permanente de la Paix (organized in 1867) the most illustrious liberal French economists of the time: Michel Chevalier, Joseph Garnier, Frédéric Passy, and Paul Leroy-Beaulieu.[35]

The only French-speaking liberal economist who in that period was opposed to the pacifist movement is Antoine-Elisée Cherbuliez.[36] Peace, he admits, is preferable to war: apart from "a dozen statesmen and old warriors"[37] no one has an interest in favoring militarism. War seems to him all the same an inevitable phenomenon in a world divided into sovereign States. While it is a necessary sanction of international law, projects of permanent peace and a European federation are only impracticable chimeras.[38] As for international arbitration, it is nothing but "warmed-up twaddle *(vieillerie renouvelée)* of the Abbé de Saint-Pierre and the philosopher Kant."[39] Cherbuliez, then, does not grant any positive value to pacifism. He even "wages a little war on the subject of peace"[40] with the *Journal des Économistes*, a liberal organ which placed itself at the disposal of pacifist propaganda.

[33] *Ibid.*, pp. 199-200.

[34] Cf. *Bibliothèque de la Paix* (1869), pp. 208-211.

[35] Leroy-Beaulieu, whose *Traité théorique et pratique d'économie politique* we have already cited, is also the author of a statistical study entitled *Les guerres contemporaines* (1869).

[36] A Genevese economist and jurist (1797-1869). Cf. the excellent book of W.-E. Rappard (1941); cf. also Silberner (1935). Let us note in passing that, according to Cherbuliez (*Précis*, 1862, vol. II, pp. 67-68) free trade cannot endanger national defense.

[37] Cherbuliez, *Le droit international* (1868), p. 22.

[38] Cherbuliez, *ibid.*, p. 18; *Congrès de la Paix* (1851), pp. 145-146; *Essai*, 1833, p. 15.

[39] Cherbuliez, *Congrès de la Paix* (1851), p. 147.

[40] *Ibid.*, p. 145.

Cherbuliez's case is, however, isolated. Most French economists gave a sympathetic reception to the pacifist movement and contributed a good deal to its progress. Their share in this movement deserves doubtless a more detailed study, which would, however, fall outside the scope of this book.

4. The Sanctification of Commercial Freedom

Bastiat found an ardent disciple in Frédéric Passy (1822-1912) who in his pacifist propaganda often uses arguments borrowed from the author of *Harmonies économiques*. The titles of some of Passy's publications[41] suffice to show the interest he has in the problem of peace.

He sees in erroneous mercantilist or protectionist conceptions the chief source of bellicism. He asserts that with their disappearance most of the causes leading to war will disappear, too. Customs barriers are also moral barriers, and by lowering the former one also reduces the latter. Every obstacle hampering the flow of goods is an impediment to the free movement of men and in the end fosters, with ignorance of one's neighbor, prejudices and hate. Thus the restrictive system creates an atmosphere favorable to war.

While restriction disunites, exchange unites and draws men together. With the multiplication of trade relations there develops a need for order without which business is impossible. Between nation and nation as between man and man in a community, trade teaches the consideration of public tranquillity, both within and without, as the greatest good.

In the beginning tribe hated tribe, yet, in the end, men united by forming great national units. This process of pacification is not yet completed. Peoples will finally extend peace beyond their frontiers, "and the day will come," says Passy, "it comes, I hope, when every European war will be a civil war, pending the time when every war, of

41 Cf. Bibliography.

whatever kind, will be banished by mankind as a crime against humanity."[42]

Nothing can contribute more effectively to this result than frequent trade relations. More than any other factor, international commerce proves the economic absurdity of military conflicts. "War," declares Passy, "is no longer merely a crime; it is an absurdity. It is no longer merely immoral and cruel; it is stupid. It is no longer merely murder on a large scale; it is suicide and voluntary ruin."[43]

He observes that it is generally economic interests ill understood which bring nations into conflict.[44] Now free trade tends to do away with these misunderstandings. "Some day all barriers will fall; some day mankind, constantly united by continuous transactions, will form just one workshop, one market, and one family."[45]

Everything in this period of modern economy seems to him to conspire to rule out war and to impose as well as to perpetuate peace. Among the causes of international concord the most active and irresistible is the extension of free trade. "And this is," he concludes, ". . . the grandeur, the truth, the nobility, I might almost say the holiness of the free-trade doctrine; by the prosaic but effective pressure of [material] interest it tends to make justice and harmony prevail in the world."[46]

With Passy we thus arrive at the sanctification of the free-trade doctrine. However, his is only the phrasing, for the concept of commercial freedom was just as holy for his master Bastiat. The disciple contents himself with following the trail blazed by the author of *Harmonies économiques*.

Bastiat develops in fact a system based on the metaphysical and providentialist conceptions of the eighteenth century. He lays down as a principle, without ever doubting

42 *Leçons d'économie politique* (1861), p. 578. Cf. also p. 577.
43 Passy, *La question de la Paix* (1894), p. 68.
44 Passy, *Les causes économiques des guerres* (1905), p. 438.
45 Passy, *La liberté commerciale* (1866), p. 251.
46 Passy, *Leçons d'économie politique*, p. 582.

it, an article of faith: the goodness of the natural laws and the harmony, established by God, of all legitimate interests. Without examining the economic world as it is, Bastiat deduces from these axioms a series of conclusions in favor of universal peace. The scientific value of such a method, which involves faith in providential laws, is very problematical. By an admission as sincere as it is eloquent, Bastiat himself recognizes the religious character of his method. "As for me," he says, "I admit it, it has so often happened to me in my economic studies, that I reached this conclusion: *God does well what He does*, that when logic leads me to a different inference, I cannot but distrust my logic."[47]

"I know," he adds, "that this faith in final causes is a danger for the mind."[48] Still, the admission of this danger does not alter at all the nature of his method. He constantly confuses religion and science, instead of separating them rigorously in the best interest of both.

This method did not permit him to notice the real contradictions existing both within each State and between nations. Consequently, he was unable to appreciate correctly the enormous difficulties which must be overcome before a durable peace among peoples can be established. The effort required appears to him only in a purely negative form: the abstention of all economic intervention by the State.

At the basis of his theory there is a postulate analogous to that of historic materialism: economic evolution determines the policy and unerringly leads the world in a definite direction. For historical materialism, this direction is called "classless society"; for Bastiat it is a society without State intervention and wars. For historical materialism, this movement is a series of natural laws pure and simple; for Bastiat it is the result of both natural and providential laws. However, while historical materialism anticipates gigantic struggles before reaching the goal it sets for man-

[47] Bastiat, *Harmonies économiques*, chap. xvi, p. 448.
[48] *Ibid.*

kind, Bastiat is convinced that social evolution will follow a wholly pacific course.

The optimism of the author of *Harmonies économiques* has all the earmarks of the old optimism of Quesnay's school. In the middle of the nineteenth century it does not mark a step forward but a retrogression: it means a return to the basic concept of the physiocrats.

5. *Some Moderate Liberals*

Our picture of the French liberal school would be incomplete without at least a brief mention of some of its less enthusiastic followers: Rossi, Chevalier, and Baudrillart. Though, like Say, Bastiat, and Passy, they are adherents of the free-trade system, they draw from it less optimistic conclusions regarding peace.

For Pellegrino Rossi[49] the national factor is not a negligible quantity. Humanity, he thinks, is, and will always be, divided into States. It is therefore "a pure abstraction to assert that the world is at bottom only one big market and one big workshop."[50] The idea of an industrial and commercial world without any political barriers, a world in which, so far as economic relations are concerned, the various nationalities would be effaced, is unfortunately only a "romantic hypothesis."[51]

"Political economy," says Rossi, "is not mistress of the world and the universal legislator of civil societies. With a few rare exceptions it demands freedom of commerce and industry: it is right within the sphere of its ideas. But there are cases where the science of wealth collides with politics, entrusted essentially with the duty of providing for the first needs of every nation, that is, for its independence, its strength, and its defense. Before knowing whether one will

[49] Rossi (1787-1848), jurist, economist, and statesman of Italian origin, became a naturalized Genevese (1820) and subsequently a French citizen (1834). In 1833 he succeeded J.-B. Say at the Collège de France.
[50] Rossi, *Cours d'économie politique* (1840-1851), 5th ed., 12th lesson, vol. II, pp. 258-259. Cf. also p. 257.
[51] *Ibid.*, vol. II, pp. 248 and 250.

be richer or poorer comes the question: to be or not to be (*il s'agit d'exister*)."[52]

There is therefore nothing strange in Rossi's favoring protection for the armament industries and, in certain special cases, for agriculture.[53]

Michel Chevalier[54] contracted a profound attachment to peace already in his youth, devoted to the propaganda of Saint-Simonism. War, according to him, is a destructive element and an obstacle to social progress.[55]

He sees in free trade a factor favoring peace and "a principle which tends to make international politics more sympathetic."[56] But, contrary to certain liberals, he does not believe that the carrying into effect of this principle would entail a pacification of mankind. On the contrary, "free-trade," he says, "presupposes peace."[57]

The pacific forces are growing daily. Scientific and industrial progress are factors of peace which one cannot but recognize. The representative system, which is taking root everywhere, and public opinion, which is more and more opposed to bellicism, likewise favor international concord.

In spite of these powerful motives making for amity among nations, Chevalier does not believe in the coming of a lasting peace. No doubt, it is desirable and advanta-

[52] *Ibid.*, vol. II, p. 278.

[53] *Ibid.*, vol. II, pp. 279-281. Rossi's description of the economic effects of war (*ibid.*, 11th lesson, pp. 242-243) resembles Ricardo's.

[54] A Saint-Simonian and editor of the *Globe*, Michel Chevalier (1806-1879) was prosecuted and sentenced to a year's imprisonment (1832). Thanks to the protection of Thiers, he served only half of this term and was subsequently entrusted with an official mission to the United States for the study of communications. In 1840 he succeeded Rossi at the Collège de France. With Cobden he was the chief negotiator of the Anglo-French commercial agreement of 1860. Cf. Nicard des Rieux (1912), and Labracherie (1929). On Chevalier as a follower of Saint-Simon cf. below, chap. xii, sect. 2.

[55] Cf. Chevalier, *Lettres sur l'organisation du travail* (1848), p. 335; *Introduction*, 1868, pp. cccxlviii; dxi f.

[56] Chevalier, *Examen du système . . . protecteur* (1852), p. 169.

[57] *Ibid.*, p. 168. For the same opinion cf. Walras (1898), p. 300, and Walras (1907), p. 169.

geous, but it seems to him irreconcilable with human nature. There is in the latter, he thinks, "an instinct, sometimes irresistible, which drives to war even the most generous and the most humane peoples. A fatal force having its point d'appui and its lever in our hearts, at certain times imposes war upon man like an inexorable necessity."[58]

"Thus political economy would go astray in the regions of Utopia if, in its plans, it would leave out of account the possibility of war. Consequently, the complete suppression of a national force for the defense of the country must be considered by it as an idea which will never materialize."[59]

"All one can do is to demand that, in the near future, armies be organized chiefly for defense and no longer for aggression."[60]

Militarism devours a considerable part of the national capital and seriously impedes social progress. The system of large armies and navies is essentially opposed to the popular interest. Unfortunately, war has long since become an art far too difficult to permit a prudent government to give up standing armies.[61] But the great nations of the European continent have exceeded all fair bounds. They all would therefore have an interest in restricting standing armies and in reducing armaments. And it is up to France, especially, to take the initiative.[62]

[58] Chevalier, *Cours d'économie politique*, 2nd ed., vol. II, p. 244. Cf. also pp. 239-240. A similar point of view is found in Storch (vol. III, p. 434).

[59] Chevalier, *Cours d'économie politique*, 2nd ed., vol. II, p. 253.

[60] *Ibid.*, p. 255.

[61] *Ibid.*, pp. 338, 345-349. For a similar point of view cf. Courcelle-Seneuil (1891, vol. II, pp. 200-201). Prior to 1871 he came out in favor of militias (1858, vol. II, pp. 204 f.; 1867, vol. II, pp. 191 f.). A witness of growing militarism, he modified his views. His fine indictment of bellicism (1891, vol. II, pp. 197-200) even now deserves being read.

According to Cherbuliez, the militia system is the least costly of all army systems; "but [he adds justly] until it is generally adopted by the nations sharing the empire of the world, the question of cost will play only a secondary role; for the objective pursued affects the very existence of each State, and savings realised only at the expense of security would not be savings." Cherbuliez (1862), vol. II, p. 371.

[62] Chevalier, *Cours*, 2nd ed., vol. II, pp. 349-350.

To reduce considerably the military budget, Chevalier also proposes to shorten the term of service. On the other hand, it seems to him impossible to diminish appreciably the military expenditures by putting the soldiers to productive labor. None the less, the partial use of the army in works of public utility would deserve a trial: one might constitute a more or less considerable fraction of the army as a reserve to be employed wherever such projects ought to be carried out.[63]

Henri Baudrillart,[64] too, has a much more modest notion than Say and Bastiat of the mission of political economy.

Economic science, he observes, deals with war because peace, together with internal security and civil liberty, is one of the elements of public prosperity. While it does not profess to solve, all by itself, the problem of war, a question too complex to be settled by any one discipline, it yet has to shed light on this grave problem and to contribute its part to its solution.

Above all, it has its own share of prejudices to combat. It turns indeed against those who sometimes try to justify military conflicts in the name of a pretended economic principle according to which war removes the surplus population when competition of working men becomes too severe. Political economy shows that war, contrary to the thought of some, does not create vacancies.

It proves furthermore that militarism and war destroy an enormous portion of the national wealth. It is evident that for its defense a nation may be obliged to expend very large sums unproductively. It would be erroneous, however, to conclude from this that war constitutes "good business," because the destruction it entails requires fresh work, to be done by the survivors.[65]

[63] *Ibid.*, lessons 11 to 18.

[64] Baudrillart (1821-1892), professor of the history of economic doctrines at the Collège de France, chief editor of the *Journal des Économistes* (1855-1865).

[65] Baudrillart, *Philosophie de l'économie politique* (1860), ed. 1883, pp. 243-245.

"In the eyes of political economy," says Baudrillart, "war is a bad business for mankind and even for the victors. Similarly, the science has shown, in another field, that slavery was in the long run disastrous even to the slave-holders."[66]

Since political economy is opposed to bellicism, some accuse it of failing to take into account the idea of nationality and even of destroying it systematically in favor of a cosmopolitanism which no longer leaves room for the diversity of peoples.

According to Baudrillart, nothing is more erroneous. As a matter of fact, political economy, by claiming a large freedom of exchange for every people, tends to restore to it its native originality, a thing apparently beyond the comprehension of protectionists.

"Those who do not consider at all the differences produced among men by climate, race, and institutions, are the very theoreticians of prohibitions who want every nation to be self-sufficient and to devote itself to all industries at the same time."[67]

"By endeavoring to maintain that division of labor which Providence itself has established among men, political economy is obviously not hostile to the spirit of nationality; it bases the alliance of peoples on the difference of characters and faculties; it wants each to excel under the conditions peculiar to it, and each to produce so as to have means of exchange. To generalize and to extend trade, it localizes industry."[68]

[66] Baudrillart in *Congress 1866*, p. 717. "L'économie politique n'a jamais élevé qu'un étendard, celui du travail libre et celui de l'échange cosmopolite; elle n'a jamais entonné qu'un *Te Deum*, le *Te Deum* de la paix!" Baudrillart, *ibid.*, p. 716. At the same congress Baudrillart objects to the keeping up of standing armies (*ibid.*, p. 717).

[67] Baudrillart, *Manuel d'économie politique* (1857), p. 299.

[68] *Ibid.* Several Spanish economists hold a similar view. "Situar bien la industria es favorecer el comercio y concertar el culto de la patria con el amor de la humanidad." Colmeiro (1865), p. 206. Free trade is not hostile to the principle of nationality (Olózaga, 1888, vol. I, p. 605); it preserves the physiognomy peculiar to each nation (Moreno Villena, 1896, p. 318). According to Carballo y Wangüemert (1855, vol. I, pp. 266

The development of production carries the nations more and more toward peace. Industry creates an international solidarity of interests which takes the place of antagonism in trade relations between peoples. The facts clearly show the impotence of military force to found anything of lasting economic utility.[69]

Political economy also proves the unprofitable character of modern wars. But because they show a deficit, can one conclude that they are going to disappear in the future? Such a prospect seems improbable to Baudrillart, or at least very remote. The economic interdependence of nations, the development of communications, and the evolution of international morality will in the end, he thinks, make wars more and more rare. But will all these factors remove this scourge forever? "That is the question. However this may be, it is not the nineteenth century, as the Abbé de Saint-Pierre imagined, nor even the twentieth, as M. de Molinari seems to believe, which will witness this great and curious spectacle."[70]

All the authors reviewed in this section express opinions much more moderate and, in certain respects, much closer to the truth than those of Say, Bastiat, and Passy.

Rossi asserts that it is impossible to consider a world divided into sovereign States as a single market. Moreover, such a division does not seem to him compatible with permanent peace; it rather implies the necessity of armed conflict. "Political economy," he says, "is not mistress of the world." Differently expressed, it means that nations do not act in conformity with the rules suggested to them by this science in order to assure them of a maximum material welfare.

---

f.), Colmeiro (*ibid.*, p. 207), Madrazo (1874, vol. I, p. 349), and Moreno Villena (*ibid.*), free trade, by uniting peoples, makes wars more difficult and more rare.

[69] Baudrillart, *Philosophie de l'économie politique*, pp. 246-248.

[70] Baudrillart, *Études* (1858), vol. II, p. 358. The ideas developed by the Italian Minghetti (1863, pp. 548-552) on the subject of war are similar to those outlined by Baudrillart.

Chevalier, too, recommends a certain moderation to the ardent enthusiasts of political economy.[71] He notes with satisfaction the pacifist tendencies which have become visible in contemporary industrial civilization; but he does not admit that free trade has the power of bringing about a lasting peace. Such an admission would be chimerical, for peoples are far from acting exclusively according to what may be considered their material interest. The risk of war being ever present, Chevalier recognizes "the advisability of continuing to cultivate the military arts in the very interest of peace."[72] He does not deny the possibility of certain military reforms favorable to peace, but he stresses their limited character.

Like all free traders, Bastiat aspires to a pacifist revolu-solution of the problem of war exceeds the limits of economic science. The latter may contribute to it in a certain measure, but nothing more. He also thinks, though rather vaguely, to be sure, that future evolution will tend to make wars more and more rare. But he nowhere asserts, as some of his predecessors had done, that the introduction of free trade is necessary and sufficient to produce lasting peace.

None of these three authors suggests the establishment of some international organization provided with coercive power to ensure peace. The only liberal economist of the nineteenth century who admits the possibility of setting up such an organization and who seriously discusses it, is, so far as we know, Molinari.

[71] ". . . l'économie politique ne possède ni l'omnipotence, ni l'omniscience. Il semble de mode aujourd'hui de réclamer d'elle des actes audessus de ses forces et de lui poser des problèmes dont elle n'a pas la solution . . ." ". . . il convient que l'économie politique, à bout d'expédients, renvoie à plus puissant qu'elle, aux seules autorités compétentes, à la morale, à la philosophie, à la religion." Chevalier, *Cours*, vol. II (ed. 1844), p. 453.

[72] *Cours*, 2nd ed., vol. I, p. 123.

VII. MOLINARI

FEW economists have devoted so much attention to the problem of war as Gustave de Molinari.[1] This question was of great interest to him throughout his career. In his *Etudes économiques* (1846, p. 25), his first publication, he already proclaims the thesis which he will defend untiringly during his entire life: "War, in ceasing to be the safeguard of civilization, has ceased to have a *raison d'être.*" His articles in the *Dictionnaire de l'économie politique* (1852-1854), his study on the Abbé de Saint-Pierre (1857), his *Projet d'Association pour l'établissement d'une Ligue des neutres* (first published in the London *Times* of July 28, 1887), and almost all his later works, particularly his *Grandeur et décadence de la guerre* (1898), attest his keen interest in the problem.

At the age of ninety-two, Molinari could say, in the preface of his last work, *Ultima verba* (1911): "It concerns everything that has filled my life: free-trade and peace."

1. *Economic Evolution and War*

From the most remote period to our own time the essential cause of wars of conquest, of unification, of succession, of trade, and of religion, according to Molinari, has always been the same: the lure of material gain. Under its multiple forms, it is always this lure which constitutes the chief motive, if not the only one, of every conflict between nations. If this motive explains the necessity and the utility of war in the past, it also explains its general noxiousness in the present.

In the early ages of mankind the imperfection of the means of production doomed peoples to the hardest priva-

[1] Molinari (1819-1912), of Belgian origin, displayed his literary activity chiefly in France. He went to Paris toward 1840 and created for himself a prominent position in the radical press. The coup d'état of December 2, 1851, compelled him to return to Belgium, where he taught political economy at Brussels and Antwerp. Toward 1860 he went back to Paris, where he became editor-in-chief of the *Journal des Débats* and the *Journal des Économistes.* Cf. Guyot (1912); Pirou (1925), pp. 104 f.

tions. The material insufficiency in which they lingered was bound to lead to conflicts. For in that period, when man depended absolutely on the food supply offered by nature, war alone gave him a means to increase it. It could not be otherwise until he succeeded in multiplying it by his industry. In the meantime war was thus useful; it vouchsafed victory to the strongest, that is to say, to those most competent to assure the existence and advancement of mankind. It was useful also because it gave rise to considerable progress in industry, both destructive and productive.

Thus Molinari finds the essential cause of war in the natural conditions of the lower species and, originally, of man himself. All species live at the expense of one another: herbivorous and fructivorous animals feed on plants and in turn serve as food for carnivora. There is perpetual war among the lower species, for they are unable to multiply the elements necessary for their maintenance: they can only seize those which nature puts at their disposal. Plants and animals are destroyers and not producers.

Such was also the original condition of mankind. In the beginning man had to fight not only other species but, multiplying at a faster rate than did his means of subsistence, he was forced to give battle also to his fellows. However, having attained a higher degree in the scale of evolution, man, thanks to his productive capacity, has reached a point at which he is able to create, to produce the goods indispensable for him.[2]

On the other hand, civilized nations no longer being threatened, as they formerly were, with barbarian invasions, war has ceased to provide for their security. It now has to its credit only the material profits accruing to the victor from his warlike expeditions. In the early ages of civilization these profits were considerable. For conquering peoples, war was the most productive of industries. Pillage, forced labor, and tributes furnished them ample means of

[2] Molinari, *Grandeur et décadence de la guerre* (1898), pp. 11-12, 57; *Comment se résoudra la question sociale* (1896), pp. 101-103.

subsistence and more than covered the cost of their military enterprises.

"Is this the case to-day? Can the profits of war still cover its cost? The history of all wars which have occurred between civilised peoples for a number of centuries, attests that these profits have progressively decreased, while the costs have no less progressively grown, and, finally, that any war between members of the civilised community to-day costs the victorious nation more than it can possibly yield it."[3]

What are the profits which civilized nations can still derive from war: territorial annexations? indemnities or tributes? But annexations, Molinari replies, augment the wealth of the producers only in so far as they expand their markets. Now this expansion can be obtained at smaller cost by the reduction or suppression of customs barriers and the construction of new communications. As for indemnities, however high they may be, and even supposing that they are increased by an annual tribute, they do not suffice to cover the cost of war and those of an armed peace. "Every war between civilised nations thus shows a deficit, and this deficit is growing in proportion as war requires a greater production of destructive power."[4]

In the modern age war is therefore superfluous and harmful: from a lucrative it has become a money-losing business. Political economy even proves that the noxiousness of war is steadily on the increase. The disturbing effect of war is growing worse with the progress of the industry of production and destruction. It makes itself felt not only on the belligerents but also, indirectly, on neutrals.

War interrupts trade between the adversaries. It reduces their revenue and hence their purchasing power. Furthermore, its repercussions, far from stopping at the frontiers of the warring countries, affect "in their means of existence the populations of all countries in direct or indirect rela-

[3] Molinari, *Comment*, p. 126. Cf. also p. 125.
[4] *Ibid.*, p. 128.

tions with the belligerents. Thus a war which breaks out in Europe or America produces in trade a perturbation the effects of which are felt even in the most remote regions of the other continents."[5]

The thesis of the money-losing aspect of modern war was reaffirmed, after Molinari, by several economists, of whom we shall mention only a few.

The Italian liberal Gerolamo Boccardo, already influenced by the early works of Molinari, asserts that war, owing to its enormous cost and more and more murderous technique, will in the end suppress itself. "For the ancient proverb *War feeds war* we to-day substitute the maxim *War will kill war*, which signifies that when the means of killing, mining, bombarding, and ruining will have attained the apogee of perfection (and we are rapidly nearing this goal), war will become almost impossible."[6] Boccardo declares himself a partisan of the pacifist movement, which in his opinion tends to favor international harmony. He does not however consider perpetual peace feasible.[7]

An admirer of Bastiat and Molinari, Vilfredo Pareto, too, expresses the thesis of the economic uselessness of modern wars though he does so in much more moderate and circumspect terms. "Often," he says, "the surviving institutions, instead of lightening their yoke, render it heavier and heavier, as they become more useless. . . . In our time, and in many cases, the same thing probably holds true for war."[8] In his "free-trade" period he stressed the bellicose nature of protectionism, as is seen in his pamphlet *La liberté économique et les événements d'Italie* (1898). In this period he also published several antiwar articles (which M. Bousquet enumerates in the bibliographical appendix to his study on *Vilfredo Pareto*).

[5] *Ibid.*, p. 211.
[6] Boccardo, *Dizionario della Economia politica*, vol. II, p. 140.
[7] *Ibid.*, vol. III, p. 728. Cf. also his *Trattato* (ed. 1879), vol. III, pp 181-193.
[8] Pareto, *Cours d'économie politique* (1897), vol. II, pp. 44-45.

The rich documentation collected by Jean de Bloch in his well-known work on *The Future of War* (1899) also tended to prove that modern military conflicts are poor business for all belligerents. Norman Angell develops the same idea in a book bearing the significant title *The Great Illusion* (1910).

According to Yves Guyot, the continuator of Gustave de Molinari's work, war no longer is the powerful means of acquisition that it was formerly, since "the victor is bound to respect private property."[9] He thus expresses explicitly what several other writers imply when they declare that modern war "does not pay." As for the idea of some future war in which the victor would respect neither the property nor the personal liberty of the conquered, it does not seem to present itself to Guyot's mind.

2. *Prospects of Peace*

Modern military conflicts being injurious both to victors and vanquished, how is one to explain the phenomenon of war in the modern age? Molinari tries to solve the problem by posing a preliminary question: Who is at the present time interested in increasing militarism and in provoking wars? In former times, he says, war was indirectly useful to all social strata of the nation, to the poor and subject classes as well as to the rich and ruling ones, because it was the only means of assuring security from barbarian invasions.[10] But it has long since lost its usefulness for the nation as a whole and for all mankind.

In modern times "only the members of the governmental and administrative personnel and of the hierarchy of professional soldiers profit from a victorious war."[11] The former find an enlargement of their "markets" in the annexed territory (a temporary enlargement, to be sure; for this territory soon supplies its quota of candidates for administrative posts). The latter enjoy more rapid promo-

[9] *La jalousie commerciale et les relations internationales* (1911), p. 23.
[10] Molinari, *Grandeur et décadence de la guerre*, p. 140.
[11] Molinari, *Comment se résoudra*, p. 128.

tions. Nor must one forget the increases of their pay in the course of hostilities and the permanent extension of their markets produced by the aggravation of the war risk. "The lure of these profits suffices to feed the warlike passions of the class from which officials and officers are chiefly recruited."[12]

Favorable to war are only "the interests of the classes supplying the paid personnel of the armies. For these classes, from among which the ruling personnel is recruited, war is a source of profit and honor. Their means of existence are assured in time of war as in time of peace. Through a happy war, they obtain an increase in power together with an extension of markets."[13] The power of making war, which rests with "the chief and the general staff of the ruling class,"[14] is exerted in the peculiar and exclusive interest of this class.

It is thus only a very small minority which provokes wars; it alone profits from militarism, the most expensive of anachronisms. Conversely, the industrious classes bear not only the calamities of war, but also the heavy burden of armaments. Militarism leads to a conscription of capital no less harmful to economic progress than the conscription of men. Though it is particularly onerous for the workers, it is just as hard on the capitalists.[15]

In all States, whatever their constitutions, power is still in the hands of a class interested in the continuance of war and of the enormous apparatus of destruction it requires.

---

[12] *Ibid*.: "L'appât de ces profits suffit à nourrir les passions belliqueuses de la classe dans laquelle se recrutent principalement les fonctionnaires civils et militaires."

[13] Molinari, *La morale économique* (1888), p. 349: "[En faveur de la guerre n'agissent que] des intérêts des classes qui fournissent le personnel rétribué des armées, pour lequel la guerre est une source de profits et d'honneurs, au sein desquelles se recrute aussi le personnel gouvernant dont les moyens d'existence sont assurés en temps de guerre comme en temps de paix, et à qui une guerre heureuse procure une augmentation de puissance avec une extension de débouchés."

[14] Molinari, *Grandeur et décadence de la guerre*, pp. 139-140. Cf. also pp. 134-135, and Molinari, *Les problèmes du XXe siècle* (1901), pp. 299-300.

[15] Molinari, *Les problèmes du XXe siècle*, pp. 218-227.

The reason is that the multitude devoted to productive industries and interested in peace has nowhere yet the influence necessary to compel States to renounce bellicism. However, the interests of the classes favorable to peace are becoming more and more powerful and are shaping a public opinion hostile to war. Like Say before him, Molinari, sees the guarantee of a future universal and permanent peace in the more and more pronounced preponderance of these interests.

The military system of antiquity and the Middle Ages had its justification in the defense against the barbarians, a danger which no longer exists. Formerly, by encouraging man to develop the industries of destruction, war also contributed, though indirectly, to the progress of the productive industries. But at the present time, Molinari asserts, such is no longer the case. War has thus lost its usefulness and, with it, its morality. Owing to the increasing losses in life and wealth produced by wars, a greater and greater number will understand their uselessness. The notion of the immorality of war will thus become implanted in the conscience of peoples.

"This notion of the immorality of war to all appearance will propagate itself only in consequence of fresh experiences more destructive and costly than the previous ones. . . . But as soon as it will have penetrated the universal conscience, the institutions necessary to prevent war and, if needful, to punish its authors and promoters will rise and impose themselves automatically; the professions and industries which make up its personnel and which supply its material will be discredited. Then war will disappear from the civilised world as cannibalism did."[16]

The classes interested in peace will finally force their will upon the State. They will in the end compel it to give up protectionism, étatisme, and socialism, which Molinari considers indistinctively as "substitutes of militarism."[17] They will finally oblige it to establish a regime of free trade.

[16] Molinari, *La morale économique*, p. 351.
[17] Molinari, *Grandeur et décadence de la guerre*, p. 175.

However, to attain this goal, the industrious classes need more than a mere will to peace. They must make a serious effort to reach this objective because the ruling class is still able to check as it pleases any progress it deems contrary to its own interests. And it would be illusory to delude oneself with the hope that it will consent voluntarily to put the general and permanent interest of the nation above its particular and immediate interest.

"If then the masses who bear the crushing weight of the old machinery of a warlike State, wish to push through its reform, they must, first, be conscious of the evils and the burdens which this machinery inflicts upon them and know [enough] to attribute them to their real cause, and, second, must acquire a power of [public] opinion capable of overcoming all resistance. For this reason such a reform will perhaps yet be a long time in coming, but it is nevertheless inevitable, since peace is the condition necessary for the existence of the present and future societies, just as war was a prerequisite for the life of those of the past."[18]

Peace will be lasting only when the industrious classes shall come to exert on public affairs an influence commensurate with their own importance.[19] This moment is bound to arrive sooner or later, and the idea of a permanent peace is therefore not chimerical according to Molinari. "Perhaps the day is not far off when perpetual peace, considered, a century ago, as the dream of an upright man (*rêve d'un homme de bien*), will become a reality, and when war in its turn will appear only as the dream of the wicked, the Utopia of the spirit of Evil."[20]

3. *International Organization of Peace*

According to Molinari, peace might be organized in two ways:

18 Molinari, *ibid.*, pp. 206-207. Cf. also his *Questions économiques* (1906), p. 383.

19 Cf. Molinari, art. *Paix-Guerre*, p. 313.

20 Molinari, *L'Abbé de Saint-Pierre* (1857), p. 67. In the same work (pp. 56-67) Molinari examines the benefits to be derived by the peoples from the establishment of a "universal concert" [of States] for the maintenance of peace.

(1) By the formation, first in Europe, of a league of neutral States which would join its forces to those of the Dual or the Triple Alliance, in case either one of these two blocks of powers should take the initiative in breaking the peace. This would, for this very reason, make war impossible.

(2) By an association of all the powers, which would commit themselves to submit their differences to a court whose decisions would be sanctioned by a collective force superior to that of the State or States against which sentence was pronounced. To all appearance, the formation of such an association would be brought about by the intervention of a League of Neutrals.[21] The establishment of the latter should then precede the foundation of a larger association.

Molinari's *Projet d'Association pour l'établissement d'une Ligue des Neutres* (1887) may be summed up briefly. War, he says, no longer is, as it was formerly, a local evil. It affects the interests of neutrals almost as much as those of the belligerents. In a period when, in spite of all barriers, trade has rendered the interests of nations more and more solidary, war has become a general evil. The neutrals have therefore the right to prevent its outbreak. Since a belligerent, by exercising the ancient right of war, inflicts on them damages which no indemnity is sufficient to cover, they may stop him from exercising this right by invoking the legitimate interest of their self-preservation. They had but a feeble interest in preventing war so long as it caused them only insignificant damage. This motive has however become more powerful since war can no longer be carried on without imperiling the interests of an ever growing portion of the neutral populations.

To take the initiative in the founding of an international peace organization should be the task of the nations to whom war may cause the greatest amount of injury, either by interfering with their economic interests (as in the case

[21] *Grandeur et décadence de la guerre*, pp. 196-197.

of England, the inaugurator of the free-trade policy) or by threatening their political independence (as in the case of the small continental States: Holland, Belgium, Switzerland, and Denmark, whose freedom is constantly menaced during the great continental wars).

Supposing, as does Molinari, that England associates herself with these small States to form a League of Neutrals, the military strength of the five States mentioned, amounting, in time of peace, to about 450,000 soldiers, might, in time of war, be increased to about 1,100,000. This army would be joined by the most powerful navy in existence. The League would also have at its disposal the financial resources of the nation enjoying the finest credit in the world. If a conflict were to come about between two continental great powers—Germany, France, Austria, or Russia—it is certain that the League, joining its forces to those of the State threatened with aggression, would assure its victory. "And would not the intervention of a pacifying power disposing of a force equal, if not superior, to the greatest military force of the continent and morally supported by universal opinion, cure the most warlike States of the temptation to disturb the peace of the world?"[22]

But if it were once felt that no State, however powerful, could henceforth trouble peace without facing a force superior to its own, there would then be produced in Europe the same phenomenon which occurred, at the end of the Middle Ages, within the States: the sovereign having become strong enough to compel the feudal lords to maintain peace, the most powerful and the most ambitious chiefs laid down their arms after finding out to their cost that they no longer could provoke military conflicts without incurring severe punishment. Similarly, the States which are now the most aggressive would finally disarm, if they were always to encounter armaments stronger than their own. "To guarantee the peace among civilized peoples and thus promote disarmament by making armies useless, such would be the aim of the institution of the League of Neutrals."[23]

[22] Molinari, *Projet d'Association*, p. 437.   [23] *Ibid.*, p. 438.

The governments will not of their own accord take the initiative in establishing such a League. Only the pressure of public opinion can induce them to do so. "That is why," notes Molinari, "we appeal to public opinion and why we found the *Association to establish a League of Neutrals.* That Association will have for special and limited aim to carry on, by publications and public meetings, an agitation, in England, Holland, Belgium, Switzerland, and Denmark, to exert on their governments pressure sufficiently strong to decide them to establish the League, which will be left open to other nations who wish to join. That end attained, the Association will be dissolved, as its elder sister, the Free-Trade League, whose work of peace and liberty it is intended to complete, was dissolved after the abolition of the Corn Laws."[24]

Such was the project formulated by Molinari in 1870. It found no echo. And how could any other result have been expected? Neither the English people nor the small neutral nations felt any call to take upon themselves the duty of a guardian of the peace. England did not think it her mission to suppress war, which constituted for her, as much as for all other powers, an important political instrument. As for the neutrals, their most ardent desire was to keep, as much as possible, out of any international conflict and to abstain from all intervention in the affairs of the great powers. English policies did not agree with those of the neutral States, and the interests of the latter were not identical either. Each of them was pursuing its own policy.

Besides, if the League of Neutrals had been formed, its power would have been too limited to prevent war. And had it had at its disposal a sufficiently strong force, it still would not have been able to assure a lasting peace to the world, for it would have been merely a sort of alliance. But every alliance, whatever its nature, is more or less fragile and susceptible of being dissolved at any moment. Molinari himself was the last to have any illusions on the practical

[24] *Ibid.*

value of his project. In 1888, for instance, he wrote: "Admitting that the classes interested in the maintenance of peace were aware of their power of public opinion [*puissance d'opinion*] and had the firm will to use it, they would find, in the formation of a League of Neutrals, an effective tool for pacification and disarmament. That is what we wished to point out in formulating this project, fully realizing that we had no chance to carry it out in the present state of things."[25]

Still, whatever the difficulties in the way of creating an international peace organization, they will be overcome, even if only in the distant future. According to its promoter, the League of Neutrals is only an intellectual construction which States might seize upon in order to carry into effect universal peace. But they may also follow other courses still open. In particular, Molinari thinks of the establishment of "international courts the enforcement of whose verdicts will be undertaken by the collective power."[26]

What motives will induce the States to create such an organization of collective security? The sufferings flowing from a new world war, replies our author. "If one examines and compares the power of the class immediately interested in the maintenance of a state of war and in the costly apparatus required by it, with the power of classes far more numerous but politically less influential, which are interested in the preservation of peace and in disarmament, one remains unfortunately convinced that only as a result of the frightful disasters of a new and great war will the peaceful interests be able to gain the upper hand and to demand from the governments the creation of an organism for peace."[27]

Such is, in brief, the theory of "the greatness and the decline of wars." The reader has doubtless noticed its re-

[25] *Ibid.*, p. 431.
[26] Molinari, *Comment se résoudra la question sociale*, p. 298.
[27] Molinari, *Grandeur et décadence de la guerre*, pp. 198-199.

semblance to Say's conceptions. In fact, Molinari borrows the chief elements of his theory from Say as well as from Saint-Simon and Comte.[28]

Molinari sees in war a factor which was necessary, useful, and moral in the past, but which is superfluous, harmful, and immoral at the present time. Such a conception, in spite of all the attraction derived from its very simplicity, is not very satisfactory from the sociological point of view.[29] Though it is not our task to criticize it from that angle, we should like to observe that it lacks historical justification. It is not exact to assume, as does Molinari, that down to the modern age war was the only or the chief means of increasing wealth, and that it was therefore necessary and useful. There doubtless were, both in antiquity and in the Middle Ages, "useful" wars as well as "useless" ones. From the fact that, in that epoch, wars were waged against the barbarians, Molinari concludes that war in general was useful to the whole of civilized society (and even to its subject classes). He proceeds as if *all* wars were directed against savages only. But such was not the case: did this epoch not witness a large number of wars carried on among civilized countries? How can one then accept Molinari's thesis?

He also does violence to the facts when he affirms that war no longer contributes even indirectly to industrial progress. He is no less arbitrary when he pretends that war was moral so long as it was useful and that, by ceasing to be useful, it becomes immoral. The utilitarian point of view alone suffices neither to establish nor to explain morality in general or the morality of war in particular.

All these observations are, however, of minor importance from the standpoint of the conclusion reached by Molinari: the noxiousness of modern wars. Admitting, as he does tacitly, that belligerents respect the right of property and the lives of the civilian populations, one does find that the

<hr/>

28 On Saint-Simon, cf. below, chap. xii, sect. i. Cf. A. Comte, *Cours de philosophie positive* (1830-1842), vols. v and vi; *Système de politique positive* (1851-1854), vol. iii, chap. i, pp. 56-67.

29 Cf. Lagorgette, *Le rôle de la guerre* (1906), pp. 490-512.

great wars in general do not seem to pay. In this one may agree with Molinari, even if one does not admit the validity of his theory of the greatness and decline of war. But it is useful to add that, when a belligerent does not respect the elementary laws of modern civilization, he can derive profit from a victorious war.

In his analysis of modern economic evolution and especially in his perspective of future peace, Molinari is influenced by Jean-Baptiste Say and his historical economism. Like him, he founds this perspective on the interests of the industrious classes. We do not wish to repeat here what has already been said, in the chapter devoted to Say, on the incongruity of this "industrialist" interpretation of the world. But it is important to us to note that in one essential point Molinari's conception diverges from Say's. The latter sets his hope on the spontaneous evolution of international relations toward peace. He does not deem it necessary, then, to organize for peace. Such, however, is not Molinari's point of view.

True enough, the latter, like all liberals, cannot imagine a lasting peace without free trade. War, which in his opinion is only a form of destructive rivalry, is certain to disappear "to make room for a higher form of competition: productive or industrial competition."[30] If war is then envisaged as a means of acquisition, it should be replaced, according to Molinari, by a system of commercial freedom. Still, though he sees in free trade one of the conditions indispensable for the realization of peace, he does not regard it as a factor which by itself is susceptible of suppressing war. War, he assures us (contrary to Say), could be abolished only by an international peace organization provided with coercive force sufficiently strong to crush any eventual aggressor.

On this point Molinari also departs from the program of the "societies of the friends of peace" of his time. The latter limited themselves indeed to demanding the interven-

[30] Molinari, *Esquisse de la société future* (1899), p. 23.

tion of the moral force of public opinion and recourse to arbitration to prevent war. Molinari does not believe moral force sufficient to establish peace between States any more than it suffices to keep the peace between individuals. He is of opinion that, to be obeyed, justice must be backed by force.

Persuaded though he is of the necessity of organizing for peace, he is opposed to a limitation of national sovereignty. An international peace organization, he thinks, should be composed of independent and sovereign States.

"The autonomy of nations," says Molinari, "implies neither isolation nor hostility. Nations are interested in unhampered communications among themselves in order to grow in wealth and power; they are even more interested in living in peace with one another."[31]

From this he concludes that the division of mankind into sovereign States does not necessarily lead to war. The political unification of the world does not therefore seem indispensable to him for the maintenance of universal peace. Furthermore, he thinks, this unification is not feasible. And even if it were he would not desire it, for he does not consider it economically advantageous. "It would certainly be a dream, and even an anti-economic dream, to wish to unify the government of nations by establishing a universal monarchy or republic."[32]

The division of the world into sovereign States, Molinari asserts, is essentially economic. Why?

To begin with, he observes, it is so because, if mankind formed only one political unit, the spirit of emulation, deprived of the stimulus of the national point of honor, would make itself felt to a lesser degree. Secondly, the political unification of mankind would have another even more serious inconvenience: the mistakes committed by the government, whose authority would extend over the entire

[31] Molinari, art., *Nations*, p. 260.
[32] Molinari, *Économie de l'histoire* (1908), p. 243. "But," he adds, "this unification which between governments would be neither practicable nor desirable, is coming to pass between nations." (*Ibid.*) •

globe, would have a much greater effect than they have under present conditions. The injury resulting from the application of an unwise measure taken by some national government remains to a certain extent localized. But if, on the contrary, all mankind should be subjected to a uniform law, this harm would be likely to become universal.[33]

Molinari's arguments would be serious if they were more convincing. But they do not quite stand up under examination. For, comparing on the one hand the debt owed by civilization to the purely national stimulus, and on the other hand the loss inflicted on mankind by the prevalence of the national viewpoint in political and economic life, it is very doubtful whether the balance would incline in favor of the national thesis. Furthermore, even in a world State the national[34] point of honor would not disappear completely. It might even conceivably take a new lease on life.

The danger to which Molinari calls attention and which would result from the blunders committed by a world State is undoubtedly serious. One may wonder, however, if it would not be largely compensated for by the advantages to be derived by mankind from the peace which this organization would secure. Why should this danger be more considerable than the injury produced by the present situation, in which a single State can often impose war upon the entire world?

Molinari admits that the establishment of a lasting peace could not be the result of the action of spontaneous forces. He realizes that peace needs an international organization provided with a coercive force. But he denies that, to create such an organization, the States must more or less renounce their sovereignty. Opposed as he is to economic nationalism, he still thinks too much in national terms to be able to admit the necessity of a limitation of national sovereignty for the purpose of establishing peace.

[33] Molinari, art., *Nations*, pp. 259-260.
[34] In the ethnical sense of the term.

BOOK TWO. The Protectionists

HAVING considered the chief liberals of the nineteenth century, let us now study the best known representatives of protectionism.

Protectionism is no less universally diffused than liberalism. It has partisans everywhere. Nor is it of recent date, for its origins go back to mercantilism. But in the nineteenth century it found an able advocate in Friedrich List, who gave it a new theoretical foundation. No other economist has so much contributed to its diffusion as the author of the *National System of Political Economy*. It goes without saying that the economic and political evolution in Germany and other continental European countries was favorable to the reception of protectionist ideas. Otherwise their spread would never have assumed such dimensions.

After List it was mainly the German historical school which propagated protectionism most systematically. It conceives protectionism not as a temporary means but as a permanent system of national economic life. It demands the application of this system in favor of both industry and agriculture. It justifies protectionist measures by the necessities imposed on nations by their history. Like List, it defends protectionism for reasons of national interest, but unlike him, it rejects completely the cosmopolitan varnish which adorns his work.

In devoting, then, the larger part of this book to German economists, we do not do so in ignorance of the existence of protectionists outside Germany or any desire on our part tendentiously to divide the economic schools according to their national origins. We do so simply because,

131

while liberalism has found its most important representatives in England and France, protectionism found its own chiefly in Germany. And since the advocates of protectionism outside Germany develop arguments which are essentially identical with those formulated either by List or by the historical school, it does not appear useful to study them here in detail. We thus devote but little space to economists such as Charles Brook Dupont-White, Henry Charles Carey, and Simon Nelson Patten, and barely mention Paul Cauwès.

The two opening chapters of the present book are given over to List, the founder of the national system of political economy. In the first we set forth his criticism of the liberal school, while in the second we analyze the constructive part of his system: protectionism conceived as a stage in the progress toward universal peace, the theory of productive forces, and the program of national expansion. We then point out some resemblances between Fichte, Dupont-White, Patten, and List, and we examine, finally, the role of nationalism and internationalism in the ensemble of List's work.

The third chapter is devoted to a survey of the German historical school. We propose to study those of its representatives who have been most interested in war: Wilhelm Roscher, Karl Knies, Lorenz von Stein, Albert Schäffle, and Gustav Schmoller.[1] The former two discuss the usefulness of war and standing armies. Stein is concerned with the economic value of the army. Schäffle engages in polemics against the partisans of military disarmament, which in his view is economic nonsense. Schmoller defends the warlike spirit.

In the last chapter of Book Two we shall study some representatives of the historical method outside Germany: Émile Levasseur, Thomas Edward Cliffe Leslie, James Edwin Thorold Rogers, Émile de Laveleye, and William Cunningham. Levasseur inveighs against the armaments

[1] Roscher and Knies, with Hildebrand, were the founders of the German historical school. Schmoller was the head of the "newer historical school."

race in Europe. Leslie poses the question as to whether peace really constitutes "the question of the age." Rogers proposes a "system of international councils." Laveleye develops a program of international collaboration preparatory to peace. Cunningham, finally, tries to determine whether the economic basis of peace is "cosmopolitan or international."

VIII. LIST

THE factor of war determines the entire thought of Friedrich List.[1] One might doubtless observe that in the last analysis his doctrine is shaped by the idea of nationality. But, since in his mind the existence of the nation is closely linked with a continuous struggle among peoples, for which every one of them must always be ready, it is none the less true and sufficient for our purpose to say that the factor of war governs and molds his conceptions. One may even add that no other great economist of the nineteenth century was as much under its influence as List.

The writings of the German economist are filled with observations on war. His capital work, *Das nationale System der politischen Oekonomie* (1841) shall be considered above all. A manuscript of List's, *Le système naturel d'économie politique*, which remained unpublished until 1927, is also of considerable interest. Among his other publications important for our study, mention should be made of his *Outlines of American Political Economy* (1827), his *Idées sur les réformes économiques, commerciales et financières, applicables à la France* (1831), and his *L'économie politique devant le tribunal de l'histoire* (1839).

It is difficult, if not impossible, to determine the authors

[1] First a simple municipal employee, List (1789-1846), a native of Württemberg, became professor of political economy at the University of Tübingen (1817). He had to resign his post (1819) for having taken part in the movement favoring the abolition of inland duties in Germany. He was expelled from the Württemberg diet for demanding liberal reforms (1821). Sentenced to ten months' imprisonment in a fortress, he fled to France (1822). Having returned to Württemberg, in 1824, he was imprisoned. After six months he was released on promising to emigrate to America (1825). After acquiring a fair fortune in the United States, he returned to Germany (1832), where he was American consul in Leipzig. He led an active propaganda in favor of the *Zollverein* and the establishment of a railway net in Germany. In his lifetime he failed to win recognition. Ruined materially, discouraged, and ill, he committed suicide. Cf. Lenz (1936); Bouvier-Ajam (1938). Among the more recent publications on List cf. Earle (1943), pp. 139-154, to which we have supplied some material.

who have unquestionably inspired the work of the founder of the national system. List himself frequently quotes, and with words of praise, two Frenchmen, Chaptal (1756-1832), a chemist of repute but known also for his economic works, and Charles Dupin (1784-1873), mathematician and economist. Their influence on List is definitely established. That of Alexander Hamilton (1757-1804) seems to be very probable but cannot be proved. That of Ferrier (1777-1861), a French neo-mercantilist, and of Raymond (1786-1849), an American protectionist, is not certain either.

However this may be, a study of List's literary sources would go beyond the scope of this book. We refer the reader interested in this subject to the excellent introduction to the fourth volume of List's *Works* published under the auspices of the "Friedrich List Gesellschaft." Let us say. in passing that of all the critical editions of great economists that of List is the best, a fact which obviously facilitates the study of this rather prolific writer.

1. The Two Economic Sciences

In the view of liberalism, economic science is not "national." It is cosmopolitan: it disregards political frontiers. Turgot best summed up this fundamental concept: "Whoever fails to forget that there are political States separated from one another and diversely constituted, will never treat well any question of political economy."[2]

In this connection it may be interesting to recall Say's views on this subject. To the question as to whether the economy of nations is the same as that of private individuals, he replies in the affirmative: "Just as it would be folly to believe that there can be two different types of arithmetic, one for individuals, the other for nations, so it is unreasonable to imagine that there can be two sciences of political economy."[3]

In other words, the liberal school proceeds as if man-

[2] Turgot, *Œuvres*, vol. III, p. 421. (Lettre à Mlle de Lespinasse du 26 janvier 1770.)
[3] Say, *Catéchisme d'économie politique*, p. 117.

kind were not divided into sovereign political units. It disregards the national factor, assuming that in principle the existence of States in no way modifies the economic laws. In its view, the concordance of the economic interests of nations is manifest: it flows from the natural order of things.

List is the most determined adversary of this cosmopolitan concept of economic liberalism. The title of his chief work, *The National System of Political Economy*, suffices to show the profound abyss separating him from the liberal school.

In his opinion, the fundamental error of the liberals is that of having confounded *cosmopolitical* and *political* economy. While the former tries to find out "how the entire human race may attain prosperity," the latter "limits its teaching to the inquiry how a given nation can obtain (under the existing conditions of the world) prosperity, civilization, and power, by means of agriculture, industry, and commerce."[4]

In List's thought this distinction between *two* political economies is of great importance. Neither Quesnay nor Smith nor even Say would have understood it. List consequently considers their work confusing and charges them with having rendered impossible all truly scientific research in the field they explore. Quesnay was the first to extend his investigations to mankind as a whole without taking into account the national factor. Smith proceeds similarly and endeavors to establish the cosmopolitan character of the free-trade system. He does not deal with political economy, that is, with the policy which each separate nation has to follow in order to further its economic development. He entitles his work *An Inquiry into the Nature and Causes of the Wealth of Nations*, but he does not discuss what the title suggests. He devotes part of his work to the

[4] List, *Das nationale System der politischen Oekonomie*, chap. xi, p. 161. [TRANSLATOR'S NOTE: We wish to acknowledge our indebtedness to the very good English translation of List's *magnum opus*, the work of Mr. Sampson S. Lloyd. The general excellence of this work notwithstanding, we have occasionally ventured to modify the text.]

various systems of political economy but only for the purpose of demonstrating their groundlessness and of proving that political or national economy should give way to universal economy.

"Although here and there he speaks of war, this only occurs incidentally. The idea of a perpetual state of peace forms the foundation of all his arguments."[5]

Jean-Baptiste Say follows in the footsteps of his predecessors. By giving his *cosmopolitical* economy the name of *political* economy he dispenses with an account of an economy of *nations*. This confusion of words produced a serious confusion of ideas. According to List, all later writers have fallen into the same error.

What modifications does List propose to make to economic science? His intention is not to reject the theory of universal or world-wide economy such as it had been created by the liberals. But he thinks that political or national economy, too, should be built up scientifically.

"To remain true to the laws of logic and of the nature of things, it is necessary to oppose social economy to private economy and to distinguish in the former political or national economy which, emanating from the idea and nature of nationality, teaches how a given nation, in the present state of the world and with due regard to its own peculiar national circumstances, can maintain and improve its economic conditions, and cosmopolitical or world economy, which proceeds from the assumption that all nations of the globe form but one single society living in permanent peace."[6]

2. *Cosmopolitical Economy*

The greater the number and wealth of those with whom the individual has free intercourse, the vaster the area open to his activity, the easier it will be for him to improve his condition. This is as true for nations as it is for individuals.

[5] *Ibid.*, p. 162. Such an interpretation of Smith is obviously erroneous. Cf. Silberner (1939), pp. 247-256.
[6] List, *Das nationale System*, p. 164.

Let us imagine an association of all the peoples in the world, and even the most vivid fancy would not be able to conceive the well-being that would result for mankind. "If, as the [liberal] school requires, we assume a universal union or confederation of all nations as the guarantee of an everlasting peace, the principle of international free trade seems to be perfectly justified."[7]

The idea of a world federation and permanent peace is an undeniable imperative both of reason and of religion. If duels between individuals are contrary to reason, how much more must armed conflicts between nations be similarly condemned? Social economy draws from the history of civilization irrefutable arguments in favor of an association of all men under a regime of law. Wherever individuals live in a state of war, their well-being is at its lowest. It increases in the same measure as human associations grow from small agglomerations of families, into cities and federations of cities, then into unions of entire countries, and finally into unions of several States under one and the same system of law.

"If the nature of things has been powerful enough to extend unification [which commenced with the family] over hundreds of millions, we ought to consider that nature is also strong enough to accomplish the unification of all nations. Since the human mind has been capable of understanding the advantages of these large unifications, we ought to assume it capable also of understanding the advantages of a total unification of all mankind."[8]

The progress achieved in the sciences, the arts, in industry, in communications, and in social organization is bringing peoples closer together. Industrial progress even goes so far as to render international armed conflict ever more difficult. "The more that industry advances, and uniformly extends over the countries of the earth, the smaller will be the possibility of wars. Two nations equally well developed in industry would mutually inflict on one an-

[7] *Ibid.*, p. 164.   [8] *Ibid.*, p. 165.

other more injury in one week than they would be able to repair in a whole generation."[9]

International collaboration, too, has made remarkable progress and is taking the place, however slowly, of the former military rivalry. List even notices signs presaging a new organization of the peoples of Europe.

"In the congresses of the great powers Europe already possesses the embryo of a future congress of nations. The endeavors to settle differences by protocol are clearly already prevailing over those which obtain justice by force of arms. A clearer insight into the nature of wealth and industry has led the wiser heads of all civilized nations to the conviction that the civilizing of barbarous and semi-barbarous nations, or of those whose culture is retrograding, as well as the foundation of colonies, offer to civilized nations a field for the development of their productive powers which promises them much richer and safer fruits than mutual hostilities by wars or restrictions on trade."[10]

The pacifism of the liberal school is therefore well founded. Science must admit that human welfare cannot reach its highest degree without a peaceful collaboration of nations. But the liberals have failed to take into account the nature of nationalities and their particular conditions, and to reconcile national interests with the idea of a universal union and permanent peace. *"The [liberal] school has assumed as actually existing a state of things which has yet to come into being.* It assumes the existence of a universal union and a state of perpetual peace, and deduces therefrom the great benefits of free trade. In this manner it confounds effects with causes."[11]

It forgets among other things that it is not commercial union which precedes the political union of nations but, on the contrary, that the latter paves the way to the former. Commercial union is thus derived from political union,

---

[9] *Ibid.*, p. 166. [10] *Ibid.*

[11] *Ibid.*, p. 167. This argument was resumed by Cauwès (*Cours*, sects. 82, 696, 710), a French protectionist inspired by List.

and not vice versa, and it would be erroneous to try to reverse this order of things.[12]

The liberal doctrine cannot, at the present time, be universally applied because hostilities among peoples have not yet ceased. The peoples of the world do not yet form a universal republic. The law of nations is as yet only the embryo of a legislative state to come. No doubt, reason orders (and their own interest advises) nations to give up their natural jealousies. The former tells them that war is no less stupid than it is brutal; the latter teaches them that eternal peace and freedom of trade would raise all peoples to the highest degree of prosperity. This notwithstanding, the world is still far from attaining international security. "Up to now only few individuals even among the most enlightened nations have understood the necessity and the usefulness of such a condition. The political and social status even of the most enlightened nations is not yet sufficiently advanced for such a reform. Besides, the civilized and cultured nations could not renounce armed protection and war so long as there are powers seeking, instead of the prosperity of mankind, the conquest and subjection of other countries and other nations."[13]

Such being the case at present and for a long time to come, a nation cannot afford to disregard the possibility of war and must prepare for it. But it will never be well prepared for it without a powerful industry whose development requires intelligent protection. It is war and the risk of war which impose a protectionist policy upon a nation. It is therefore from national necessity, and not because of an aversion for peace, that List thinks himself obliged to side with protectionism.

In this he differs from the "romantic school," whose two chief representatives, Adam Heinrich Müller (1779-1829) and Carl Ludwig von Haller (1768-1854) glorify war for its

12 *Das nationale System*, p. 167.
13 List, *Système naturel*, p. 182. Cf. pp. 178, 180.

own sake.[14] Such is not the case with List whose work contains no apology of war.

He does not blame the liberals in principle for their internationalism, for he, too, considers "nationality only as a stage on the road to cosmopolitanism."[15]

"We, too," he says, "are cosmopolites, except that our cosmopolitanism rests on a solid basis, on nationality. We, too, arrive at a point at which the free-trade system is more advantageous to a nation than a system of restrictions; but we arrive there by quite a different route than Smith and Say. We are citizens of a State before being citizens of the world. Our efforts and faculties are devoted to the civilization, the prosperity, the glory, and the security of our nation. We strive for the same goal, in regard to humanity; but its welfare must be compatible with that of the nation, and the latter must not suffer in order to hasten the prosperity of the former."[16]

In defending protectionism List, of course, believes he does so in the name of free trade. In demanding the military strengthening of the nation, he does so in the name of pacifism.

"Though partisans of the free-trade theories," he declares, "we believe in the necessity of a wise protection for national industry; cosmopolites in principle and filled with faith in the utopia of eternal peace, nevertheless, we cannot persuade ourselves that, in the present condition of the globe, a nation acts prudently by dismantling its fortresses and by neglecting all its means of defense."[17]

Et la patrie et l'humanité, such is List's motto. His system of national economy, he thinks, is destined to conciliate the interests of the nation with those of mankind.

---

[14] Müller (1809), vol. I, pp. 94-124; vol. III, pp. 271-272; Haller (1821), vol. III, chap. xlix. Conversely, Fr. von Gentz (1797, pp. 17-18), another "romantic," sees war only as a necessary evil to be avoided as much as possible: "Es giebt keinen *positiven* Vortheil, der nicht durch einen Krieg viel zu theuer erkauft würde." (*Ibid.,* p. 17.)

[15] List, *Système naturel,* p. 538.

[16] *Ibid.,* p. 396.

[17] List, *Idées sur les réformes économiques,* p. 72.

3. *National Economy*

In the matter of international trade, political economy must draw its lessons from experience and, considering the present interests of the nation, must take into account the requirements of the future and of mankind as a whole. It thus leans on history, on politics, and on philosophy.

History teaches the necessity of certain protectionist measures for States desirous of attaining a superior degree of power and of material and intellectual progress. In the interest of each nation politics demands guarantees for its independence and security.

"In the interest of the future and of mankind as a whole, philosophy demands: an ever increasing rapprochement of nations, the avoidance of wars so far as possible, the establishment and development of an international state of law (*Rechtszustand*), transition from what is now called law of nations to a federal law, freedom of international intercourse, both intellectual and material, and, finally, a union of all nations under one and the same system of law—the universal union."[18]

According to List, both practice and theory had been thus far too narrow and too unilateral. Practice, in other words, the mercantile system, attributes an absolute character to protectionism, which is useful and necessary only for certain nations and only in certain periods of their evolution. Mercantilism fails to see that protection is only a means, while liberty is the end. Considering only the nation and the present time, and never mankind and the future, it is exclusively political and national; it lacks philosophic perspective and cosmopolitan tendency.

The liberal doctrine falls into the opposite extreme. "The prevailing theory . . . as dreamt by Quesnay and elaborated by Adam Smith, has in view exclusively the cosmopolitan demands of the future, nay, those of the *most distant* future. It considers the universal union and absolute freedom of international trade, a cosmopolitan idea

[18] *Das nationale System*, Einleitung, p. 41.

which at present is perhaps realisable only after centuries, as realisable even now. Failing to understand the needs of the present and the nature of nationality, it ignores even the existence of the nation and hence the principle of the *education of the nation to independence (Selbständigkeit)*. With an exclusively cosmopolitan orientation it everywhere considers only mankind as a whole, the welfare of the entire species and nowhere the nation and its welfare; it despises politics and declares experience and practice a mere contemptible routine."[19]

This cosmopolitanism renders Smith's doctrine as chimerical as that of the Abbé de Saint-Pierre. This is why politics does not and cannot take its cue from the teachings of the liberal school. The utopianism of the liberals is responsible for the abyss separating the economic policies of States from economic theory. How could a statesman act in conformity with Smith's principles?

Protectionism is one of the forms of war, and the latter is nothing but a duel between nations. One may doubtless condemn war, as one condemns duels, and admit its unreason and immorality. It is permissible to consider it "a postulate of reason, that nations should settle their differences by law, as now the United States do among themselves."[20] But what would one say, List asks, of a minister of war who, a partisan of the Quakers, should refuse to construct fortresses, to train soldiers, and to found military academies, because humanity would be happier if there were no wars? Yet such a course would not be more unreasonable than that of Smith's disciples who, in the imperfect condition of the present-day world, forsake the immediate interests of their nations because in a more perfect but completely imaginary state of the human race freedom of trade would be more advantageous to mankind.[21]

The liberals overlook that in *political* economy there is

[19] *Ibid.*, p. 42.
[20] List, *Outlines of American Political Economy*, p. 102.
[21] *Ibid.* Cf. also *Das nationale System*, p. 215; *Briefe* (1819), p. 575; *Dr. Bowring* (1841), p. 191.

as much politics as there is economics. They forget that political economy must not be confused with cosmopolitical economy. Politics being essentially national, political economy is identical with national economy. While private and cosmopolitical economy deals exclusively with wealth, political economy has for its object of study national power as well as national wealth, two factors which are interdependent. Indeed, "national wealth is increased and secured by national power, as national power is increased and secured by national wealth."[22] Of these two factors, List thinks, "power is of more importance than wealth because a nation, by means of power, is enabled not only to open up new productive sources but to maintain itself in possession of former and of recently acquired wealth."[23]

While political economy concentrates its attention on national prosperity and power, cosmopolitical economy does not have to pay much heed to the real condition of nations. "It has for its aim only to show how freedom of trade would raise the world republic to the highest degree of prosperity and how governments, to attain this goal, have merely to suppress tariff duties and to let the individuals act and manage their affairs with complete freedom."[24]

Cosmopolitan economy ignores the division of mankind into nations and supposes the nonexistence of war. But in so doing it keeps aloof from the reality of things. It thus renders all its conclusions useless and inapplicable to practice which, obliged to follow a national goal, must take into account and prepare for international hostilities. By departing in its speculations from the facts of the real world, the liberal system has become impracticable.[25]

When trying to reconcile theory and practice, liberal economy arrives at contradictory conclusions. The concessions it makes to practice are of a nature to involve, much against its will, the admission of the protective system as a

22 List, *Outlines*, p. 105. Cf. also p. 104.
23 *Das nationale System*, chap. iv, p. 100.
24 List, *Système naturel*, p. 210.
25 *Ibid.*, p. 520.

whole. Thus Smith permits the State to protect the industries contributing to national defense.

"Now," List observes, "it is quite evident, and we undertake to prove it, that nothing contributes more strenuously to defense, that is, to the independence and power of a nation, than an evenly developed and equally vigorous agricultural and industrial force combined within the State. One sees that to admit this exception of Smith means to admit the principle of protection."[26]

List wishes to free political economy from these contradictions. According to him, it cannot ignore the existence of war and neglect all the problems resulting from it for the nation.

4. War and Industrial Development

Like struggles between individuals, wars are explosions of the savage nature in man.[27] International animosity and wars have their prime cause in man's efforts to get rid of his toil and to devolve it upon others.[28] Men wage war, among other reasons, in order to capture booty, occupy lands, and subject their former owners,[29] to maintain or acquire commercial supremacy, or to shake it off.[30]

War is particularly harmful to the country on whose soil it is waged. It inflicts injury on its agriculture and manufactures.[31] It may lead to the decay of national industry as a whole or of some of its branches.[32]

Though war is "the greatest scourge of civilized nations,"[33] it would be erroneous to regard all its economic consequences as baneful. Certain countries, England for example, have grown very rich as a result of wars waged

---

[26] List, *L'économie politique devant le tribunal de l'histoire*, pp. 101-102. Cf. also *Das nationale System*, p. 331.

[27] List, *Die Staatskunde* (1818), p. 303.

[28] List, *Arbeit* (1834), p. 41.

[29] List, *Die Ackerverfassung*, p. 421.

[30] List, *Système naturel*, p. 420; *Die Freiheit* (1839), p. 331.

[31] List, *Das nationale System*, chap. iv, p. 106.

[32] *Ibid.*, chap. xxiv, p. 310.

[33] List, *Ueber den Wert . . . einer Allianz* (1846), p. 274.

far from their national soil.[34] Even countries which carry on wars on their own soil, in certain circumstances, may derive from it a good deal of economic benefit. Such was the case, for example, with the United States whose economic development was favorably affected by the War of Independence.[35]

War exerts a destructive action on international trade. It breaks the ties which bind the agriculture of one people to the manufactures of another. The farmer no longer can sell his corn to the manufacturer of the enemy country, nor can the latter ship his goods to the foreign agriculturist. To satisfy their needs, nations must fall back on their own resources.

This is the time when the industrialist, overwhelmed by foreign competition, begins to raise his head. In the beginning he is not able to sell to the farmer of his country industrial products as cheaply as the foreign manufacturer, nor of equally good quality. But given time, he will manage it by improving his methods.

To begin with, it is true, the farmer is not compensated by the industry of his own country for the losses he suffers from the interruption of foreign trade. He does not sell as much as formerly and, besides, he must pay more for industrial goods of inferior grade. He thus loses both ways.

However, he soon sees that competition becomes more marked between the domestic manufacturers; in the long run he also makes larger sales in the domestic market owing to the development of national industry; he then realizes that, as time goes on, the establishment and progress of national industries offer him advantages vastly superior to those of foreign trade and which furthermore are exempt from pernicious interruptions resulting from war. If the latter lasts long enough, it ensures industrial progress sufficient to convince agriculture that it is in its interest to see domestic industry protected from foreign competition.

[34] List, *Die grosse Gewerbsrevolution* (1843), p. 362; *Die politisch-ökonomische Nationaleinheit* (1845-1846), pp. 476-477.
[35] List, *Das nationale System*, chap. ix, p. 141.

Such is the economic development of an advanced agricultural nation in wartime.

At the return of peace, the merchants engaged in foreign trade begin to shout *laissez faire, laissez aller.* The industrialists, on the contrary, demand that the privilege given them by the war through the exclusion of foreign competition, be continued for their benefit even after the cessation of hostilities. They prove that a restoration of free trade would ruin the national industry and render useless the sacrifices made, during the war, by both agriculturists and capitalists. In the case of a new war the agricultural nation would be obliged to make once again the same sacrifices, whereas, if it continues to grant the necessary protection to industries, the latter as time goes on become strong enough not to be apprehensive of foreign competition.

As for agriculture, it will henceforth derive large benefits from its relations with a perfected national industry which future wars will no longer be able to disturb and which, for this reason, will grow more and more. The farmers must choose between the apparent advantages of the present and the real advantages of the future. On the one hand, the present freedom of trade permits them to buy manufactured goods more cheaply. On the other hand, the future offers them an enlarged and assured domestic market. Wisdom and some patriotism advise them to decide in favor of protectionism which lays the foundations of the future prosperity and grandeur of the nation.

Such is List's point of view, developed in 1837, in his *Système naturel d'économie politique.*[36] His conclusion is that "the protective and prohibitive systems of nations are not the invention of some speculative minds, but the natural consequence of wars and enmities among nations."[37] Protective tariff duties, he asserts, must be considered as a "natural and inevitable outcome of international struggles and hostilities."[38]

In the *National System of Political Economy* (1841) we

[36] List, *Système naturel*, pp. 246-250.
[37] *Ibid.*, p. 252.   [38] *Ibid.*, p. 362.

find again the same ideas. In this work, however, List does not explain the origin of protectionism by war alone. *"Previous progress made by other nations, foreign tariff systems, and war* have compelled less advanced nations to look to themselves for the means of effecting a transition from the agricultural to the manufacturing stage and to restrict, by a customs system of their own, trade with more advanced nations striving for an industrial monopoly—so far as this trade is in their way.

"The customs system is thus not, as has been asserted, an invention of speculative minds; it is a *natural consequence of the striving of nations for guarantees of their permanency and prosperity* or predominant power."[39]

In another place, List sums up his point of view as follows: "History is there to prove that protective regulations originated either in the natural efforts of nations to attain prosperity, independence, and power, or in consequence of wars and of the hostile trade policies of predominating manufacturing nations."[40]

Between 1837 and 1841 List thus enlarged his interpretation of protectionism. Whereas in 1837 he finds the origins of the protective system in international hostilities, in 1841 he mentions another basic cause of this system: the tendency of peoples to ensure their prosperity. From the texts just cited one might conclude that, in his view, these two causes are equally important. This is undoubtedly true so far as the theoretical justification of protectionism is concerned. In the *National System* he justifies in effect the necessity of protection both by the possibility of war and by the drive of nations for their economic and cultural progress.

When it is however a question of explaining protectionism on a purely historical basis, he appears to think it has its origin in war rather than in national effort to t-tain prosperity. Two passages of his *National System* suggest this interpretation:

[39] *Das nationale System*, p. 50.   [40] *Ibid.*, chap. xv, p. 214.

"Thus history shows that restrictions are not so much the inventions of speculative minds as the natural consequences of the diversity of interests, and of the strivings of nations after independence or overpowering ascendency, and thus of national jealousy and wars, and that therefore they can cease only with the cessation of this conflict of national interests, that is to say, as the result of the union of all nations under one and the same system of law."[41]

The other text, though shorter, is all the more trenchant: "War has called into existence the modern systems of protection."[42]

The liberal school, according to List, has failed to understand this truth. It takes no account of the influence of war on the economic life of nations and on economic policy. Especially, it fails to perceive that war of necessity calls forth the prohibitive customs system.[43]

War operates upon a fairly civilized agricultural nation like a prohibitive system. Judged from this point of view, the effects of war on the national industry are most favorable.[44]

It is the design of Providence, List thinks, to improve the condition of mankind and to raise its power and faculties by an eternal strife, both moral and physical, between opinion and opinion, interest and interest, nation and nation. Though philosophers believe that perpetual peace and the union of peoples would produce the highest degree of human happiness, it is none the less true that combats between nations, pernicious to civilization though they frequently are, have often been the reason for the uplift of peoples fighting for their freedom and independence. By developing all the faculties of nations, wars have con-

[41] *Ibid.*, chap. x, p. 156.

[42] *Ibid.*, chap. xv, p. 216: "Der Krieg hat die neueren Schutzsysteme hervorgerufen."

[43] *Ibid.*, chap. xxvii, p. 329.

[44] *Ibid.*, p. 216. Chaptal (1819, vol. II, p. 37) and Raymond (1823, vol. II, pp. 91-95) had expressed, before List, a similar view. List knew and appreciated Chaptal. On the other hand, he does not quote Raymond. On the latter, cf. Neill (1897).

tributed to the advancement of the human race toward greater perfection.[45]

List is not one of those who defend useless expenses occasioned by war and the maintenance of large armies, or who claim the absolute utility of a considerable public debt. But neither does he agree with the liberal school which depicts as wholly harmful all consumption not directly reproductive, for instance, that of war.

"The equipment of armies, wars, and the debts contracted for these purposes, may, as the example of England teaches, under certain circumstances, very greatly conduce to the increase of the productive powers of a nation. Strictly speaking, material wealth may have been consumed unproductively, but this consumption may, nevertheless, stimulate manufactures to extraordinary exertions, and lead to new discoveries and improvements, and to an increase of productive powers in general. This productive power then becomes a permanent acquisition; it will increase more and more, while the expense of the war was incurred only once."[46]

It follows that war is not exclusively destructive. By contributing to the industrialization of a country, it may, from the purely economic point of view, be favorable to the nation.

"A war favoring the change of the purely agricultural State into an agricultural-manufacturing State is therefore a blessing to a nation, just as the War of Independence of the United States of North America, in spite of the enormous sacrifices it required, has become a blessing to all future generations. But a peace which throws back into a purely agricultural condition a nation fitted to develop a manufacturing power of its own, becomes a curse to it, and is incomparably more injurious to it than war."[47]

Peace is then not necessarily favorable to national economy. If it is accompanied by a simple return to the pre-

45 List, *Outlines*, pp. 130-131.
46 *Das nationale System*, chap. iv, pp. 106-107.
47 *Ibid.*, pp. 216-217.

war economic status, that is, to free trade, it may, in a country that is poorly industrialized, lead to the ruin of the new national industries which had just been created in consequence of the hostilities and isolation. The whole national manufacturing power runs a risk of being broken, the more rapidly, the more active and redoubtable foreign competition happens to be in the period immediately following the conclusion of peace. It is therefore natural that a nation should prefer to maintain the state of things which subsisted during the war, and to isolate itself, so far as possible, from competing nations, rather than to venture on free-trade experiments to the detriment of the prosperity of its citizens.[48]

[48] List, *Système naturel*, p. 368.

1. Protectionism as a Stage in the Progress toward Universal Peace

A UNIVERSAL union whereby all nations would recognize one and the same system of law and would renounce self-redress is feasible according to List. But it can be carried into effect only at some future period when many nations will have attained to a nearly equal, and high, degree of industry, of civilization, and of power. Freedom of trade can expand only through the gradual formation of this world association which is alone able to ensure to all peoples those great advantages of which politically united provinces and States today offer a shining example.

In List's opinion, the protective system is the only way to lift States less advanced in civilization to a higher level. It is therefore also the most powerful promotor of the final union of nations and of true free trade. From this point of view political economy appears as the science which, taking into account the special interests of nations, teaches how each of them may attain to this stage of economic development at which an association with other peoples of an equally high civilization, and hence freedom of commerce, will become both possible and advantageous. Yet the liberal school has failed to recognize this mission of protectionism.[1]

According to List—and this feature constitutes his originality—protectionism is a system which should lead to true free trade. He admits with the liberals that freedom of commerce is profitable to all nations. Unlike them, however, he points out that free trade presupposes the non-existence of wars and the establishment of a world federation. But the latter cannot be formed before a majority of nations has attained to approximately the same high level of civilization, wealth, and power. Now, it is just the na-

[1] List, *Das nationale System*, chap. xi, pp. 167-168.

tional system which indicates to the peoples the road they must follow to arrive at this level of social evolution. It is this system which must lead them to the supreme goal of rational politics, "the union of nations under one and the same system of law."[2]

Having passed the protectionist stage and attained a high degree of economic development, each people will have an interest in practicing free trade and in joining with others in order to establish a world federation. Conversely, the immediate introduction of freedom of commerce would prove injurious to a number of poorly industrialized nations and would not advance mankind along the road of industrial, cultural, and peaceful development.

"That under the existing conditions of the world," List says, "the result of general free trade would not be a universal republic but, on the contrary, a universal subjection of the less advanced nations to the supremacy of the predominant manufacturing, commercial, and naval power, is a conclusion for which the reasons are very strong and, in our view, irrefragable."[3]

The immediate carrying into effect of the maxim *laissez faire, laissez passer* would actually lead to a universal monopoly by England, to her supremacy, to the permanent predominance of agriculture within all other nations, and to their degradation to a state of vassalage. It would render impossible a true world federation of free nations one of whose main purposes should be to secure freedom of trade. Under contemporaneous circumstances, such a policy would then be contrary to a genuine cosmopolitanism.[4]

This tendency to justify protectionist measures by cosmopolitan considerations is quite characteristic of List and differentiates him from the traditional protectionists. To

[2] *Ibid.*, p. 406: "die Vereinigung der Nationen unter dem Rechtsgesetz."
[3] *Ibid.*, chap. xi, p. 167.
[4] List, *Wesen und Wert einer nationalen Gewerbsproduktivkraft*, pp. 360-361.

quote but one example, let us take Ferrier. He, too, fears that freedom of commerce tends to the political and economic enslavement of industrially backward nations. "Without the commercial system," he observes, "there would be in Europe only one manufacturing people. All other nations would depend on it. Their means of exchange would be reduced to the produce of their soil. They would thus lose both their industry and their fleet. They would become subject."[5] But, whereas List envisages protectionism as a means for arriving at universal peace, Ferrier thinks that "all these projects of union embracing the whole world" are chimerical.[6]

For List protectionism is an historical necessity. It is an indispensable means for the industrialization of a country, though only a temporary one, a passing necessity. The mercantilists were wrong in believing in an eternal opposition of the economic interests of peoples and in recommending, consequently, protectionism as a permanent system. List blames them for utterly ignoring the cosmopolitan principle and for not recognizing "the future union of all nations, the establishment of perpetual peace and of general freedom of trade, as the goal toward which all nations have to strive and which they should more and more approach."[7]

Nothing has injured more the freedom and welfare of peoples than the mercantilist folly which pretends to base the liberty and wealth of one nation upon the oppression and poverty of others. The mercantilist system owes its origin to this folly. It fosters, among nations which under the plan of Providence are meant to alleviate and render more pleasant each other's burdens, a war without respite for the prosperity of each to the detriment of all others. Thanks to the progress of political insight in the nineteenth century, this folly has been unmasked in all its hollowness and all its horror, and no power can now save it. One

[5] Ferrier, *Du governement* (1805), pp. 396-397.   [6] *Ibid.*, p. 15.

[7] List, *Das nationale System*, chap. xxix, pp. 349-350.

may rejoice in this, for "the world has not been created to be ruined by customs barriers."[8]

2. *The Theory of the Productive Powers*

List justifies his protectionism by the *theory of the productive powers*. He builds this theory on the obvious difference existing between wealth and its causes or, if one prefers, between wealth itself and the power producing it. A nation may be rich in exchangeable values, but if it does not develop its *productive powers* its wealth will not increase and may even diminish. On the other hand, a nation, poor but able to produce beyond its consumption, may grow in wealth.

"*The power to create wealth* is thus infinitely more important than *wealth itself*; it ensures not only the possession and the increase of what has been gained, but also the replacement of what has been lost."[9]

A nation would be wrong in taking into account only present interests and in neglecting the future. It is of more importance to it to increase its productive powers than to gain in wealth by an accumulation pure and simple of exchangeable values. It is worth a nation's trouble to develop its productive powers, even at the price of a temporary diminution of its material wealth. Nor will it hesitate to do so, although it is aware of the fact that a full yield of productive powers is possible only in the long run. "The nation must sacrifice and give up material goods in order to acquire moral or social powers; it must renounce present advantages with a view to securing future ones."[10]

The prosperity of a people does not depend upon the quantity of its wealth but upon the degree of development of its *productive powers*, by which List means both the power to create wealth *directly* and the power to increase it *indirectly*. Among these powers he counts factors as heterogeneous as manufacturing industry, the Christian

[8] List, *Briefe* (1819), p. 574. Cf. also p. 571.
[9] List, *Das nationale System*, chap. xii, p. 173.
[10] *Ibid.*, p. 183.

religion, hereditability of the throne, technical inventions, means of transport, freedom of thought, of conscience, and of the press, parliamentary government, publicity of the administration of justice, trial by jury, etc.[11] The most life-giving of these is doubtless manufacturing industry, for it develops the mental and moral powers of the nation to the highest degree. "In a country devoted to mere raw agriculture, dullness of mind, awkwardness of body, obstinate adherence to old notions, customs, methods, and processes, want of culture, of prosperity, and of liberty prevail. The spirit of striving for a steady increase in mental and bodily acquirements, of emulation, and of liberty characterize, on the contrary, a State devoted to manufactures and commerce."[12]

Manufacturing industry makes possible a better utilization of the natural resources of the country: water, wind, minerals, and fuels. It stimulates the sciences to constant research, it calls forth inventions, and contributes to the development of the net of railways and canals. It creates the need for trade and necessitates the building of a merchant marine. It is at the origin of maritime and colonial power.[13]

It also strengthens the national defense. And this political aspect of modern industry is of capital importance.

"At a time when technical and mechanical science exercise such an immense influence on the methods of warfare, when all warlike operations depend so much on the condition of the national revenue, when successful defense greatly depends on the questions whether the mass of the nation is rich or poor, intelligent or stupid, energetic or sunk in apathy; whether its sympathies are given exclusively to the fatherland or partly to foreign countries; whether it can muster many or but few defenders of the country—at such a time, more than ever before, the value

11 *Ibid.*, p. 178. 12 *Ibid.*, chap. xvii, p. 228.
13 *Ibid.*, bk. ii, chaps. xvii to xxv.

of manufactures must be estimated from a political point of view."[14]

List insists on the economic and political inferiority of mere agricultural countries as compared with nations which are both agricultural and industrial, for the following reasons. The former are always more or less dependent on those foreign nations which buy their agricultural produce and sell them their manufactured goods. They thus cannot determine the volume of their production but must wait and see how much foreigners will buy from them. On the other hand, a nation which is both agricultural and industrial produces itself large quantities of raw materials and provisions, while as a buyer it takes from agricultural countries just enough to cover its own deficiency. The latter, then, depend for their sales on the more or less abundant crops of nations which are both agricultural and industrial. What is more, they have for competitors other agricultural countries, so that a market in itself very uncertain becomes still more problematic.

"Lastly, they are exposed to the danger of being totally ruined in their trading with foreign manufacturing nations by wars, or new foreign tariff regulations, whereby they suffer the double disadvantage of finding no buyers of their surplus agricultural products, and of failing to obtain supplies of the manufactured goods which they require."[15]

It is thus not surprising that List compares a purely agricultural people to "an individual with *one* arm, who makes use of another's arm, but who cannot be sure of its use in all cases."[16] Conversely, "an agricultural-manufacturing nation is an individual who has at his disposal two arms *of his own*."[17]

It is then of great moment that every large nation should endeavor to become both agricultural and industrial, and furthermore, if possible, commercial. It can attain to this

[14] *Ibid.*, chap. xvii, p. 238. Cf. also List, *Die gegenwärtige Lage*, p. 257.
[15] *Das nationale System*, chap. xv, p. 214.
[16] *Ibid.*   [17] *Ibid.*

high "degree of culture" (or this supreme form of economic constitution) solely by a wise protection of its industry.

The protective system is justified only when its goal is the *industrial education* of the country, and not mere self-sufficiency, to which List is opposed in principle. It must therefore not be applied to a nation whose education is already completed, nor to peoples which, like those of the tropics for example, have neither the aptitudes nor the resources indispensable to industrialization. It should protect only industry, education in agriculture having been long since an accomplished fact.[18]

Industry as a productive force is of such importance to the country that it deserves being favored and protected by the State even at the price of temporary discomfort. To the objection that this industrialization might be carried out without governmental intervention, List retorts: "Quite true, experience teaches that the wind carries the seed from one region to another, and that in this way waste moorlands have been transformed into dense forests; but would it on that account be a wise policy for the forester to wait until the wind in the course of centuries effects this transformation? Would it be unwise on his part, if by sowing of waste lands he seeks to attain the same object within a few decades? History teaches us that whole nations have successfully accomplished what we see this forester do."[19]

Protectionism should aid the nation to attain to the supreme stage of its development, but it is justified only so far as it is not opposed to "the higher goal of mankind, the future world federation."[20] Just as nations should see in the prohibitive system only a means for arriving quickly at the protective system, so the latter is useful and reasonable only in so far as it favors and prepares the widest possible freedom of commerce.[21] World federation and free

18 *Ibid.*, chap. xiii, p. 198; chap. xv, p. 220; chap. xviii, p. 241.
19 *Ibid.*, chap. x, p. 153.   20 *Ibid.*, p. 50.
21 List, *Système naturel*, p. 374.

trade thus constitute for List the final goal of protectionism.

Apart from the industrial education of peoples, List
mentions still another means for bringing the nations
nearer that goal: trade agreements. Based on reciprocal advantages, they should ensure and favor the industry of
both signatory powers. To the extent that they vouchsafe
industrial prosperity, they hasten the realization of free
trade and of a world federation.

The best way to improve international economic relations would be to institute "a commercial world congress
to which all nations would send experienced, competent
and well-versed men, a congress which would have no other
mission and no other purpose than to consult and to de-
liberate on the common and mutual interests of all nations."[22]

Prior to the publication of his *National System*, in which
he is no longer interested in a commercial world congress,
List attributes much importance to such a congress. He
speaks of it for the first time in a memoir addressed, in
1820, to the congress of the German States assembled in
Vienna. "Europe," he says in this document, "will see the
meeting of a commercial congress which will again gradually loosen the fetters with which one has contrived so artificially to load oneself."[23] Fifteen years later, List, then
American consul in Leipzig, elaborated a plan for convok-
ing a commercial world congress.[24] He submitted it,
through the Department of State, to President Jackson,
but did not obtain the slightest success.

3. *The Program of National Expansion*

We have already drawn the reader's attention to several
passages in which List protests his attachment to peace. In
fact, he declares himself "a cosmopolite in principle and
filled with faith in the utopia of eternal peace."[25] This

---

[22] *Ibid.*, p. 404. Cf. also p. 402.   [23] List, *Denkschrift*, p. 546.
[24] Reproduced in Notz (1925), pp. 170-174. Cf. List, *Werke*, vol. VIII,
p. 527.
[25] List, *Idées sur les réformes économiques*, p. 72.

pacifist credo, though repeated by him more than once, is however not very convincing when confronted with his other conceptions. To seize this, it is sufficient to compare the program of territorial expansion he suggests for Germany with the pacifist superstructure he gives to the *National System.*

Let us note first that List has little sympathy for the "small" nations. From the intellectual point of view, he thinks they are inferior to the "great" nations: A nation restricted in the number of its population and in territory, especially if it has a separate language, can only possess a crippled literature and crippled institutions for promoting art and science.[26] It is even astonishing that he should have given to his doctrine the name of "national system." For only the "great" nations (which List calls "normal") are able to apply the policy recommended by him. In other words, his system is meant only for nations able to carry on a policy of expansion.

List was striving for a greater Germany and was anxious to see it become a "normal nation," that is, a nation possessing, among other things, "an extensive and well rounded territory endowed with manifold natural resources and a large population."[27] To become "normal," the German nation cannot be satisfied with the political unification of the German lands. According to List, Germany should also include other countries: Holland, Denmark, Belgium, Southeastern Europe, and Switzerland.

First: He regards Holland as a German country. By its geographical location, its commercial relations, the origins of its inhabitants, and their language it is, in his opinion, a German province. If Germany does not incorporate it, she will resemble a house whose door belongs to a stranger. So long as Holland forms a separate State, the independ-

---

26 *Das nationale System*, chap. xiv, p. 210. Cattaneo (1843, p. 190) was one of the first to point out this contempt of List for small nations. In a passage which has become famous, to which he adds, besides, no commentary, Cattaneo (1849, p. 306) sets forth an entire pacifist program: "Avremo pace vera, quando avremo li Stati Uniti d'Europa."

27 *Das nationale System*, p. 210.

ence and power of Germany will be as unreal as would have been those of France had Brittany and Normandy remained in the hands of the English.[28] Without the annexation of the Netherlands, Germany will never attain the highest degree of her economic development. In return, by incorporating them, Germany would acquire not only the mouths of the Rhine but also colonies and a powerful fleet.

It goes without saying that List prefers a peaceful incorporation of Holland into Germany to an annexation by force. He is convinced that it is in Holland's interest to join the German Confederation. But should the Dutch refuse and should they continue, as they have done in the past, to favor England commercially, he finds no fault with the exerting of economic pressure, which would be "the most effective means of inducing Holland to join the German *Zollverein*."[29]

Second: List also advocates the "admission" of Denmark "into the German nationality."[30] The *Zollverein*, he says (and in using this word he frequently thinks simply of Germany) cannot be considered a perfect institution so long as it does not extend over "the whole coast from the mouths of the Rhine to the frontiers of Poland, including Holland and Denmark."[31] Besides, Danes as well as Dutch "belong, as respects their descent and whole character, to the German nationality."[32]

Third: Belgium which, according to List, is but the fraction of a nationality, runs the danger of falling a prey to France. It is therefore of importance for Germany to forestall France at the mouths of the Rhine and the Scheldt.[33]

Fourth: German penetration should extend also to Southeastern Europe. The colonization of that part of the continent should be undertaken in full accord with Hun-

[28] *Ibid.*, chap. xxxiv, p. 404.
[29] *Ibid.*, chap. xxxvi, p. 421. The Germans (says List) should understand that it is within their power to compel Holland to join the *Zollverein. Ibid.*, p. 405.
[30] *Ibid.*, p. 211.   [31] *Ibid.*   [32] *Ibid.*
[33] List, *Unsere Fortschritte*, p. 96; *Belgien und der Zollverein*, p. 183.

gary. The union of the Hungarians with the Germans would amount to nothing less than the "formation of a powerful Germano-Magyar State in the East, washed on the one side by the Black Sea, on the other by the Adriatic, and animated by the German and Hungarian spirit."[34] "We can grow like North America, and do so soon and quickly, without sea, fleets, and colonies: we have backwoods as well as the Americans—the lands along the lower Danube and the Black Sea, the whole of Turkey, the entire South-East beyond Hungary are our *hinterland.*"[35]

Such is List's conception of the natural frontiers of Germany. To be complete, we should add that he also desires the disappearance of Switzerland as a sovereign State. By annexing Holland, Belgium, and Switzerland, Germany would be able to ensure a long peace to the European continent.[36]

List is well aware that the carrying into effect of such a program of national expansion may provoke wars. He is less interested in avoiding them than in making Germany understand that she should do whatever is necessary to be well prepared for such an eventuality. The idea of war, he says in his polemics against the London *Times*, is not foreign to the preoccupations of the partisans of a "national German commercial system." The future, he asserts, speaking in their name, will know only national wars, and it is of importance to prepare in time of peace all the material and moral forces of the nation, and to adapt the national economy to such an emergency.[37]

Except when using vague and evasive formulas, List does

[34] List, *Die Ackerverfassung*, pp. 499-500.
[35] *Ibid.*, p. 502.
[36] *Das nationale System*, chap. xxxv, p. 409. Also, according to Wagner (1871, pp. 32-33; 1870, pp. 83-84), Germany's natural frontiers include Holland and parts of Switzerland and Belgium. On the possibility of wars being caused by overpopulation, cf. Wagner, 1902, p. 83; cf. also pp. 155-156.
[37] List, *Die Times und das deutsche Schutzsystem*, 1846, pp. 693-694. We owe our knowledge of this article, which is little known and not reproduced in List's *Werke*, to Sevin (1910), pp. 217-218.

not conceive of a peaceful world. He first considered the formation of a "continental system," that is, a bloc of continental States turned against the economic and political supremacy of Great Britain. Germany was to form the vital center of this system. Subsequently, he changed his mind. Convinced that Germany would have more to gain by an alliance with England against the continent, he did not fail to formulate a project in this sense.[38] In either case he pursues the same objective, the aggrandizement of Germany.

Such was List's outlook for what lay immediately ahead. For a more distant future he foresees even more grandiose struggles: inter-continental wars. In the twentieth century, he thinks, the power of the United States will grow to such an extent that a clash between England and her former colony is bound to occur.

"Thus in the not very distant future the natural necessity which now dictates to the French and Germans the establishment of a continental alliance against British supremacy, will impose on the British the necessity of founding a European coalition against the supremacy of America. Great Britain will then be compelled to seek and to find in the leadership of the united powers of Europe protection, security, and compensation against the predominance of America, and an equivalent for her lost supremacy."[39]

A few years later List reverts to the same subject but treats it in a spirit less sympathetic to Great Britain.

There is not the slightest doubt, he asserts, that another war is necessary to make England recognize the full power of the United States. He wishes this final struggle between two world giants to be decided as quickly and as unequivocally as possible. The Americans would do well to begin at once to prepare for it, so that they may win it at one stroke and without internal convulsions.[40]

[38] Cf. List, *Ueber den Wert* (1846). Cf. also Bahr (1929).
[39] List, *Das nationale System* (1841), chap. xxxv, p. 417.
[40] List, *Die pol.-ökon. Nationaleinheit* (1845-1846), p. 493.

4. Fichte, Dupont-White, and Patten

In the part dealing with national territory, List's definition of a normal nation recalls the conception of Johann Gottlieb Fichte (1762-1814) on natural frontiers. It is therefore of some interest, perhaps, to point out this resemblance which does not seem to be wholly accidental, since in all probability List had studied Fichte.

According to the German philosopher, certain parts of the globe are by nature clearly predestined to form political units. They are separated from the rest of the earth by large rivers, seas, and impassable mountains or, in other words, by *natural frontiers*. In using this term, "one must not only think of frontiers militarily well covered and solid, but far more still, of a certain productive autonomy or self-sufficiency."[41]

In reality the political boundaries of States are not drawn according to a rational plan, but are due to blind chance. In these circumstances, States will always fight with one another and will sign peace treaties only in order to again prepare for war. The necessity of *rounding out* their territory, that is, of expanding within the limits of their natural frontiers, thus imposes itself.[42]

Unless this is done, the realization of a "closed commercial State" (we should call it today an *autarkic* one) is impossible. And since, according to Fichte, peace can be lasting only in a world divided into closed commercial States, that is, among nations which are completely isolated from one another, it follows that peoples will live in war until they establish natural frontiers to separate them.

The same fundamental idea is found in List: a nation is "normal" only when it possesses a well-rounded territory, that is, one marked by frontiers which it may regard as satisfactory from the military and economic point of view. Like Fichte,[43] List[44] realized that the drive toward "natural

[41] Fichte, *Der geschlossene Handelsstaat* (1800), p. 480.
[42] *Ibid.*, p. 481.
[43] Cf. *ibid.*, p. 502.
[44] List, *Die Times und das deutsche Schutzsystem*, pp. 693-694.

frontiers" would lead to armed conflicts. Neither one of the two was frightened by this prospect.

"It has at all times been the privilege of philosophers to deplore wars. The present author does not love them more than anyone else; but he thinks he realizes their inevitability in the present circumstances and deems it useless to complain of what is unavoidable. If war is to be abolished, it is necessary to abolish its causes. Every State must receive what it intends to obtain through war and what alone it can reasonably have in view, namely its natural frontiers. Henceforward it has no further claims on any other State, for it now possesses what it had sought. No other State has any claim on it, for it has not stepped beyond its natural frontiers and encroached upon those of another."[45]

So far Fichte. Let us now see what List has to say on this subject: "It must not be ignored that the rounding out of the national territory must be reckoned among the most important requirements of nations, that striving to attain it is legitimate, that in some cases it is indeed a justifiable reason of war."[46]

Fichte thinks that, if the world were divided into States each of which would be delimited by its natural frontiers, universal peace would be established automatically. According to List, such a state of things would not lead automatically to a pacification of the world. Mankind, divided up into "normal nations," bounded by their "natural frontiers," in his opinion is only a means to bring the culture of each to its full bloom, a prelude to the establishment of a world union, of peace, and of free trade. The economic objectives assigned by Fichte and List respectively to their "ideal" States are different: the former recommends autarky with national socialism as its aim, the latter a protectionism which is to lead to freedom of commerce. But the goals of both have this in common that they imply a program of national expansion inviting war. The fact that the ultimate

[45] Fichte, *Der geschlossene Handelsstaat*, p. 582. Cf. on this passage the commentary of Rappard (1936), pp. 16-17.
[46] List, *Das nationale System*, chap. xxxv, p. 407.

aim of their ideals is pacifist does not change their bellicose character.

Warlike tendencies appear also in the works of Dupont-White (1807-1878), a French economist and publicist whose views singularly resemble List's national system. A precursor of State socialism, Dupont-White develops ideas which might serve as a model for any system of economic nationalism. He notes that free trade is neither a condition nor a guarantee of universal peace. Friendship among peoples can dispense with commercial relations. Moreover, "in the life of nations trade does not play such an important role that, completely free and unhampered, it imposes upon them peace as a permanent and imperative need."[47] The liberals are wrong in condemning war unconditionally. "War is a scourge not in itself but only when victory falls to the Barbarian. . . . To repudiate war means considering the peoples as satisfied and progress as everywhere accomplished."[48] Standing armies and colonies are part of progress and, for a nation, a new manner of defending and extending its territory.[49]

Inspired by List, the American protectionist Patten (1852-1922) is frank to admit that the carrying out of his national economic program would give the United States such power that it could "expect to exert a commanding influence upon the development of other nations, and force them to break away from their present economic conditions and adjust themselves to a higher social state."[50]

---

[47] Dupont-White, *Le libre-échange* (1851), p. 233.

[48] *Ibid.*, pp. 233-234. Cf. also Villey (1936), pp. 617-622.

[49] Dupont-White, *L'individu et l'État* (ed. 1865), p. 63. On the other hand, Carey (1848, pp. 261, 414, 427), whose doctrine resembles greatly List's, is very much attached to peace. In his opinion, "commerce" (direct exchanges between men) is peaceful, while "trade" (exchanges carried out by professional merchants) is always bellicose. *Principles of Social Science*, vol. I, pp. 210 and 214; vol. II, p. 253.

[50] Patten, *The Economic Basis of Protection* (1890), p. 141. It goes without saying that the dominant nation would be the one to decide what that "higher social state" would be.

Commenting upon this passage, Professor Rist observes that here, as often happens, protectionism is confounded with nationalism or imperialism.[51]

In his critique of the American economist, M. Bouvier-Ajam reaches the conclusion that "economic nationalism as conceived by Patten has no other objective than to foster a conquering imperialism, absolutely opposed to List's desires.[52] But such an interpretation of List seems to us erroneous. For if Patten's imperialism is well established, List's is no less so. The latter's program of German territorial expansion attests it sufficiently.

5. *List's Nationalism and Cosmopolitanism*

List's theory of the productive powers is a serious contribution to economic science. It substitutes a dynamic conception for the former static point of view of the liberals. It shows that temporary protectionist measures, though opposed to the rigid free-trade doctrine, are none the less in the last analysis reconcilable with the *spirit* of Liberalism.

List contents himself with demanding protection for industry only, and he recommends it merely as a measure calculated to further the industrial education of the nation. Thanks to this moderation, the theory of productive powers had found adherents even among the liberals such as, for example, John Stuart Mill. Without expressly mentioning List, perhaps because he does not consider him original enough, Mill implicitly admits his point of view. "The only case," he says, "in which, on mere principles of political economy, protecting duties can be defensible, is when they are imposed temporarily (especially in a young and rising nation) in hopes of naturalizing a foreign industry, in itself perfectly suitable to the circumstances of the country."[53]

The theory of the productive powers is of considerable

51 Gide and Rist, *Histoire des doctrines économiques* (1920), p. 334.
52 Bouvier-Ajam, *Frédéric List* (1938), p. 275.
53 John Stuart Mill, *Principles*, bk. v, chap. x, sect. 1, p. 922.

interest for the economy of war. Even before List, economists admitted some exceptions to free trade in order to
strengthen the national defense. For example, Adam Smith
recognizes the cogency of measures such as the Navigation
Acts and in general all those favoring a particular branch
of industry necessary for the defense of the country.[54]
Hamilton goes further: he stresses the importance of industrialization in general for national security.[55] But List
was the first to set forth systematically a general theory of
the development of the economic and military resources of
a nation. By setting up freedom of commerce as the final
aim of his system, he gives a solid basis to the temporary
protectionist measures which he recommends as favorable
to the industrial development of the nation and to the
strengthening of its defense.

While List's theory of productive forces enriches economic science, the same cannot be said of his attempt to
give a synthesis of what he calls "cosmopolitical economy"
and "national economy." List's starting point, namely the
distinction between two economic sciences, is in itself de-
batable, for the basic economic laws are the same all over
the world, whether it is politically united or not, and it is
thus difficult to see the necessity for two economic *sciences*.
But much less sound and far more artificial seems List's
conviction of having theoretically reconciled the interests
of the nation with those of mankind as a whole.

List affirms categorically his attachment to the idea of a
world federation and peace. On the other hand, he works
out, for Germany, a program of national expansion which
is necessarily warlike. This contradiction between his cosmopolitanism and his imperialist tendencies must be obvious to anyone who attentively reads his works.

Thus an important question comes to the mind: what
role are we to attribute to List's cosmopolitanism? In his
work taken as a whole cosmopolitanism seems to us to have

[54] *Wealth of Nations*, bk. IV, chap. ii, pp. 429-431. Sismondi (*Nouveaux principes*, vol. I, p. 441; *Études*, vol. II, p. 310) also advocates the encouragement of industries necessary for the national defense.
[55] Hamilton, *Report on Manufactures* (1791), pp. 227-228.

only one function: the moral justification of protectionism. His profession of pacifist faith has only one purpose, and a highly practical one: to furnish an ethical foundation for his protective system, to justify it, even from the liberal point of view, and to try to make it as invulnerable as possible theoretically. By his pacifist and free-trade credo, he tries to reconcile, in the last analysis, the national system with the liberal doctrine which was then in vogue. In attacking the liberal school, he is convinced he has accomplished a duty toward his German fatherland.[56]

Even on the supposition that in his youth List sincerely believed in a world federation—which is problematical—we must admit that he gradually lost this faith.[57] Nowhere in his work does he desire to substitute, at the time of his writing, a new pacifist orientation for the ancient mode of thought. He is not really bent on a pacific transformation of the world. The pacification of mankind is much less important to him than the aggrandizement of his country's power. He wants to be above all, and he effectively is, the champion of a national program to which he subordinates everything.

But it would have been difficult for him, without a cosmopolitan superstructure, to furnish an ethical basis for his doctrine, just as he would have found it impossible to present it to the public as a new *system*. For him cosmopolitanism is thus chiefly a means for defending morally and justifying philosophically his conception of economic policy. It is a philosophical frame and a moral ornament of his national program. But it is also a means of propaganda meant to make his protectionism popular.[58]

[56] "Wir haben es getan [scil. die Smith-Sayische Schule angegriffen] in der Ueberzeugung, unsere Pflicht gegen unser deutsches Vaterland zu erfüllen." List, *Unsere Gegner* (1843), p. 433.

[57] Cf. Sommer (1927), pp. 190-191, and Sommer (1930), p. 516.

[58] In general List was fond of using pacifist arguments to make his ideas more attractive. His propaganda in favor of railway construction is a characteristic example of this. A well developed railway network (he says) would make standing armies superfluous or would at least permit an enormous reduction of their size. A country having the possibility to concentrate the militia (*garde nationale*) at the danger points, in a few days, would become virtually unassailable. Wars of invasion would cease.

The objectives of List's national system may be summarized in the following schema:

(1) Happiness of individuals; ways of attaining it:

(2) a world federation of peoples and free trade; prerequisite for accomplishing them:

(3) an equal degree of civilization and power among the "normal nations";

(4) protectionism as a means to lift such nations to the same level of civilization and power.[59]

Having thus fixed the aims of his system, List thinks he has given a fruitful synthesis of cosmopolitical economy and national economy. However, on looking more closely, we do not find a true synthesis. One clearly recognizes that List tends to increase the power and wealth of Germany, but it is difficult to see how, once the same degree of civilization is reached by the "normal" nations, peace should come about. For List this is a postulate, but for the reader an enigma. For one fails to understand—and List hardly explains it—why the same degree of civilization and power should do away with the causes of international conflicts. Equality of civilization and power among States may doubtless dispel many misunderstandings and much distrust. But does it suffice to make them give up national sovereignty and induce them to form a world federation?

Again, is it not illusory to believe that peoples *can* attain the same degree of civilization and power? And supposing it possible (though the very supposition conflicts with common sense), how are we to measure and compare the degree of civilization and power of different States so as to know whether they are equal? To ascertain this equality is no less difficult than it is to attain it.

List often speaks of a world federation. But he nowhere considers it as an objective close enough and sufficiently realizable to be able to inspire contemporary politics. Nor

(*Ueber ein allg. Eisenbahnsystem* [1832], p. 566). The railways would thus be transformed, finally, into an instrument that would destroy war itself. (*Deutschlands Eisenbahnsystem* [1834-1836], p. 267.) Cf. also List, *Idées sur les réformes économiques*, pp. 63-64.

59 Cf. Sommer, *Friedrich Lists System* (1927), p. 184.

does he say anything about the political and economic structure of this world federation. Finally, he fails to specify how he imagines its formation, though he mentions it whenever he professes his pacifist faith. When on one occasion he happens to use the term "congress of nations"[60] he attributes to it no precise meaning. One does not learn what he means by "congress." Is it a permanent organization or an occasional meeting of a diplomatic character? Is it the organ of a world federation of nations or a conference of sovereign and independent States?

A federation of nations is not feasible without a renunciation, or, at least, a limitation of national sovereignty. In this connection List, shortly before his death, recommends however the following precept: As long, he says, as there are wars, great nations must endeavor to become political bodies perfect in themselves; they must rely on their own strength and carry into effect cosmopolitan ideas only so far as not to suffer therefrom any limitation of their national independence and power.[61]

Can such a policy, in practice, mean anything but the abandonment of true cosmopolitanism? Evidently we are here caught in a vicious circle. For as long as there are sovereign States there will always be fear of war, and this fear will prevent them, if they follow List's counsel, from embarking on a real pacifist policy. It is impossible to see how the policy recommended by List could lead to a union of peoples and to free trade. If one is opposed to a limitation of national sovereignty, one cannot aspire to, nor arrive at, a federation of nations. Federalism and intransigent nationalism are irreconcilable principles.

[60] "In the congresses of the great powers Europe possesses already the embryo of a future congress of nations." *Das nationale System*, chap. xi, p. 166.

[61] "Solange es aber noch Krieg auf dieser Erde gibt, werden die grossen Nationen streben müssen, in sich selbst vollkommene politische Körper zu bilden, auf ihren eigenen Füssen zu stehen und kosmopolitische Ideen nur insoweit zu verwirklichen, als es geschehen kann ohne Beeinträchtigung ihrer Nationalselbständigkeit und Nationalmacht." List, *Letzte Abrechnung* (1846), p. 164. Cf. also List, *Cobden* (1846).

X. THE GERMAN HISTORICAL SCHOOL

AS early as the opening of the nineteenth century, Sismondi wrote in the preface of his *Richesse commerciale*: "Political economy is based on the study of man and of men; one must know human nature, the condition and fate of societies in various periods and in different places; one must consult historians and travelers; one must see for oneself."

List, too, wanted political economy to draw its lessons from experience. For him, history is one of the elements on which economic science must found its reasonings. Yet in addition it must largely take into account both politics and philosophy. To express it differently, historical analysis, however important, is in his opinion only an auxiliary method of political economy.

The economists of the German historical school went much further. Up in arms against the classical method which, according to them, was too abstract, they were not satisfied with demanding that political economy make use of history as an instrument of demonstration. Their avowed aim was to reform radically economic science by basing it on a new, an *historical*, method. No doubt, they had notable predecessors in this new departure: Sismondi, List, socialists of various shades, and especially the Saint-Simonians had provided their economic works with thorough historical analyses.

"But none of these authors," writes Professor Rist, "had deliberately sought in history and observation a means of reconstructing political economy as a whole. It is in this attempt that the originality of the German historical school must be looked for."[1]

The latter was founded toward the middle of the nineteenth century. One used to distinguish the older historical school (Roscher, Hildebrand, Knies) from the younger, headed by Schmoller. However, this obsolete division is

[1] Gide and Rist, *Histoire des doctrines économiques*, p. 452.

based on no fundamental criterion. For in the last analysis the differences separating the older school from the younger are of no greater importance than those one usually finds among partisans of the same doctrine.[2] All the followers of the historical school are agreed on the prime importance of the historical method in political economy; all admit the necessity of a specifically national policy; all demand State intervention in order to give the desired direction to national economic life.

In the present chapter we propose to consider the followers of the historical school who concerned themselves with the problem of war (Roscher, Knies, Lorenz von Stein, Schäffle, and Schmoller), ignoring those among them who, to our knowledge, paid no attention to it (Hildebrand, Bücher, Knapp, and Held) or those who made no pronouncement on the subject during the historical period under discussion (as for example Lujo Brentano).

As for Werner Sombart, who is connected by intellectual tics as much with the historical school as he is with Marx, he is the author of a study on war and capitalism (*Der Krieg und der Kapitalismus*, 1913). One would however vainly look, in this work, for a synthetic view on the relations between war and the economic. He is content with bringing together materials favoring his pet thesis on the origin of capitalism. He asserts, as is known, that capitalism could never have come into being without the existence of armies and wars which, in the course of history, have been the first to create a vast demand for goods, which is the essential condition of capitalist production.

1. War and Standing Armies: Roscher and Knies

A trained historian, Wilhelm Roscher[3] pays close attention to the phenomenon of war. In studying the history of economic doctrines, he notes the opinions of the econo-

---

[2] Cf. Schumacher (1931), p. 371.

[3] Roscher (1817-1894) was professor of political economy at the universities of Goettingen and Leipzig.

mists on armed conflict.[4] He even manages to save from oblivion a pacifist project (in which, it is true, the economic factor plays only a secondary role): that of the free-trader Lips[5] who proposes the organization of a Council of the European nations (*Völkerrat von Europa*).

Roscher shows up the losses resulting from war. Apart from material damage, it causes indirect injury by the diminution of production. The latter is reduced not only because of the removal of an increasing number of men from productive labor, but also because of the economic crises which usually accompany an abrupt passage from peace to war and from war to peace.[6]

From the international point of view war involves large-scale destruction. The victor wins less than the vanquished lose. To give an example, Roscher thinks that by the contributions imposed on France, in 1871, Germany hardly gained one sixth of what the former country lost. And even this last is true only if one disregards the production and speculation crises which occurred as a consequence of the Franco-German war of 1870-1871, which at that was for Germany so happy and so short.[7]

But however great the losses entailed by war, it would be illusory to regard them as factors which, by their very excesses, favor the permanent pacification of mankind. When after a long war a conflict seems to be definitely settled, doctrinaires without a sufficient knowledge of history and of man believe they perceive the premonitory signs of perpetual peace. This was the case, for example, after the Thirty Years' War, after the Seven Years' War, and after the Napoleonic Wars. Yet nothing is more erroneous than such a belief, since it has no sound basis in fact. It is all the more dangerous because it may prompt

[4] *Zur Geschichte der englischen Volkswirtschaftslehre* (1851), pp. 35, 49, 89; *Geschichte der Nationalökonomik in Deutschland* (1874), passim.

[5] *Der allgemeine Friede* (1814). Cf. Roscher, *Geschichte*, p. 992.

[6] Roscher, *System der Volkswirtschaft*, vol. I, sect. 186, p. 451; vol. III, sect. 172, pp. 810-811; vol. IV, pt. 2, sec. 119, p. 188; *Ansichten der Volkswirtschaft*, 1861, pp. 339-349; 372-373.

[7] Roscher, *System*, vol. IV, pt. 2, sect. 120, p. 197.

governments to an unjustified reduction of the military budget and thus imperil the national defense. Nor should it be forgotten that a considerable armament is always the best means for the maintenance of peace.[8]

Nor should one imagine that a democratic form of government renders men peaceful. Democracies often are more bellicose than monarchic or aristocratic regimes, even if only from motives of vanity.[9]

Looking upon war as an historical fact destined to last, Roscher is careful not to describe only its favorable aspects. He is very critical of the economists tending to exaggerate the blessings of war. Thus he does not spare irony in discussing Lueder who, he says,[10] is not satisfied with stating that war often plays a beneficent role in human society, a role resembling that of a thunderstorm, but who declares furthermore that war favors national industry by an increase of capital and labor.[11]

Are war expenditures productive? From the national viewpoint they are so only when the war is just and victorious.[12] From the international point of view they can be so only if in both hostile camps the armed conflict fa-

---

[8] *Ibid.*, sect. 119; *Geschichte*, pp. 115, 590; *Grundriss*, p. 139.

[9] Roscher, *Politik* (1892), p. 392.

[10] Roscher, *Geschichte der Nationalökonomik*, p. 620.

[11] Lueder, *Ueber Nationalindustrie* (1800-1804), vol. III, p. 18. War, he claims furthermore, stimulates work and savings, increases demand, and augments the national income. Perpetual peace—which is, besides, but a dream—would be no less detrimental than an everlasting war. Like Dohm, to whom he refers, he attributes a wholesome influence to standing armies, for the soldiers, in spending their pay, accelerate the circulation of money and goods. (*Ibid.*, pp. 8, 17-19, 39, 137-138.) Cf. also Saint-Chamans (1852, vol. II, p. 225): the production of arms and munitions enriches the country by giving work to the laborers and profits to the producers.

[12] "The powder that explodes when a powder magazine burns is consumed unproductively; but the powder shot away in war may be productively consumed just as that used to explode a mine may be unproductively consumed; namely, when the war is a just and a victorious one and the mining enterprise has failed." Roscher, *System*, vol. I, sect. 211, p. 520. According to Wirth (1861, vol. II, p. 545) the expenses entailed by war are the most productive of all, provided that the war is a defensive one.

vors certain virtues[13] or improves certain unwholesome conditions.

A short war sometimes lays the basis for a long peace. Unsound conditions in the interior of the country, too, may be abolished thanks to the danger of some conflict with a foreign country: the prospect of a coming war may dispose a government more readily to offer to national or religious minorities fair concessions which in normal times it would not have granted. Athens after the Persian wars, the Netherlands after their war with Spain, England after her victory over Napoleon, all attained the acme of their economic evolution, certainly not in spite of these wars but, at least partly, thanks to them. Unfortunately, one might quote as many examples to prove the contrary. To cite but one: the Romans, who regarded the profession of arms as the most lucrative, by their very conquest of the *Orbis Terrarum* struck with blight the political structure of their empire.

If carried on reasonably and economically, all preparations for war are productive, first, because they develop skill, order, and discipline, qualities indispensable to civilized people; second, and chiefly, because they ensure peace, an object of the greatest interest for society both from the economic and the cultural point of view.[14]

With the perfecting of the technical and military arts the superiority of the nation which is the best prepared for war becomes more and more marked. In principle this is true for every aggressor. There is then no more unwise economy than that which delays the preparations for a war which has become inevitable. The United States, whom the Civil War cost three billion dollars, would have saved three fourths of this sum if, instead of militias, they had had a

[13] Roscher quotes with approval the famous letter of the chief of the German general staff, Von Moltke (1880, p. 80). "War," says the latter, "is an element of the world order established by God. It fosters the noblest virtues of man: courage and self-denial, obedience to duty and the spirit of sacrifice; the soldier gives his life. Without war the world would stagnate and sink into materialism."

[14] Roscher, *System*, vol. IV, pt. 2, sect. 120, pp. 196-200.

standing army. Quite true, Christendom has abolished the ancient barbarian principle, applied by both Greeks and Romans, of considering as war booty the total of persons and goods of the vanquished. But it is true none the less that the conquered is obliged to pay, on demand of the conqueror, more than the maintenance of a large army would have cost.

Roscher thus comes out against certain writers such as Say, Bastiat, and Rotteck,[15] who, he observes, advocate false economies in the military department. He thinks that negligence in the construction or modernization of ships, fortresses, and arsenals is particularly serious. A large part of the products necessary for war cannot be manufactured during hostilities. At all events, a sudden demand would raise their price exorbitantly, while in spite of this the need could not be satisfied in time. In a period when technology is improving daily it is very costly to fall behind in the field of armaments. It is therefore necessary to do all one can to be the best equipped for war.

One may also make unwise economies by paying insufficient attention to the preparation of the human material: deficiency of officers and men and inadequate length of military service. Savings in this department are no less disastrous than in the domain of matériel. At present the most efficient, and at the same time the most economical, procedure, if we are to believe Roscher, seems to be the division of men, according to their ages, into three classes: the army, the reserve, and the *landwehr*. In this way men are trained in their youth, whereas in mature age, the most productive from the economic point of view, they may devote themselves to their callings, while profiting from the aptitudes acquired during their military service (punctuality, cleanliness, courtesy, and discipline).[16]

[15] The German publicist Rotteck (1816, pp. 157, 202-216), influenced by Say, is a partisan of militias. Roscher might also have quoted Arnd (1868, pp. 210 f.). This German economist (who occupies an intermediary position between the classics and the historical school) likewise advocates militias.

[16] Roscher, *System*, vol. IV, pt. 2, sect. 119, pp. 189-192.

It would be equally erroneous to be excessively sparing in the expenses indispensable for diplomatic representation, expenses a large part of which must be considered as a necessary sacrifice either in the preparation for war or for the purpose of avoiding it. It is truly absurd, even from the economic point of view, to make use of wealthy but stupid ambassadors merely in order to reduce the costs of representation.

The technique of military and naval armaments must be entrusted to specialists. It does not concern political economy. Nevertheless, its warning against unwise military economies must not be interpreted in the sense that the taxpayers are bound to consent blindly to every demand made by some great military leader. Louis XIV would often have done better had he followed Colbert's rather than Louvois's advice. In the present epoch, Roscher thinks, statesmen, though they are not specialists, are likely to have enough military knowledge to subject the judgments of military experts to judicious criticism.[17]

War, Karl Knies[18] states, has a tendency to reduce in two ways the total quantity of capital: on the one hand it destroys goods, on the other it diminishes their production. It may none the less favor the economic interests of one country to the detriment of another. In every period there have been wars arising from economic motives: carried on, first, for the conquest of territories, they were later waged for commercial reasons, and finally for the sake of industrial interests. Even if a military conflict is not provoked by economic causes, the belligerents endeavor to benefit from it materially. After a victorious war one may seize rich territories and exact indemnities from the vanquished. One must however not lose sight of the fact that contributions paid by the conquered cover only the expenses of the vic-

[17] *Ibid.*, sect. 120, pp. 197-198.

[18] Professor of political economy at Freiburg im Breisgau and Heidelberg, Knies (1821-1898) represented the university at the diet of Baden (1861-1865) where he was a leader of the liberal party.

torious *State*. Now these expenses are less than the total loss incurred through war by the *national* economy of the conquering country. At any rate, there can be no doubt that the accumulation of capital will be more rapid in a country enjoying lasting peace than in one exposed to numerous conflicts.[19]

When a neighbor is evidently animated by a warlike spirit, he forces other States to ward off this danger by all means including aggression. Wars of aggression are legitimate if they forestall an attack contemplated by the enemy. But Knies does not condemn en bloc even wars of pure aggression, for they, too, may be advantageous to the national economy.

The productive service of the army in time of peace consists in preventing an eventual aggression or, in other words, in ensuring peace. In time of war it defends the country and its wealth. In consideration of the necessity of national defense, military expenses, if they do not go beyond what is necessary, must be regarded as the most productive of all expenditures of the State.[20]

Knies favors compulsory military service and standing armies, the militia system being inadequate for large countries such as Germany. The peacetime strength of armies, however, and the length of service should be reduced as much as circumstances permit. In his critical observations on the system of conscription Knies suggests that the State should fully compensate each soldier for the material loss he incurs by military service. He is convinced that as time goes on this rule of elementary justice will finally impose itself.[21]

With the increase in wealth and the perfecting of the military art the ravages of war have a tendency to grow

[19] Knies, *Die politische Oekonomie* (1853), pp. 85-87.

[20] Knies, *Die Dienstleistung des Soldaten* (1860), pp. 5-11; *Das moderne Kriegswesen* (1867), pp. 3-4. The army constitutes an eminently productive body also according to Wagner (*Grundlegung*, p. 325; *Flottenverstärkung*, p. 50) who advocates the maintenance of standing armies (*Finanzwissenschaft*, 1883, p. 418).

[21] Knies, *Das moderne Kriegswesen*, p. 28; *Dienstleistung*, pp. 60, 70.

in seriousness. Happily, Knies notes, growing civilization counterbalances this tendency by inclining nations to peace and by improving international law as applied in time of war. International credit, too, favors solidarity among nations.[22] Yet though he mentions these pacificatory tendencies Knies, on the whole, does not attribute very much importance to them. He leaves it to the distant future to discuss the question as to whether or not a lasting peace among nations is possible. War is a frequent phenomenon in history, and nothing justifies one in foreseeing its disappearance. Even if military conflicts are regarded as a pathological phenomenon, it must be considered as chronic.[23]

Knies is not interested in the therapy of war, or at least does not speak of it. Indeed, he discerns no method for settling peacefully serious international conflicts.

2. *Economic Value of the Army: von Stein*

For Lorenz von Stein,[24] too, war is a permanent phenomenon. Fundamentally, he says, it is merely the exteriorization of the propensity for domination, which is deeply rooted in human nature.[25] War flows from the human character and is thus a natural phenomenon. A cultivated nation will always regard war as a misfortune and will oppose it in the name of humanity. This notwithstanding, after a victory a people will but rarely regret its price. The very

22 *Ibid.*, p. 15, and Knies, *Geld und Kredit* (1879), vol. ii, pt. 2, p. 186.
23 Knies, *Das moderne Kriegswesen*, p. 23.
24 von Stein (1815-1890) was born in Schleswig, where he spent his youth. Appointed professor at the University of Kiel (1846), he took an active part in the agitation of which the Duchies were then the scene. After the restoration of Danish authority von Stein was dismissed (1851). Professor of political economy at the University of Vienna (1855-1885), he became a naturalized Austrian (cf. Schmoller, 1888, p. 115). Among German economists and writers he occupies a rather isolated position. In spite of this he may be classified among the followers of the historical school (cf. Bonar, 1923, p. 203; Espinas, p. 316; Ingram, 1923, p. 202).
25 von Stein, *System der Staatswissenschaften* (1856), vol. ii, p. 132. Dühring (1866, pp. 433-434) ascribes war to the combative instincts of man. According to Wagner it is due to profound and unsurmountable conflicts [*Grundlegung*, 1879, p. 331; *Finanzwissenschaft* (1883), p. 419; Wagner in Rau (1872), p. 161].

triumph seems to be worth its cost in sacrifices. That is why there have always been, and always will be, military institutions.[26]

According to von Stein, an army costs the nation what its members, officers and men, are prevented from producing because of their military service. How is one to compute the real cost of the army? By multiplying the number of soldiers by the average wages, he thinks. However high, this charge must be considered as a national premium of insurance. For without this premium the nation would be defenseless and run the risk of losing its whole wealth. In certain respects one may go so far as to assert that the economic "value" of the army is far superior to its cost of upkeep.

By the "value" of an object von Stein means what would be in danger of being lost or destroyed but for the object in question. For instance, the "value" of a dike is equal to the probable loss which would result from floods had the dam not been constructed. The "value" of a lighthouse equals the losses which would occur in shipwrecks if the lighthouse were not there.

From the strictly economic point of view the use of any product is rational if its "value" is higher than its cost (of production). Now, it is obvious that the army is an "economic" institution in that it preserves from destruction values greater than its own upkeep. One may admit that even in a case highly favorable to the vanquished the latter must pay the victor a contribution which would have allowed him to cover the maintenance cost of a strong army had he possessed the wisdom to organize it in time. For even a "humane" victor will endeavor to deprive the conquered of that part of his wealth which would be necessary for the rebuilding of his military power.

To conclude from the military budget alone that the great powers approach economic ruin would be a grave error. Nothing warrants such a supposition. Von Stein ob-

[26] von Stein, *Die Lehre vom Heerwesen. Als Theil der Staatswissenschaft* (1872), pp. 33, 35.

serves in this connection that Austria was losing annually (1861) from sixty to seventy million guldens in consequence of the economic inactivity of her soldiers, while her tobacco monopoly yielded a profit of some thirty millions. From this fact it follows that the Austrian army of 300,000 men cost the nation about twice as much as the latter was spending on cigars and cigarettes. Pessimism on the subject of military expenses, von Stein concludes, would thus be exaggerated.[27]

It is useless to speak of the blessings of a perpetual peace, which has never existed and which will never come to pass. It is an old truth that he who wishes to live in peace must be prepared for war. If a country does not have strong armies capable of defending it effectively, it may be forced, directly or indirectly, to pay some enemy more than the upkeep of such armies would have cost.[28]

In short, the most economic and most rational way of guaranteeing the security of a country is the maintenance of armies. This is the viewpoint of the entire historical school. Von Stein affirms it repeatedly. It is therefore surprising to find, in one of his brochures, the assertion that the epoch of conquests is gone, to make way for a period of humanitarian and peaceful evolution.[29] But this is an isolated passage which slipped from his pen we do not know how, and which, in the total perspective of his work, is devoid of all deeper significance.

3. *Economic Senselessness of Disarmament:* *Schäffle*

War losses are considerable and are becoming more and more so. Though, thanks to modern progress, they are overcome in a relatively short space of time,[30] it is important to determine under what regime mankind could at present

27 von Stein, *Volkswirtschaftliche Studien über stehende Heere,* 1861.
28 von Stein, *Lehre vom Heerwesen,* p. 21.
29 von Stein, *Grundlagen und Aufgaben des künftigen Friedens* (1856), p. 2.
30 Schäffle, *Das gesellschaftliche System der menschlichen Wirtschaft* (1873), vol. I, pp. 265-266.

live in security and do so at the cheapest cost possible. A European federation? Albert Schäffle[31] attaches no importance whatever to it. He limits himself to recommending the federal principle to Austria-Hungary, who might thus save herself and, with her, Europe.[32]

The political unification of the world? No, the dream of a world State (*Weltstaattraum*) at present offers no practical solution. The creation of such a State is more than doubtful. If sometime in the future, however, it were to come into being, that day would certainly be very far off.[33]

International disarmament? According to Schäffle it offers no more satisfactory a solution.

The chief error of the "friends of peace" consists in believing that military disarmament is sufficient to prevent war. It is based on an erroneous idea they have of peace. They wrongly imagine it to be a manifestation of universal harmony between individuals and peoples. They forget that foreign wars are merely one of the many forms of the destructive social struggle going on within the human race. The prevention of war would thus constitute only part of a vast social reform having for objective the general abolition of all destructive forms of social strife. Now, such a reform cannot be accomplished by means of disarmament. On the contrary, it is feasible only on the basis of a complete armament of men affording them a possibility of defending themselves against their enemies.[34]

[31] Schäffle (1831-1903) was journalist, professor of political economy at the University of Tübingen (1860), and a member of the Württemberg diet (1861-1865). From 1868 to 1872 he lived in Austria, where he became naturalized. He taught at the University of Vienna (1868) and for a few months, in 1871, was Austrian minister of commerce. In the same year he retired from politics and teaching to devote himself entirely to his scientific labors. In 1872, he returned to Germany. Schäffle is chiefly known by his sociological works, of an organicist tendency. His numerous ties of affinity with the historical school justify his being considered as one of its followers, though he is not directly connected with it (cf. Bonar, 1923, p. 203; Ingram, 1923, p. 201). Cf. Schäffle, *Aus meinem Leben*, 1905.

[32] Schäffle, *Kapitalismus und Socialismus* (1870), pp. 295, 278 n.

[33] Cf. Schäffle, *Deutsche Kern- und Zeitfragen* (1894), pp. 105-111.

[34] Schäffle, *Zur sozialwissenschaftlichen Theorie des Krieges* (1900), pp. 220-224.

The causes of foreign wars are manifold: overpopulation, greed, thirst for military glory, religious fanaticism, etc. All these causes cannot be suppressed by simple military disarmament. Even an enlightened public opinion is not sufficient to guarantee peace which, to be lasting, must rest on two factors: the mutual adaptation of nations (or international division of labor), on the one hand, and on a military superiority so great that it discourages and intimidates any possible adversary, on the other.[35]

It is of course possible to sign an international disarmament agreement. But it would be truly naïve to believe in its observance so long as there is no international executive power. This means in practice that the control of disarmament is impossible so long as States remain sovereign.

Nor must one forget the great technical difficulty of defining the exact meaning of military terms (arms, munitions, warships, etc.) which figure in a disarmament treaty. This difficulty alone would be sufficient to make such a treaty ineffective, even admitting the good will of the signers.

Bellicism does not depend exclusively on the armed force at the disposal of States but also on their political constitutions, which may be more or less favorable to the warlike spirit. This element renders disarmament precarious, for it would be illusory to admit the possibility of giving to all States the same form of government. The partisans of disarmament forget, too, that it is impossible to disarm in an atmosphere of war. Now, our time is charged with a continual threat of war, which does not promise to disappear.

The advocates of disarmament take for their starting point the present ratio of the military strength of States, and would like to stabilize it. However, this ratio, while advantageous to the strong States, is not so to the weak ones. The latter have an interest in, and often the power of, increasing their strength more than proportionately with respect to other nations.

[35] Schäffle, *Bau und Leben des socialen Körpers*, vol. I, pp. 463, 471, 474.

The stabilization of the present ratio of the military strength of States would thus favor the predominant nation, leaving it always free to take up arms again.[36] Though it is true that general disarmament would reduce the military expenses of all States, this reduction would be obtained only at the expense of the external security of relatively weak nations.

It would moreover be utopian to believe it possible to stabilize the relative ratio now existing between the military forces of the various States. Social evolution does not know fixed and immutable proportions. It is therefore impossible to maintain forever a given ratio of armed forces. Such a stabilization, even if it were feasible, would not be desirable at all, for in certain cases war leads to progress, for example, when it presents the only possibility of suppressing an intolerable state of things. Wars would doubtless be avoidable if men were made differently. But given their nature it is erroneous to attribute only baneful results to war.[37]

The defenders of disarmament frequently invoke two arguments which seem to them particularly cogent, viz., (1) that military expenses are unproductive, and (2) that they are one of the chief causes of economic crises. According to Schäffle, the very opposite is true.

(1) The thesis of the unproductivity of military expenditures is untenable. In Schäffle's opinion it is based on purely declamatory arguments. No doubt, military expenses are not productive if by productivity we mean the faculty of creating material goods: neither soldiers nor sailors produce. But neither are a large number of other expenses productive in this sense. Yet they are of the greatest social importance: priests, artists, scholars, professors, statesmen, and sovereigns, though they do not devote a single day of their lives to the production of material goods, render

---

[36] "Die Abrüstung . . . leistet nicht dem Weltfrieden, sondern dem Weltkrieg, nicht dem friedlichen Verkehr aller Völker, sondern der Welteroberung Vorschub." *Zur sozialwissenschaftlichen Theorie des Krieges*, pp. 260-261.

[37] *Ibid.*, pp. 227, 238 f., 251, 253, 256 f.; *Bau und Leben*, vol. I, p. 470.

nevertheless the most useful services to the community. The expenditures incurred in the struggle against the elements (floods, fires, and epidemics) are no more "productive" in the sense given to this term by certain authors. The same observation, Schäffle notes, applies to the sums set aside for the protection of persons and property against the enemy within: police, prisons, courts, etc. And yet the "friends of disarmament" do not propose to abolish these institutions to prevent civil war or to have more peace within the country itself.

Just as long as there is danger (without or within), protection is necessary no matter what its price. Now, this danger exists in our time. As for the future, no one can foresee if and when all danger of foreign aggression will disappear.

The military expenses allowed by the State to ensure the security of the whole nation offer the most economic solution of certain problems of offensive or defensive warfare, for one thus obtains a maximum of protection and security with a minimum of sacrifices in capital and labor.

There are enemies outside and inside against which the nation must have an armed force at its disposal. If it gave up collective defense assured by the State, by leaving to each citizen the task of defending himself against anybody and everybody, security would be unattainable or at least much less perfect and much more costly than it is today. The abolition or withering away of the armed force, in other words, disarmament, is therefore economically senseless.[38]

Monetary disarmament is likewise inadvisable. The State must keep a war chest to be able to meet sudden expenses imposed by a military conflict.[39]

As long as there is the harmful action of the elements and of men it is unreasonable to hope to suppress all ex-

---

[38] Schäffle, *Zur sozialwissenschaftlichen Theorie*, p. 233. Prior to Schäffle a similar thesis was upheld, though more briefly, by Jakob (1814, pp. 333-334). Wagner (1883, p. 418), too, is opposed to disarmament.

[39] Schäffle, *Die Steuern* (1895), pp. 229, 236.

penditures not productive in the strictest sense of the term. It would be folly to disarm. It is a quite different question whether the present universe is the best of all possible worlds and whether or not another social order, one without disputes and without strife, is possible. The world such as it is knows not only harmony but also clashing interests, conflicts, and contests. In this state of things, military expenses are inevitable and of the greatest utility.[40]

(2) According to Schäffle, the second argument invoked by the partisans of disarmament, namely, that extreme armaments produce economic crises, is no more serious. Economic depressions may doubtless come about before, during, or after a war, in close connection with military events. But it is exaggerated to claim that a large number of these crises are the result of excessive armaments. For one thing, most production and credit crises have occurred in times of profound peace, when armaments were not excessive. In the second place, it is erroneous to assert that such economic crises as have really been produced by war are ultimately the result of the armaments required for it. On the contrary, war breaks out all the more easily when the enemy is tempted to it by the inadequate armaments of a nation. When war comes, such a nation must make up for what it had neglected to produce long before it became a victim of aggression, and this very thing is the reason for

---

[40] Like Schäffle, but before him, Cournot (1863, p. 503) speaks of ". . . grandes nations qui se tiennent, comme on dit, en échec, en entretenant des flottes, des forteresses, des armées immenses et qui coûtent bien cher. . . . Il vaudrait mieux sans doute que la nature de l'homme permît de s'affranchir de telles nécessités. Cependant, si à la faveur de pareilles sacrifices on prévient, on rend de plus en plus rares des révolutions, des guerres bien autrement ruineuses, et par ce qu'elles détruisent, et par ce qu'elles empêchent de produire, la philosophie le plus décidément cosmopolite sera bien forcée d'approuver des sacrifices qui tournent effectivement au plus grand avantage économique de toutes les nations, lors même qu'ils ne semblent faits que dans un but d'agression ou de défense nationale."

The question of European disarmament is one which to all appearances can be solved only in consequence of far-reaching social transformations, of which it is for the present impossible to form a correct idea. (Cournot, 1872, vol. I, p. 230.) Cf. also Ruyer (1930), pp. 99-101.

the economic crisis eventually produced by the war. The nation is suddenly forced to cover all sorts of gaps which would not exist if the armament had been distributed over a sufficiently large number of years. Planned and complete armaments (*die planmässig vollzogene Vollrüstung*) are thus less likely than disarmament to disturb the economic equilibrium of a nation.[41]

Apart from this, more or less temporary crises in the national economy are always preferable to the dangers arising from military inferiority to an enemy who, in spite of his pledge to disarm, secretly continues to carry his armaments to extremes.

While neither the argument of "unproductivity" of armaments nor the so-called danger of economic depressions can justify disarmament, it is possible to prove that adequate armaments are the most economic (and the only possible) means of ensuring security.[42]

In showing up the wholly utopian nature of disarmament projects, Schäffle maintains that, though opposed to the advocates of disarmament, he is not hostile to the "friends of peace." On the contrary, like them he desires the peaceful settlement of international conflicts and is firmly convinced that social evolution is strengthening the peaceful tendencies. It is inexact to see in social life nothing but strife. To conceive thus a complex reality is simply distorting the facts. Schäffle is therefore opposed to the "theoretical brutalization" of social strife which some authors, Schopenhauer for instance, have elevated to the dignity of a philosophic system.

Examples of cooperation are no less numerous than examples of fight to the death. To deny in advance all possibility of a peaceful settlement of conflicts between States is unscientific. The aim of the struggle for life is to ensure

[41] *Zur sozialwissenschaftlichen Theorie*, pp. 234-237.
[42] "Die militärische Vollrüstung ist gegen äussere Feinde, wie Polizei und Justiz gegen innere Feinde, die wirtschaftlichste, überhaupt die einzig mögliche Art der Sicherstellung des äusseren, bezw. inneren Friedens." *Ibid.*, p. 238.

to the fighters the best possible conditions of existence. However, this goal cannot be attained by a war *omnium contra omnes,* but, on the contrary, through a transformation of armed strife into a mutual adaptation useful to all, by means of division of labor and peaceful cohabitation. The cost of war rises more and more, making victory less and less profitable. The international division of labor, on the other hand, tends to lessen international tensions. The presence of peaceful tendencies in the modern epoch is thus understandable. Yet the best means of strengthening them is not disarmament but the integral armament of the State. It is by arming to the utmost that States hold one another in check, neutralizing each other's forces and thus diminishing, so far as possible, the danger of war.[43]

Schäffle concludes that it is power which constitutes the basis of international harmony.[44] The dissolution of the States, or of their armies, would lead, not to peace, but to anarchy and to war of all against all.[45]

4. The Warlike Spirit: Schmoller

Gustav Schmoller[46] does not conceal his hostility toward liberal pacifism. He severely criticizes Herbert Spencer who, as is well known, sees the sense of history in the evolution of society from a warlike type to a peaceful one. This reasoning, by which the English sociologist is linked to Saint-Simon and to Comte, cannot, according to Schmoller, be denied a certain amount of truth.

"Spencer," he adds, "is not wrong in saying that in the

[43] Schäffle, *Abriss,* pp. 169-171; *Bau und Leben,* vol. I, pp. 471, 477; *Zur sozialwissenschaftlichen Theorie,* pp. 262 f. Already Canard (1801, p. 235) observes: "la paix [entre nations] n'est que l'équilibre de leurs forces opposées et égales."

[44] "Macht ist die Grundlage und Grösse auch der internationalen Harmonie." Schäffle, *Abriss,* p. 200.

[45] *Ibid.,* p. 184. Apart from the writings we have already cited, the following publications likewise bring out Schäffle's opposition to disarmament: *Pas de guerre!* (1887); *Der nächste Krieg in Zahlen* (1887); *Die Friedenskonferenz im Haag* (1899).

[46] Schmoller (1838-1917), professor of political science at Halle, Strasbourg, and Berlin. In 1884 he was named a member of the Prussian *Staatsrat.* Cf. Brinkmann (1937).

warlike type [of society] authority and subordination dominate, whereas in the peaceful type personal freedom prevails; in the former, the individual exists for the sake of
the whole, in the latter, on the contrary, the whole is there
for the sake of the individual. But he forgets to add that
the peaceful type with its individualism also dissolves and
weakens States and lets individuals decay in their egoism.
He overlooks the other causes concurrent in the formation
of States and societies. Nor is he aware to what extent he
simply remains stuck in the current views of the English
Manchester school in thus glorifying the peaceful type of
society."[47]

For Schmoller war is an element as necessary in international life as social strife is in national life. The idea of
perpetual peace between nations is no less illusory than is
the notion of social peace. It would be erroneous to believe that political liberty or democracy contributes to
international peace. English and American imperialism
rather prove the contrary.[48]

Schmoller admits the baneful effects of wars, especially
if the latter are protracted. He is convinced, however, that
technical progress tends to shorten wars, thus rendering an
enormous service to human civilization.[49]

He does not believe in the possibility of doing away with
military conflict. The old mercantilist bellicism, to be sure,
is a thing of the past. It has given way to a commercial
policy inspired by other principles and to a new morality
in the law of nations. The national spirit, however, has not
disappeared, and there is nothing to announce its disappearance. Now, as long as there are nations and national

---

[47] Schmoller, *Grundriss* (1900), sect. 274, p. 1337. Cf. Spencer, *Principles
of Sociology*, vol. II, chap. xvii-xviii.

[48] Schmoller, *Die soziale Frage* (1874), p. 39; *Die wirtschaftliche Zukunft
Deutschlands* (1900), p. 26.

[49] Schmoller, *Der moderne Verkehr* (1873), p. 28. For a similar viewpoint cf. Wagner (1879, p. 330; 1883, p. 424). Hamélius (1891, p. 198),
curiously enough, mentions still another capital advantage of modern
military conflicts: "La supériorité des guerres modernes sur les anciennes
réside dans le fait qu'elles durent moins longtemps et qu'elles font périr
plus d'hommes qu'elles ne détruisent de choses."

economic life, States are likely to have special economic interests susceptible of provoking wars, as was frequently the case, for example, in the mercantilist epoch.[50]

Free-trade and pacifist illusions, which were fostered particularly after the Napoleonic wars, began to disappear in the last quarter of the nineteenth century, to make room, as Schmoller thinks, for a synthesis of mercantilism and free trade. In the present-day world (that is, on the threshold of the twentieth century) he observes that three immense States, Great Britain, the United States, and Russia, have seized huge territories and wealth, and have a good chance to capture what is still left. To ensure her demographic and economic growth, Germany must retain her colonies and, if possible, acquire additional ones, as well as develop and defend her foreign commerce, tasks which she cannot carry out without a navy whose construction he advocates. Germany cannot (and does not wish to) build a navy as powerful as that of Great Britain any more than she can become a true naval power. She wants only to preserve her stature as a continental and military State. None the less she can build a navy important enough to help her increase her political influence. This is of the greatest consequence for foreign trade which, unless backed by military and naval force, cannot attain its apogee.[51]

Far from regretting what he considers as inevitable, Schmoller rather endeavors to see whatever advantages militarism might present. Compulsory military service, he notes, demands sacrifices of society and imposes upon it loads which only the necessity of being prepared for aggression justifies. Other economists stress above all the economic loss resulting from conscription. Schmoller is less severe with regard to military institutions, for in them he discerns also elements favorable to national economy. In the compulsory military service which weighs heavily on

[50] On the wars at that period cf. Schmoller, *Das Merkantilsystem* (1884).
[51] Schmoller, *Die Wandlungen in der europäischen Handelspolitik* (1900); *Die wirtschaftliche Zukunft Deutschlands* ([1900], cf. especially p. 33: "Wir wollen ein Kontinental- und Militärstaat bleiben.")

all classes he finds the best corrective imaginable for an excessive division of labor. At the same time, "it is an educational means for the whole nation and a sure antidote against the abuses of class rule."[52]

[52] Schmoller, *Grundriss*, sect. 114, p. 356. Hamélius (1891, p. 199) goes further: "La guerre rend égaux devant la force matérielle des hommes qui, en temps de paix, se trouvaient dans les conditions les plus inégales. Elle fait plus *pour la fraternité des hommes et des peuples* que la meilleure législation."

XI. THE GERMAN HISTORICAL
SCHOOL AND THE HISTORICAL
METHOD OUTSIDE GERMANY

HAVING originated in Germany, the historical method has found followers in other countries. We propose to examine several among these, who have discussed more or less at length the relations between the economic and war, namely Cliffe Leslie, Thorold Rogers, Laveleye, Levasseur, and Cunningham. We shall not consider here those who say very little or nothing on the subject, Bagehot for example, who looks at war from the Darwinian standpoint, and Toynbee, who looks upon peace as a religious ideal.[1]

The partisans of the historical method outside Germany do not form a school properly speaking. What they have in common is not a uniform body of doctrines but only the application of this method, in which they find a valuable instrument of economic research. Thus there is no historical school outside Germany: there are only economists adhering to the historical method. Nor is it surprising, therefore, that a number of them arrive at conclusions differing from those of the German historical school.

Levasseur deals briefly with militarism in his well-known work *La population française* (1892). Cliffe Leslie devotes more attention to it in several studies: *The Military System of Europe Economically Considered* (1856, inaccessible to us), *The Question of the Age—Is it Peace?* (1860), *The Future of Europe Foretold in History* (1860), *The Military Systems of Europe in 1867*. Thorold Rogers treats war in some of his publications, especially in *Cobden and Modern Political Opinion* (1873). Laveleye is the author of *Des causes actuelles de guerre en Europe* (1873). Among

---

[1] Bagehot (1872), chap. ii; Toynbee (1879), p. 252. In a very interesting article, *Count Your Enemies and Economise Your Expenditure* (1862) Bagehot comes out against all military expenses not really indispensable for national defense.

the works of Cunningham we note *Nationalism and Cosmopolitanism in Economics* (1892) and *The Economic Basis of Universal Peace—Cosmopolitan or International?* (1912).

1. Liberal Followers of the Historical Method outside Germany

The partisans of the historical method outside Germany, to whose ideas this section is devoted, are free traders. Cliffe Leslie prefers economic interdependence to independent national economies. Thorold Rogers considers protection by tariff barriers as a theft perpetrated by the State for the benefit of certain private citizens.[2] For Levasseur the protectionist policy is merely an "economic absurdity."[3] Laveleye, too, is a believer in freedom of commerce: "The cause of free trade," he notes, "is a cause already won. The unity of the species is manifestly in the designs of Providence. Free trade, which leads to this unity, is therefore a providential fact. All resistance will be vain. What is to be will be. Such is the will of history and of the good of mankind."[4]

The question may be asked, Why do we discuss these free traders in Book II, devoted as it is to a study of the protectionists? The reason is simply to show that there are, outside Germany, a number of followers of the historical *method* who do not share the *doctrines* of the German historical school. This divergence of views touches economic policy as well as the problem of war.

(A) THE ARMAMENTS RACE: LEVASSEUR

It is while studying the demographic consequences of the military system that the French economist Émile Levasseur[5] speaks in passing of the economic effects of the growing militarism. Europe, he observes, is stricken with, and ruined by, the contagion of what he calls the "fever of

---

[2] Rogers, *Economic Interpretation of History*, p. 375.

[3] Levasseur, *La population française*, vol. III, p. 275.

[4] Laveleye, *Études historiques* (1857), avant-propos, p. iv.

[5] Levasseur (1828-1911), professor of geography and economic history at the Collège de France. Cf. Guyot (1911).

armaments." "The burden of armed peace, which was heavy already in past centuries, has never been so onerous as it is today, by the number of men serving with the colors and by the expenses of armaments."[6]

To prepare for war, the large States enroll millions of men. Military service may present certain advantages in the forming of citizens; it has none for the formation of workmen: "The soldier, who is unproductive, lives on the tax-payers' money, and lives so dearly, because it is not only necessary to feed him but to maintain the war matériel; he thus contributes in two ways to the impoverishment of his country, since he does not produce wealth but consumes part of it."[7]

(B) THE QUESTION OF THE AGE—IS IT PEACE?—CLIFFE LESLIE

To this question, which is the title of one of his studies,[8] Cliffe Leslie replies negatively and, contrary to many of his contemporaries, foresees wars on a large scale. It would be erroneous to believe in the near reality of permanent peace only because war is injurious to peoples. Nations do not always act in conformity with their own material interest, not because they do not know it, but because to economic advantage they prefer other ideals.

Cliffe Leslie denies that the number of wars has diminished in his time. He shows, by a long chronological list of wars, that between 1816 and 1860 there was not a single year of peace. The bellicose policy of Napoleon III belies the dawn of a new era of peace. Whether this policy is due to the national character of the French or to the militarist spirit of Europe is only a secondary question, for either explanation presages a gloomy future. The militarist spirit

6 Levasseur, *La population française*, vol. III, p. 249. Le Play (*L'organisation du travail*, p. 436) remarks on this subject: "La paix armée de notre époque est devenue aussi funeste aux peuples que l'étaient autrefois les guerres prolongées. Un tel état de choses ne saurait se perpétuer en Europe sans amener la décadence."

7 Levasseur, *La population française*, vol. III, p. 255.

8 Cliffe Leslie (1827-1882), professor of political economy and of law at Belfast. Cf. Bastable, 1897.

of the times, the imperfection of the mechanism for adjustment of international rights, the unsound organization of continental polities, the impending repartition of Europe, and an alarming situation in other parts of the globe constitute a political atmosphere charged with war clouds. There follows, for the British Empire, the necessity of being well armed: a national militia is imperative, and it should be supplemented by a standing army of volunteers.[9]

Must one despair of the future? No, for it is economic interdependence and peace and not independence and war which seem to be the ultimate destiny of mankind.

At the beginning, humanity was divided into tribes, continually fighting one another. In the Middle Ages the lords of adjacent territories were often at war with one another. Subsequently nations were formed and large States came into being. But progress did not stop there. A new idea, a superior unity, already appears on the horizon: Europe. Some day this idea will materialize.

International law has a great future, though there is as yet no supreme power able to impose respect for it. Law did not arise spontaneously from the sentiment of what is right. Law is compulsory justice. It often has its source in violence, in quarrels, and in the need for putting a stop to them. One can even now conceive the formation of a "European Senate," and the rudiments of European law are already discernible. Wars are becoming more and more disastrous, and nations will finally understand that it is to their advantage to avoid them by submitting to certain rules of law and equity.[10]

Two preliminary international measures are necessary to put an end to war: the establishment of free institutions and the substitution of national militias for standing armies. But the danger of war will disappear completely only

[9] Cliffe Leslie, *The Question of the Age—Is it Peace?* (1860); *The Military Systems of Europe in 1867*, p. 145.

[10] Leslie, *The Future of Europe Foretold in History* (1860), pp. 101, 109-110. Cf. also Laveleye, *Cliffe Leslie* (1881), pp. 626-627.

when the civilized world has a common legislature and a common tribunal for international affairs.[11]

(c) "A SYSTEM OF INTERNATIONAL COUNCILS": THOROLD ROGERS

For Thorold Rogers,[12] an enthusiastic follower of Cobden, "an armed peace, if prolonged, is more destructive of economic prosperity than open warfare for a time."[13]

The advantage derived from free trade is not only material but also, and even to a higher degree, moral. Freedom of commerce binds nations and thus favors peace between them. The time when it was believed that the wealth of one country is conditioned by the poverty of the others is definitely past. Men have learned that the welfare of their country is intimately connected with the moral and material progress of other nations. Every reasonable man knows that war is becoming more and more of a folly and a public crime. With the disappearance of the erroneous commercial and political theories of past ages, war, which is getting to be increasingly irrational and injurious, at the same time becomes less and less possible.[14]

As time goes on, it will become an institution as ridiculous and anachronistic as the divine right of sovereigns and the duel. Thorold Rogers has confidence in international arbitration and sees in public opinion the power able to make the decisions of a court of arbitration duly respected. At the present time it is improbable that nations will give up their armies and the study of military science. But it is quite possible that under different international conditions they will employ their power and science to preserve peace and, if necessary, to compel arbitration.[15]

[11] Leslie, *The Military Systems of Europe in 1867*, pp. 131-132.

[12] Carried along by his friend Cobden, James Edwin Thorold Rogers (1823-1890) left the Church to devote himself to university teaching and to politics. He was a Member of Parliament from 1880 to 1886. Cf. Castelot (1892).

[13] Rogers, *The Economic Interpretation of History* (1888), p. 294.

[14] Rogers, *A Manual of Political Economy* (1876), p. 250; *The Free Trade Policy of the Liberal Party* (1868), pp. 23-24.

[15] Rogers, *Cobden and Modern Political Opinion* (1873), pp. 138-139, 141.

In a study on colonies, in which he asserts that they do not offer any economic advantage to the mother country, Thorold Rogers also touches on the question of an international organization and recommends a "system of international councils," whose form and composition he fails, however, to define more closely. "That system of international councils which shall discuss the general good of all those whom political science affirms to have common interests, whatever may be the accidental difference in their form of government, should have its initiative in a close alliance between Great Britain, the American Union, and the free colonies of this country. It should commence by according without difficulty to those citizens of these countries who may change their residence from one of these independent communities to another, civil rights as full as those which an Englishman enjoys in Scotland or Ireland. It should affirm that all those persons who belong to any of these countries have a common nationality, and should have a common commercial law, a common currency, a common postal system. It should make the intercourse between all these communities as free and as easy as possible."[16]

(D) A PROGRAM OF INTERNATIONAL COLLABORATION: LAVELEYE

Émile de Laveleye,[17] a well-known Belgian economist and writer, in 1873 published a study on the present causes of war in Europe and on arbitration (*Des causes actuelles de guerre en Europe et de l'Arbitrage*).

Some twenty years ago, he says at the opening of this work, a large number of intelligent men, by no means utopians, most of them economists, began to hope that the civilized nations had finally come to understand that by war they had everything to lose and nothing to gain. This hope has however been vain.

Everywhere preparations for war are on the increase,

[16] Rogers, *The Colonial Question* (1871), pp. 458-459.
[17] Laveleye (1822-1892), professor of political economy at Liège. Cf. Goblet d'Alviella (1895), especially p. 60.

and one might think oneself on the eve of a general conflagration. "Among the sad things of our time," Laveleye notes, "I know nothing more distressing and more calculated to confound reason than the contrast we behold between the advance of international solidarity and the revival of bellicose ideas."[18]

The causes of modern wars are numerous and manifold: thirst for conquests, religion, the maintenance of the European balance of power, interventions abroad, historical rivalries, colonies, quarrels over spheres of influence, hostilities between races, the inadequacy of political institutions, and the theory of natural boundaries. It is however in the principle of nationalities that we must seek the main cause of future conflicts.

Apart from the bloodshed and the sorrows it causes, war always costs more than it yields. It is a scourge for all nations, victors and vanquished. On the other hand, protective tariffs by which, in view of a possible war, one intends to make a State economically independent of foreign countries are likewise very costly, aside from the absurd aim they pursue.

No foreign territory and no colony are worth conquering. If peoples were enlightened enough to discern their true interest, there would no longer be wars, for, none of them deriving an advantage from attacking and conquering, none would be under the necessity of defending itself.[19]

"Economists," says Laveleye, "are quite right: if nations had only the instinct of animals, which pursue their interests, there would no longer be wars. Unfortunately, the prejudices, the grudges, the rivalries, the ambition of rulers, and the stupidity of the ruled still hide from view this undeniable truth, that peace is for States not only the most sacred of duties, but the first of their interests."[20]

[18] *Des causes actuelles de guerres en Europe* (1873), p. 9.
[19] *Ibid.*, pp. 13, 21, 153, 18-19, 57-59; cf. also Laveleye, *Éléments* (1882), p. 252.
[20] Laveleye, *Cliffe Leslie* (1881), p. 626.

Nations no longer have any interest in fighting. The sooner they understand that conquest is harmful to them, the less frequent wars are likely to become.[21]

Some day war between nations will cease, as it has ceased between citizens of one and the same State. "What is required to abolish wars between nations? An international code of law, an international court of justice, and an international executive power."[22]

Mankind is obviously advancing toward the realization of this ideal. But meanwhile it is at least necessary to reduce the causes of war, that is, reduce their number. With this end in mind one must favor everything tending to establish common views and common interests among peoples. Laveleye enumerates the following measures to bring this about:[23]

(1) Reduce and, so far as possible, completely abolish tariff duties, for everything separating men disposes them to war, while everything facilitating their intercourse inclines them to peace.

(2) Reduce freight rates and postage in order to multiply as much as possible the exchange of both merchandise and ideas.

(3) Adopt a universal system of coins, weights, and measures as well as of commercial law, not only with a view to promoting business transactions but also in order to bring home to peoples the strength of the tie which binds them to one another.

(4) Concede equal civil rights to foreigners and citizens, so that man may find his country everywhere and a sentiment of universal brotherhood may gradually take the place of that of exclusive nationalism.

(5) Promote the teaching of foreign languages, of geography, and of all subjects relating to the situation of foreign countries.

(6) Encourage the distribution of books fostering love

21 Laveleye, Des causes, p. 153; Le Gouvernement (1892), vol. I, p. 51.
22 Laveleye, Des causes, p. 149.
23 Ibid., pp. 159-160, and On the Causes of War (1872), pp. 29-31.

for peace and proscribe those which instill admiration for war.

(7) Support everywhere all that gives strength and efficiency to the representative system, and especially shear the executive of the power to declare war and to conclude peace.

(8) Encourage the exportation of capital so as to make it cosmopolitan, and to create a solidarity of interest among all capitalists.

(9) Following the example of the Quakers, the clergy should inspire all men with that horror of war which, being the very essence of Christianity, would at last differentiate Christians from savages.

If we have reproduced, in addition to the economic measures suggested by Laveleye, his pedagogical and political precepts, we have done so to bring out better the importance he attributes, in the whole framework of his pacifist program, to economic factors, especially freedom of trade. All his economic recommendations are founded on the liberal thesis according to which "international exchange leads to international dependence resulting in universal solidarity."[24]

2. *A British Protectionist Follower of the Historical Method: Cunningham*

The English protectionist William Cunningham[25] develops ideas which recall singularly those of the German historical school.

Cunningham started out as a free trader. He claimed that everywhere in the world cosmopolitan economic tendencies would in the end gradually abrogate national ex-

---

[24] Laveleye, *Des causes*, p. 155. [Le libre-échange] "prépare la confédération fraternelle des peuples; en cela consiste sa grande, sa réelle importance." Laveleye, *Études* (1857), p. iv.—Henry George thinks that free trade would lead to an Anglo-American federation, a first step toward the universal federation of nations. Cf. his *Protection or Free Trade* (ed. 1891), p. 354.

[25] Cunningham (1849-1919), a clergyman and professor of economic history at the University of Cambridge. Cf. Scott.

clusivism. He also stressed the necessity of considering the world as a unit, for economic interests are henceforth no longer as narrowly national as they were in the past; he believed in the victory of cosmopolitanism and expressed his satisfaction with it.[26]

Even in defending British imperialism he gave his apology a free-trade justification. England, he said, in all her colonial possessions applies the principle of commercial freedom. Though assuring for herself in this way an important market, indispensable to her growing industry, she debars from it no other nation.[27]

In his *Essays on Western Civilization* (sect. 133), published in 1900, Cunningham, like List before him, comes out in favor of economic nationalism as a transitory stage on the road to the "cosmopolitical" system. Subsequently he gives up altogether the cosmopolitan point of view and declares himself an ardent partisan of the protectionist policy of Joseph Chamberlain, who wrote the preface of his antiliberal pamphlet *The Case against Free Trade* (1911).

Criticizing the free-trade doctrine, Cunningham blames it for having ascribed to international trade faculties which it hardly possesses. Just as competition between private individuals does not lead to social concord, so competition between nations does not produce international solidarity. It is a pure illusion to believe that international exchanges necessarily give rise to friendly sentiments between peoples. Ashley, another partisan of the historical method, shares the same point of view. He recalls Cobden's surprise when the free traders of Yorkshire and Lancashire supported the imposition by force of the Open Door Policy upon China.[28]

Whatever the intentions of the free traders, their attitude is causing irreparable damage to the British Empire, which should defend itself against the growing protection-

[26] Cunningham, *Nationalism and Cosmopolitanism in Economics* (1892).
[27] Cunningham, *English Imperialism* (1899).
[28] Cunningham, *The Rise and Decline of the Free Trade Movement* (1904), pp. 164-165; *The Progress of Capitalism in England* (1916), p. 120; *The Case against Free Trade* (1911), p. 76. Ashley, *The Tariff Problem* (1903) (ed. 1920), p. 196.

ism of foreign countries. For a number of reasons, among others from military necessity, Cunningham demands that Great Britain should no longer trust the old maxim of laissez-faire, but should adopt a "conscious economic policy," that is, protectionism. War may prevent grain imports from abroad, a danger all the greater for England because in this respect she depends more and more on foreign markets. She should therefore tighten her economic links with the members of the Empire by means of preferential tariffs, so as to develop the productive forces of that immense territory which, of all States in the world, has the best chances of becoming self-sufficient.[29]

It is easy to exaggerate, according to Cunningham, the progress accomplished by economic cosmopolitanism. The nation as an independent political unit can still do plenty to improve the welfare of its members. It is moreover erroneous to believe in the coming extinction of national units. Even if militarism were to disappear completely, mankind would none the less remain divided into sovereign nations.

Every one is interested in those nations living in a state of mutual peace. The whole question resolves itself into finding out how this peace is best served, by "cosmopolitanism" which ignores, undermines, and denigrates national economic life, or by "internationalism," based on a group of strong and vigorous nations. Cunningham does not define further this "internationalism" which might be qualified as *patriotic* internationalism. But he considers it the best road toward universal peace.

To him it seems to serve the cause of peace better than learned dissertations on the identity of the interests of all belligerents, dissertations which in practice lead nowhere. They appear to him quite as ineffective as those which, while asserting the existence of a harmony of interests be-

29 Cunningham, *The Case against Free Trade*, pp. 19, 41-45, 132. International arbitration and universal peace have very little chance of being realized, according to Cunningham (*Prospects of Universal Peace*, 1899).

tween social classes, are all the same unable to prevent the constant rise of clashes between capital and labor.[30]

There are writers who, contemplating the world, deplore the existence of militarism and the horrors of war. Seeing the nations in incessant conflicts, they are inclined to consider the division of mankind into separate nations as vicious in itself. They would do everything in their power to suppress the distinctive features of peoples and to promote a cosmopolitan orientation of the human mind. Such an animosity against nationalities easily degenerates into a peevish antipatriotism which habitually presents one's own country to the world in a garb of penitence. But the suppression of all national barriers and organizations would not efface racial differences; it would not offer a true equality of opportunity to everybody; it would not put an end to the struggle for life, which is the chief reason for all human conflicts. A nation has a positive function. The rise of large nations has suppressed private and provincial wars. It is in their mutual understanding and in their intervention in world affairs that Cunningham finds the best hope for the maintenance of universal peace. Mankind will attain its fullness of life not by weakening the distinctive traits of nations, but on the contrary by granting to each a possibility of developing its own inner character.[31]

A collaboration, conscious and as close as possible, among nations is doubtless desirable in their own interest. If there is, however, any chance at all of the various States forming some day a world union, its basis will not be the coincidence of their material interests. Only in religion and in the recognition of one omnipotent God to Whom each individual would feel responsible, will one find, according to Cunningham, the most favorable condition for the establishment of a universal federation.[32]

[30] Cunningham, *The Economic Basis of Peace—Cosmopolitan or International?* (1912).
[31] Cunningham, *The Case against Free Trade*, pp. 15-16.
[32] Cunningham, *The Progress of Capitalism in England*, p. 135.

3. The Historical Method and War

From time immemorial war has been playing havoc with the human species. From early days, peoples, both primitive and civilized, have not ceased to butcher one another. Prompted by hunger or hate, by greed or pride, by faith or superstition, by the desire for adventure or excessive stupidity, by vanity or honor, by poverty or sloth, or by any other serious cause or specious pretext, they expend the best of their strength in fighting, in ruining, in destroying one another. Assailants or assailed, they know peace only as an interval between two wars.

Man in the end thus has come to believe that war is inseparable from human condition, that it is a "normal" fact, a phenomenon that will always be with us. The philosophers who showed its necessity, the sociologists who described its utility, the theologians who pointed to its divine nature, all have strengthened men in this conviction. In short, ideas as much as circumstances have contributed toward spreading the general belief that war is a fact in conformity with human nature and a thing unavoidable.

Among social phenomena war is not the only one to be generally considered as "eternal."

The most powerful intellects of antiquity saw in slavery, for example, an eternal institution. They could not imagine a civilized world without slaves. As late as the nineteenth century the emancipation of woman was regarded as no more than a socialist's dream. The introduction of the twelve (!) hour working day was fought in good faith by many nineteenth century economists, convinced as they were that such a measure would be likely to ruin the economic life of nations. For this reason, and for many others, the industrial protection of the worker seemed to them no less utopian than the abolition of slavery appeared to the ancients or the abrogation of serfdom to the men of the feudal ages. Examples might easily be multiplied.

Nothing is more common in human society than to regard a temporary phenomenon as a permanent one, for a number of reasons. Human knowledge and creative imagination are limited, and material interests have a way of preventing all too often the seeing of things as they really are. The relativity of human knowledge, far from justifying the presentation of any absurdity as realizable, imposes however the duty to proceed with much caution, especially in the social sciences, before declaring a given phenomenon necessary and immutable. The very teachings of history dictate such circumspection. For history, in effect, warns us not to confound a traditional phenomenon with one which is unchangeable.

Now, on this score, the attitude of the German *historical* school in regard to the problem of war seems ill-founded and in contradiction to the method advocated by this school. Its pessimism on the possibility of organizing for peace is certainly traditional but not very scientific.

Roscher views war as a fact bound to stay but fails to explain why the pacification of mankind should be only a pure illusion.

Knies sees in war an event chronic in history and asserts that nothing warrants our looking toward its probable disappearance. But he does not even attempt to defend his point of view by a thorough analysis.

This is equally true of von Stein who, without any explanation whatever, declares in a few words that war is the consequence of the propensity for domination ingrained in human character, and that a lasting peace will never be realized.

Schäffle is right in his opinion that in the present-day world such as it is peace is but an equilibrium of opposing forces which hold one another in check. But from this he concludes too hastily that a dissolution of the sovereign States would lead, not to peace, but necessarily to anarchy and to war *omnium contra omnes*.

Schmoller asserts with good reason that there will be war as long as there are sovereign nations. But since he does not seem to be interested in peace, the possibility of the disappearance of sovereign States or of a limitation of their sovereignty does not elicit any attention from him.

By such isolated, detached, and nonsystematic observations the German historical school believes it has proved the impossibility of organizing a lasting peace. Such are the arguments or, better said, the preconceived ideas which are at the basis of its pessimism. The latter is not deduced from a thorough analysis of social tendencies or from the discovery of an economic (or other) law necessarily driving men into war. The school confines itself to drawing this inference from its belief in the widely held idea that, since there have always been wars in the past, there will always be wars in the future. Such a mode of viewing things is, of course, basically opposed to the true historical spirit; what is even more interesting, it is contrary to the method advocated by the school itself. And this contradiction of the German historical school would seem to deserve pointing out.

The deep rooted pessimism of this school as to permanent peace is surprising if one takes seriously its promise to abstain from generalizing data valid only in a limited time and over a limited social space. In its reasonings on war, however, the historical school does the very opposite: it generalizes and "eternizes" certain opinions commonly called "old truths."

Yet one of the founders of this school, Hildebrand, already voiced warnings against such a method. "One should not forget," he said, "that man as a social being is always a child of civilization and a product of history, and his needs, his education, and his relations to both material goods and to men never remain the same but differ geographically and constantly change historically, advancing with the entire culture of the human species."[33]

If such is the case, why should war, an essentially social phenomenon, be an exception to this law and be regarded as a permanent institution? Why concede a priori that rea-

[33] *Die Nationalökonomie der Gegenwart und der Zukunft* (1848), vol. I, p. 29.

son, which revolts against war, not as an historical but as an eternal phenomenon[34] only reflects a utopian turn of mind?

Essentially evolutionist, the historical school asserts that the economic life of nations tends toward higher forms. The same Hildebrand notes that not only national economic life but also the economy of mankind as a whole is developing toward more and more perfect forms.[35] One wonders then why economic nationalism, which is evidently incompatible with peace, should constitute the last degree in economic development and form an impassable barrier in the social evolution of mankind.

The conclusions of the German historical school (largely shared, we saw, by Cunningham) do not flow from the method which it thinks it applies to the social sciences. It is therefore not surprising that several followers of this method outside Germany reach conclusions opposed to those of the German historical school. Levasseur, Cliffe Leslie, Thorold Rogers, and Laveleye indeed reject its protectionist ideas and its militaristic spirit, but they remain all the same faithful to the historical method. They come out in favor of the liberal and pacifist thesis without giving up the method referred to. Contrary to the historical school, they do not regard universal peace as an unrealizable chimera. Cliffe Leslie sees in political freedom, in the system of militias, in international legislation and in an international court instruments susceptible of ensuring peace to the world. Thorold Rogers for the same purpose proposes a "system of international councils" and an Anglo-American alliance as its trail blazer. Laveleye, who declares himself in favor of an international code of law, an international court of justice, and an international ex-

---

[34] "Nicht gegen den Krieg als historische Erscheinung, nur gegen den Krieg als ewige Erscheinung erhebt sich die Vernunft, empört sich unser Gefühl und unser Glauben an Perfektibilität." Lips, *Der allgemeine Friede* (1814), p. 8.

[35] *Naturalwirthschaft, Geldwirthschaft und Creditwirthschaft* (1864), p. 24.

ecutive power, also works out a complete program of immediate cooperation among nations.

The assertion of the German historical school that war is a phenomenon destined never to disappear cannot be explained by the application of the method it sponsors. The explanation, it seems to us, lies elsewhere, namely in the supreme goal to which that school subordinates everything: to serve above all the German fatherland. The historical school feels therefore obliged, not only to justify the past of its country, but also to take up the defense of the conceptions which were favorable, at that time, to the German Empire. A witness of its birth and flowering, the school is convinced that Germany's growth cannot continue without a solid and ever expanding military foundation. Whence its economic justification of militarism. The fate of Europe, not to speak of other continents, leaves it more or less indifferent. What matters to it is the power of the Reich. As for von Stein, he is animated by the same spirit as the German historical school, with this difference that he is preoccupied with the military power of Austria-Hungary, his adopted country.

In considering war as a perpetual phenomenon, the German historical school proceeds too hastily, generalizes too quickly, and puts itself in contradiction with the very method it recommends and which it believes it applies correctly. In its concrete appreciation of the economic and social effects of wars, however, it remains faithful to its method. It is careful not to see in war only destruction. While pointing out its harmful effects, it also notes its favorable consequences. Roscher observes that a short war sometimes creates the basis of a long peace; that war may oblige the government to make fair concessions to national or religious minorities; that it may contribute to the economic development of the victorious country. Knies remarks that it may favor the economic interests of one country to the detriment of another. Schäffle admits that in certain cases it leads to progress, namely, when it offers the only possibility of abolishing an intolerable state of things.

The historical school views without any prejudice army and military expenses. In the present political structure of the world a State can have confidence, so far as its security is concerned, only in its own defense and its own army. If it withholds part of the outlay necessary for the upkeep of a well-trained army, it may find itself attacked and beaten, and the enemy can then extort not only what has been saved, but even more. In such circumstances it would be absurd to deny the utility of military expenditures. Whether or not one calls them "productive" (as several members of the historical school do) is only a terminological question of secondary importance. It goes without saying that if by "productive" one means the faculty of producing directly material wealth, military expenses will be classed as "unproductive." If on the other hand this term is used as a synonym of social utility, military outlays will be called "productive." In any case, what matters is not the term but the fact that these expenses are (or at any rate may be) socially useful and will continue to be so as long as there is international anarchy in which an inadequately armed State runs a constant risk of being plundered.

This consideration explains why von Stein declares that economically speaking the "value" of the army exceeds the cost of its upkeep; why Knies sees in military expenditures, if they do not go beyond what is really necessary, the most productive of all State expenses; why Schäffle (who correctly foresaw the fiasco of disarmament conferences) is opposed to disarmament and calls it an economic absurdity.

The historical school also understood, as did, by the way, certain liberal economists (for instance Chevalier, Cherbuliez, Courcelle-Seneuil) the inevitability of standing armies in a world in which nationalist tendencies predominate and where a single State organizing such armies forces the others to imitate it. It proves that in a world in which an inadequately armed nation runs a risk of being devoured by its neighbors, standing armies are worth keeping up, even from the economic point of view. It also realizes (particularly so von Stein) that the wealth of modern nations is so vast and the technique of production so advanced that the military expenditures of the great powers are still far from having attained the highest limit possible.

It fails, however, to warn the world of the dangers conjured up, in the long run, by an armed peace and a militarism running wild. Circumstances may compel every State to arm to the teeth and thus to safeguard its independence. But there cannot be the slightest doubt that such a regime entails a terrible impoverishment for each nation and for mankind as a whole, though the baneful consequences it produces are, in a certain measure, compensated for by technical progress and a growing production.

The dangers of militarism are not all of a material order. There are others, of the moral kind, the most important of which is a degradation of mind and character, a factor which, obviously, is bound more or less to affect economic life. And this danger is not outweighed by some advantages of the pedagogical kind which certain adherents of the historical method ascribe to standing armies. Roscher praises the army as a school of skill, order, and discipline, qualities indispensable to civilized nations. He forgets, however, to point out that it is no less a school of servility, and that the great powers such as Great Britain and the United States have reached a very high degree of industrial civilization without the system of standing armies. Schmoller regards compulsory military service as the best corrective imaginable of an excessive division of labor. This is an evident exaggeration. A large number of men, with an imagination a little more vivid and creative than his, can conceive a better corrective (physical education, sport, travel, rational recreation, reduction of the number of working hours, etc.). He affirms that compulsory military service is a means of education for the entire nation and a sure remedy against the abuses of class rule. It doubtless *is* a means of national education, like any other. But one simply fails to understand how it can be a remedy, and even a sure remedy, against the abuses of class rule. For whatever the appearances of military discipline, obligatory for all, nowhere are these abuses, when there are any, more obvious than in the very armies. One must be very fond of such discipline not to see that.

However this may be, the historical school, an enthusiastic witness of the tremendous upswing which was then coming over Germany, is full of confidence in the national future and is not worried about the remote consequences of a militarism unleashed. In its narrow patriotism it closes its eyes on the economic, political, and moral danger which militarism holds in store for mankind.

THE liberals and the protectionists study the relations between war and the economic on the assumption that the economic regime or, more exactly, the economic basis, of society, is fixed and not subject to change. Not that they consider society as something static: on the contrary, they talk a good deal about economic and social progress and about its determining factors. The liberals see in free trade the system most suited to peace and social progress, from the national as from the international point of view. The protectionists believe that national progress is best served by an intelligent protection given to national production, even at the risk of such protection strengthening hostility between nations. But in their research on the relations between war and the economic neither one of the two schools is concerned with the social problem. Private property being, according to them, a condition *sine qua non* of every civilized society and of all economic progress, collectivism naturally could appear to them only as a retrograde current, incapable of solving the problem of war.

The very opposite view is held by the socialists. For them the problem of war is closely linked to the social question, of which it forms a relatively small part. It is thus not independent of the status of property. On the contrary, it takes on a different complexion according to whether property is private or collective, free or regulated by certain rules. Like any other social problem, it cannot be solved without the abolition or, at least, without a fundamental reform of the institution of private property.

An introduction of the socialist order, by doing away with the chief sufferings of human society, would *ipso facto* annihilate war.

The notion of socialism, to be sure, varies with its proponents who, as is well known, are not agreed on its interpretation. Classification is therefore difficult; but fortunately, division into homogeneous groups is not necessary for our purpose. For us it is sufficient to regard as socialists all those who advocate the substitution of a collectivistic economy for a capitalistic one, a total suppression or a very far-reaching limitation of private property.

Socialist literature of the nineteenth century is so voluminous that it is impossible to analyze here all its manifestations. Among the socialist writers of the period we must then choose those who are the most outstanding and at the same time the most representative.

The first chapter of this book (Chapter XII) is devoted to a study of Saint-Simonism (Henri de Saint-Simon, Augustin Thierry, Michel Chevalier, Gustave Biard, etc.). In the second we propose to examine the most important spokesmen of the other currents of idealist socialism in the nineteenth century: Robert Owen, Charles Fourier, Victor Considérant, André Godin, Constantin Pecqueur, François Vidal, and Louis Blanc. The third chapter will deal with the two founders of modern socialism: Karl Marx and Friedrich Engels.

HENRI DE SAINT-SIMON is not a socialist in the proper sense of the term. In the economic field he ties up with Jean-Baptiste Say, whose liberal and industrialist doctrine he reaffirms. He does, however, blaze the trail for socialism by his critique of the economic order of his time. His disciples, scholars and mystics, grouped after his death in a religious sect, draw from his ideas socialist consequences, which are, by the way, quite reconcilable with his industrial system.

The Saint-Simonian school—one of the first and most interesting manifestations of nineteenth century socialism —advocates the abolition of inheritance and the socialization of the means of production. By these measures it does not propose doing away with private property but recommends the distribution of wealth in accordance with the capacities of individual men. Private property, it asserts, is legitimate only by one's function; it should be conceded on the basis of one's capacity. Saint-Simonian society is therefore a "capacitary" hierarchy.

Saint-Simon examines the problem of peace from a two-fold point of view. He studies first its political aspect in a brochure of considerable interest, published in 1814 in collaboration with Augustin Thierry and entitled *De la réorganisation de la société européenne ou de la nécessité et des moyens de rassembler les peuples de l'Europe en un seul corps politique en conservant à chacun son indépendance nationale.* He next examines the economic and social aspect of the problem in some of his numerous writings: *L'Industrie ou discussions politiques, morales et philosophiques dans l'intérêt de tous les hommes livrés à des travaux utiles et indépendants* (1817), *Lettres de Henri Saint-Simon à un Américain, Le parti national ou industriel comparé au parti anti-national* (1819), *Essai sur la politique qui convient aux hommes du XIXe siècle* (1819), and *L'Organisateur* (1819-1820).

The publications of the Saint-Simonian school are very numerous. In addition to the exposition of the *Doctrine de Saint-Simon*, we have drawn on the writings of "Père" Enfantin, the "Apostle" Michel Chevalier,[1] and several other members of the sect: Charles Béranger, Gustave Biard, Auguste Comte, L. Delaporte, Paul Rochette, and P.-I. Rouen. Among the sources of the present chapter let us mention further: *Le Producteur*, a Saint-Simonian periodical, and the *Globe*, a liberal paper of great renown, transformed by its former editor in chief Pierre Leroux, after his conversion to Saint-Simonism (1830), into the official organ of the sect.

Leroux's essay, *De l'Union européenne* (1827), written at a time when its author was still a liberal, has not been considered in this chapter.[2] The doctrine of peace he there propounds contains nothing specifically socialist but is most genuinely liberal: Leroux defends the thesis of political economy tending to create a new spiritual unity, the universal society, which will have no material organization and will not need any.

1. A Precursor of Socialism: Saint-Simon

(A) REORGANIZATION OF EUROPEAN SOCIETY

Taking the English constitution as a model for all others, Saint-Simon[3] proposes to have all nations of Europe governed by national parliaments and to have them collaborate in the formation of a general parliament entrusted with the common interests of European society. "Europe," he says, "would have the best possible organization if all her

[1] On the "liberal" period of Chevalier, cf. chap. vi, sect. 5.

[2] Leroux did not become a Saint-Simonian until 1830. Cf. Isambert (1905), p. 210. Cf. also Thomas (1904), chap. ii.

[3] Claude Henri de Rouvroy, comte de Saint-Simon (1760-1825), fought for the independence of the United States. After his return to France, in 1783, he traveled. During the Revolution he was not interested in politics but in business, speculating in national properties and making a fortune. In 1797 he returned to his studies and then began once more his travels abroad. Having returned to France, he led a worldly and ostentatious life, lost his money, and lived in great misery. Cf. Weill (1894).

nations, each being governed by a parliament, were to recognize the supremacy of a general parliament above all national governments and invested with the power to judge their disputes."[4]

This European parliament, like the English one, would have two houses, a House of Representatives and a House of Peers, whose constitution and functions Saint-Simon sets forth in detail.

The first step toward the establishment of a European parliament should be the formation of an Anglo-French parliament, an object attainable, since both England and France enjoy a parliamentary form of government. This Anglo-French parliament would have a twofold task: to adjust the interests of both nations and to endeavor, by the voluntary adherence of other nations, to transform itself by degrees into an institution embracing the whole of Europe.

The difficulties in the way of such an organization are many, and the time of its foundation is certainly still far off. "This epoch," Saint-Simon states, "is still remote, and frightful wars and numerous revolutions are bound to afflict Europe in the interim."[5]

But a time will doubtless come when all the peoples of Europe will feel the necessity of arriving at an understanding and of organizing themselves internationally. Then the evils will lessen, and military conflicts will gradually disappear. It is to this splendid future that we must look for the full flowering of human civilization. "The golden age of mankind does not lie behind us; it is in front of us; it must be sought in the perfection of the social order."[6]

In his project of European reorganization Saint-Simon does not examine economic problems. He notes however that "all enterprises of general utility for European society will be managed by the great parliament: thus, for example, it will join by canals the Danube with the Rhine, the Rhine with the Baltic, etc.

4 Saint-Simon, *De la réorganisation européenne*, pp. 43-44.
5 *Ibid.*, p. 57.   6 *Ibid.*, p. 97.

"Without activity abroad there is no tranquillity within. The surest means to maintain peace within the confederation will be to expand it continually and to keep it busy all the time with vast internal public works. To people the globe with the European race, which is superior to all others; to open it up and to make it inhabitable like Europe, this is the undertaking by which the European parliament should keep Europe continually busy and on the alert."[7]

Such is Saint-Simon's project. It contains few observations of an economic order because its author proposes to draw up an essentially political plan. It resembles the future League of Nations so much that Saint-Simon is regarded as one of its illustrious precursors. A comparative study of this project and the Genevese institution would doubtless be interesting but would go beyond the scope of the present book. None the less, it is perhaps not superfluous to observe that the League recalls Saint-Simon's project in its aims as well as in the unlimited sovereignty of its members.

Saint-Simon thus foresaw the formation of the League of Nations and the leading role played in it by England and France. But it is important also to note what this genius, in his time, was unable to foresee, namely the inherent weakness of any international political body whose member States retain their full national sovereignty.

One can easily understand that, writing at the beginning of the nineteenth century, Saint-Simon should have limited himself to outlining a project of international association embracing only the European States. One can also understand, at least in part, that he should have wanted to "people the globe with the European race," for several continents were then largely uninhabited. But it is surprising to meet, in a mind as powerful as his, the vague notion of a "European race" which he considers, without saying why, "superior to all other human races." However erroneous it is, we cannot discuss here an idea the study of which is no part of political economy.

[7] *Ibid.*, pp. 51-52.

Saint-Simon could not imagine—and with good reason, it seems to us—a powerful organization of international peace which would limit its activity strictly to politics. In his view such an organization is viable only when it combines political functions with economic activity aiming at an improvement of the welfare of the masses. That is why he attributes such great importance to projects designed to transform the globe, "to open it up and to make it inhabitable like Europe."

(B) REAFFIRMATION OF SAY'S INDUSTRIALISM

Saint-Simon, who, as we have observed, shares the economic doctrines of Jean-Baptiste Say, pays a ringing homage to the latter. "M. Say's *Traité d'économie politique*," he notes, "seems to me a book in which one finds the greatest number of coordinated positive ideas."[8]

The divergences of view between Say and Saint-Simon do not touch the principles of political economy but only its relations to politics. While Say regards the latter as independent of economic science, Saint-Simon, agreeing on this point with Dunoyer, sees in it "the true and only foundation of politics."[9] There is, he thinks, only one true policy: the one which identifies itself with economics. "Politics," he says, "therefore is, to sum it up in a few words, *the science of production*, that is, the science which is concerned with the order of things most favorable to all kinds of production."[10]

Among Say's ideas Saint-Simon subscribes particularly to the irreconcilable opposition existing between welfare and bellicism. Like Say, he thinks "that men can never turn their forces against one another without injury to production; that for this reason wars, whatever their object, inflict harm upon the whole human species; that they injure even the victorious nations."[11]

One of the greatest prejudices fostered by ignorance is the desire to increase national wealth by violence. For it is

[8] *Lettres de Saint-Simon à un Américain* (1817), pp. 182-183.
[9] *Ibid.*, p. 185.   [10] *Ibid.*, p. 188.   [11] *Ibid.*, p. 187.

of paramount interest to an industrial people to live in peace, since war impedes production and interrupts commerce.

"To wage war in order to promote trade is to work against one's very objective; it is to fall into a contradiction. Trade can neither be won nor preserved by arms; it is the reward of industry and is maintained by industry; all wars are harmful to industry, for they hinder production; they are therefore injurious to commerce.

". . . Monopoly, colonies, and prohibitions have drenched with blood land and sea, devoured the fruits and sustenance of industry; and what profits have ever been derived from them?"[12]

Industry and war are then opposed and incompatible activities. While force is at the basis of war, utility and a common interest constitute the foundation of industry. "Everything gained in industrial *value* is lost in military *valor*."[13]

Industry requires security and liberty of trade. The producers of all classes are therefore essentially friends. Nothing prevents their uniting in order to give industry all the influence it can enjoy. It is in this predominance of the "industrial spirit" that Saint-Simon sees the best guarantee of future peace. "It is because the industrial spirit does not yet dominate that national animosities continue to exist. But as soon as industry has gained the ascendancy, these hates will disappear and give way to feelings of brotherhood based on an awareness of an identity of interests.[14]

When experience finally convinces nations that their only means of acquiring wealth consists in productive activity, which is exclusively peaceful, the conduct of tem-

[12] *L'Industrie*, vol. I, pt. II, pp. 54-55 and 79. Saint-Simon entrusted his secretary, Augustin Thierry, with the writing of this part. Though it is signed by Thierry "the adoptive son of Saint-Simon," it is the latter who is its spiritual author.

[13] *L'Industrie*, vol. I, pt. II, p. 102.

[14] *L'Industrie*, vol. II, p. 63. Cf. also p. 47.

poral affairs will naturally pass to "industrial capacity," and military force will gradually disappear.[15]

The world will thus change its appearance as soon as the "industrialists" assume power. One must not forget that Saint-Simon puts in this category all those he considers as productive workers, in contrast to the idle consumers. Thus the "industrialists" comprise laborers, artisans, and farmers, as well as entrepreneurs, bankers, scholars, and artists. Among the "idle" appear: the nobles, priests, owners of real property, judges, soldiers, etc.[16]

In his *Essai sur la politique qui convient aux hommes du XIXe siècle*, which appeared in an ephemeral Parisian review (*Le Politique*, 1819), Saint-Simon summarizes his viewpoint as follows: "Freedom, peace, and economy will be solidly established only when the main political power passes into the hands of the 'industrialists'; now, if this passage has not yet been accomplished, the 'industrialists' have only themselves to blame, their lack of firmness and political activity: for today there is no longer any other real obstacle capable of slowing up the progress of civilization, at least in France. . . ."[17]

The idea of the substitution of an industrial society for a military one, which Saint-Simon, following Say, develops with so much fervor, was taken up again by Proudhon (1809-1865) in *La guerre et la paix, recherches sur le principe et la constitution du droit des gens* (1861), "a sort of historical study of the manner in which civilization, setting out with war, is tending toward a universal pacification."[18]

Though this idea is common to Saint-Simon and to

[15] Saint-Simon, *L'Organisateur* (1819-1820), pp. 81-82.
[16] Cf. *ibid.*, pp. 17-26, and Saint-Simon, *Le parti national ou industriel*, pp. 202-204.
[17] Cited according to Puech (1921), pp. 42-43.
[18] Proudhon, *Correspondance* (May, 1859), vol. IX, p. 84. "Le but de mon livre, *La guerre et la paix*, est, très positivement, de détourner les esprits de la guerre, de les affermir dans la paix, en dirigeant les forces et les courages, non plus vers les conquêtes et les combats, mais vers le travail, ou ce que j'ai appelé métaphoriquement les *luttes industrielles*." *Ibid.*, vol. XII, p. 366 (March 16, 1863).

Proudhon, one must not conclude an identity of their views on war. Proudhon[19] regards pauperism as the main factor of bellicosity, which cannot be said of Saint-Simon. On the other hand, he does not approve of the Saint-Simonian project of a reorganization of European society.[20]

We have seen in this section that Saint-Simon essentially restates the industrialist doctrine of Jean-Baptiste Say. Like Say, he is persuaded that political power will finally pass into the hands of the "industrialists," and that this regrouping of social forces will ensure world peace. In spite of all the differences separating the two thinkers, this basic conception is common to both. It would therefore be superfluous to repeat here, in connection with Saint-Simon, our critical remarks on "industrialism" as set forth in the chapter on Say.

2. *Universal Association: The Saint-Simonians*

(A) "CAPACITARY" HIERARCHY AND INTERNATIONAL PEACE

The Saint-Simonians appraise war as their master had done. A cahier of the *Religion saint-simonienne*, written by Ch. Béranger, bears a title which sums up their point of view very well: *La guerre détruit tout commerce et toute industrie* (1832). By wishing to conquer by force some trade privilege one proves one's own failure to understand the very essence of industry, which is by nature a wholly pacific power. At the present time military conflicts have become particularly costly, for war no longer feeds, as it did formerly, on war.[21]

The Saint-Simonian school often opposes the feudal and warlike to the industrial and peaceful order. In his *Considérations sur l'organisation féodale et l'organisation industrielle*, Enfantin shows "how the *spirit of association* is gradually taking the place, in social relations, of the

---

19 *La guerre et la paix*, bk. IV. Cf. also Duprat (1929, 1932).

20 Cf. Puech (1920), and Puech (1921), chap. vi.

21 Cf. *Doctrine Saint-Simonienne*, ed. 1854 (Exposition, 2e année, 12e séance), p. 467. On the Saint-Simonian school, cf. Charléty (1931); Weill (1896); Halévy (1908).

spirit of conquest."[22] "The *temporal* fact," he says, "has become chiefly an *industrial,* instead of being above all a *military* one."[23]

Saint-Simon's disciples think that "all the efforts of mankind, which have thus far been instinctive, have for their aim to substitute, some day, *association* for *conquest,* the *industrial* for the *military* order."[24] They wish to strengthen these efforts and make them conscious. It no longer suffices to desire peace; one must know how to establish it on a secure foundation. The only effective means of inaugurating it is to change the present social order based on private property capriciously distributed, to a regime organized on the principle: "To each according to his capacity, to each capacity according to his works." In this new order each individual would be classed according to his capacities and remunerated according to his work; a predominant influence would be assured to the "workers" (*travailleurs*), a category in which the Saint-Simonians include artists, scholars, and "industrialists" (both entrepreneurs and workmen). Society thus organized would be peaceful, for "the workers are never interested in isolating themselves and in fighting."[25]

The Saint-Simonians consider their doctrine as the continuation and perfecting of the work of the early Christians; "but it essentially differs from the latter in this twofold respect that, contrary to the law of Christianity and of all its sects, the Saint-Simonians proclaim the association of industry (*l'association de l'industrie*) and the emancipation of women."[26]

We naturally ignore here the question of the emancipation of the fair sex, and we also disregard, in general, the religious and mystical aspect of Saint-Simonism. But we do

[22] In *Le Producteur,* vol. III, May (1826), p. 66.
[23] Enfantin, *Correspondance philosophique et religieuse* (1843-1845), p. 12.
[24] Enfantin, *Économie politique et politique* (ed. 1832), p. 59.
[25] *Ibid.,* p. 101.
[26] Biard, *Aperçu des vues morales et industrielles des Saint-Simoniens,* 1832, p. 4.

wish to state precisely what the sect means by the "association of industry."

"In the association as conceived by the Saint-Simonians, each member, after receiving education and training, will exercise a function of which the enjoyment of the entire usufruct will, under the same right, be guaranteed to him as to any other member of the association.—The most capable, in the professional hierarchy of this member, will be his successor after his death, as in military rank the colonel succeeds the general, the captain the colonel, the lieutenant the captain, and so on, always choosing, to succeed a member departed, the one most capable of replacing him in his function."[27]

That is what the Saint-Simonians mean by "classifying each according to his capacity and by remunerating each according to his works." The association will be a vast hierarchy based upon capacity and function, in principle similar to the organization of modern armies.

"The Saint-Simonian association, whose *religious, political*, and *moral* aim will be to assure to each of its members *education, function*, and *retirement pension*, will be composed not only of a more or less important fraction of humanity; it will comprise mankind as a whole, and mankind is the universality of men inhabiting the world."[28]

The progress of civilization and, in the first place, of industry, is teaching men the secret of prospering simultaneously without injuring each other. "Men and nations," says Auguste Comte, "are continually driven to form associations which are becoming more and more extensive and more and more peaceful."[29]

The infinite perfectibility of human society, which Saint-Simon affirms and raises to the dignity of a law, is the surest pledge of the coming of a peaceful era. Social evolution is characterized by an alternate succession of apparent rises and falls. It is tending however toward a definite goal. "This goal is *universal association*, that is, the association of all

[27] *Ibid.*, pp. 4-5.   [28] *Ibid.*, p. 6.
[29] Comte, *Considérations sur le pouvoir spirituel* (1826), p. 324.

men on the entire surface of the globe, in all their rela-
tionships."[30]

The Saint-Simonians endeavor to "explain and popular-
ize at once the new order toward which mankind is advancing, the *universal association* of all peoples, in which
idleness, chicanery, and war will no longer rule, having
given way to industry, to science, and to all the peaceful
virtues."[31]

What exactly is meant by "universal association,"[32] an
expression of such frequent occurrence in the literature of
the sect? In the *Doctrine saint-simonienne*[33] we find the
following answer to this question:

"Universal association, whose very name is the equivalent of a definition [sic], means a state in which all human
forces, being engaged in the path of peace, will be combined for the purpose of making mankind grow in *love*,
in *knowledge*, in *wealth*; in which individuals will be *classified* and remunerated in the social hierarchy *according to
their capacity, developed as much as possible by an education placed within reach of all.*"

It follows that by "universal association" the sect does
not mean a definite international organization but a stage
in social evolution in which the peoples, organized according to the precepts of the Saint-Simonian religion, would
necessarily live together in peace. The "universal association" is thus something altogether different from a simple
confederation of nations.[34]

[30] "Ce but c'est *l'association universelle*, c'est-à-dire l'association de tous
les hommes, sur la surface entière du globe, et dans tous les ordres de
leurs relations." *Doctrine de Saint-Simon, Exposition, Première année
1829*, 4e séance, pp. 203-204.

[31] Enfantin, *Économie politique et politique* (ed. 1832), p. 102.

[32] Saint-Simon did not formulate himself the idea of the "universal association" preached by his disciples. (Cf. Puech [1921], p. 35 n.) The
latter deduced it from his industrialist system and from his philosophy
of history.

[33] Ed. 1854, p. 336 (Exposition, 2e année, 1829-30, première séance).

[34] "La politique est tout entière dans le sentiment de l'*association universelle*; mais il ne faut pas l'entendre seulement d'une confédération de
peuples ou d'un traité de commerce entre les cabinets." Chevalier, *Politique d'association* (1832), p. 32.

When the Saint-Simonians say that humanity must work toward the realization of this universal association, they have in mind chiefly that it must set about to change education, legislation, the organization of property, and all social relations, so as to attain in the quickest possible manner its future condition as imagined by the sect.[35]

The latter makes the permanent maintenance of peace depend upon the realization of the highest ideals of man. "Universal association," says Michel Chevalier, "will not be accomplished until justice has been done to all, parties, classes, races, and sexes; until each temperament is recognized and assigned a role in the common work."[36]

Is such a solution, necessarily hypothetical and remote, the most practical and the most economical? Could the Saint-Simonians not have asked themselves the question whether it is not more advantageous for mankind to seek a solution closer to the problem of war and to try to organize for peace, even in a world less perfect than that which they advocate? A prey to a profound mysticism and animated by a new faith, they fail to pose these questions. They believed in the universal expansion of the new religion and looked to it for an automatic solution of all human problems including war.

Consequently, contrary to their master, they do not outline a plan of international organization. To our knowledge, only one among them touches upon this problem: Ange Guépin, a second-rate writer. He sees in an international congress the future political and economic directory of our globe. With the improvement of communications and the progress of industry and commerce, the world, he thinks, will change its appearance and prejudices will disappear. Soon a "central congress" will preside over the government of the world, superimposing itself upon all member States of "the great federation" of nations. Hu-

---

[35] *Doctrine de Saint-Simon, Exposition, Première année, 1829, 6e séance,* p. 236.
[36] Chevalier, *Politique d'association* (1832), p. 32.

manity as a whole will form only one family of peoples associated for the utilization, in common, of the earth.[37]

(B) THE PEACEFUL ROLE OF BANKERS

Resuming an idea dear to Saint-Simon, his disciples assign to the bankers an important function in the pacification of the world. They rejoice at seeing the strength and influence of this group of "producers" increase. Cosmopolites by the nature of their business, the bankers, according to the sect, constitute a power friendly to peace, always ready to back up constructive work and quick to move away from regions where violence and idleness predominate. They link all parts of Europe into a common financial system and replace the old social order by the "fruitful seeds of the European federation."[38]

The international collaboration of bankers presages a new peaceful world. It proves that the industry of one nation is not the enemy of that of others but, on the contrary, is their natural ally and support.[39]

The social importance of bankers, moderate formerly, has grown immensely thanks to the development of the industrial establishments relying on credit. The very monarchs are more and more depending on financial power. It rests only with the will of the bankers themselves to transform their economic strength into political power.

"On the very day," says Chevalier,[40] "on which bankers, too, will wish to form their holy alliance, on the day when they will be united in a congress, their political power

[37] Guépin, *Traité d'économie sociale* (1833), p. 7. Cf. also Picard (1925), pp. 491 f.

[38] Enfantin, *Des banquiers cosmopolites* (1826), p. 211. Cf. also p. 210.

[39] Rouen, *Société commanditaire de l'industrie* (1825), p. 121.

[40] *La paix est aujourd'hui la condition de l'émancipation des peuples* (1832).—A quarter of a century later he will say: "L'importance extraordinaire qui, dans les Etats modernes, est acquise à une classe particulière de commerçants, les banquiers, est aussi un gage de paix. . . . Par position, par instinct, par son intérêt le plus absolu, cette classe influente est nécessairement ennemie de la guerre." Chevalier, *Cours* (2nd ed.), vol. II, p. 239.

will be founded; on that day all chances of war will vanish like smoke."

Such are the sect's ideas on bankers. It is hardly necessary to say that they are not based on an analysis of economic and social facts. As the reader has doubtless noticed, the sect deduces them from its purely speculative premise that bankers are cosmopolites because their business embraces the entire world.

Among the queer ideas one finds in the annals of the history of social thought, the one which expects from the bankers the organization of international peace is certainly not the least strange.

(C) INDUSTRIAL ORGANIZATION OF THE ARMY

Adversaries of war, the Saint-Simonians are opposed to the maintenance of armies in the traditional sense of the word and advocate an "industrial organization of the army."[41]

According to Biard,[42] the army should be transformed from an instrument of war into a practical and theoretical school of artists, scholars, and industrialists, in which all members of the most numerous and the poorest class would enroll for general education and professional training in harmony with their natural vocation.

A complete transformation of the army is suggested also by Chevalier. He wants men to be recruited in order to be taught not the art of destroying and killing, but that of producing and creating. In the new military organization, regiments will become schools of arts and crafts, to which all could be admitted at the age of sixteen. "Artillerists will be mechanics and smelters; the gun-foundries will be turned into factories of fire-engines and steamboats; the cavalry will form the corps of farmers, wagoners, and of the public mail and coach service; the soldiers of the engineer corps will be miners; the pontoniers will span the rivers

41 Cf. Chevalier, *Organisation industrielle de l'armée*, 1832.
42 Biard, *Aperçu*, 1832.

with steel bridges; the infantry of the line will take up a vast variety of trades. . . ."[43]

For the time being, target practice would be kept up as a gymnastic exercise. Military uniforms, music, and festivals, too, will be retained. But it is clear that the "regiments of peaceful workers"[44] will have nothing in common with regiments in the current sense of the term. These "workers-soldiers" (soldats travailleurs)[45] will in effect be nothing else but workers.

An industrial organization of the army would be very beneficial from the economic point of view. It would be the best means of inaugurating a true peace policy.[46] It would lead to disarmament, of which France should set the first example.[47]

As for the organization of national defense, in a world not yet enjoying perfect peace, the sect is not interested in it.

(D) THE "MEDITERRANEAN SYSTEM"

"Universal association" (treated in a previous section) is a constant preoccupation of the Saint-Simonians. We have already quoted one of their definitions of it. We add another, from the pen of Chevalier: "From the strictly political viewpoint," he observes, "the universal association is the organization of a system of industrial works embracing the entire globe, which supposes an enterprise general in scope, in which all peoples will have a share, and a secondary one particular to each people."[48]

As a first element of the enterprise general in scope, Chevalier outlines what he calls the "Mediterranean System" (le système de la Méditerranée). This plan, which was to unite Occident and Orient and constitute the first

---

[43] Chevalier, Aux hommes politiques (1832), p. 15.

[44] Religion saint-simonienne. L'armée guerrière et l'armée pacifique, p. 1.

[45] Chevalier, Aux hommes politiques, p. 16.

[46] Cf. Delaporte, De l'application des armées aux travaux (1832).

[47] Rochette, Du désarmement de la France (1832).

[48] Chevalier, Politique d'association, pp. 33-34.

step toward the universal association, is essentially nothing but a vast project of railway construction. Railways, however, in the eyes of the Saint-Simonians are more than a means of communication. "In the material order [of things] the railway is the most perfect symbol of the *universal association.* . . . The introduction on a large scale of railways on the continents and of steamships on the seas will be not merely an industrial but a political revolution."[49]

These important results expected of railways by Chevalier explain the boldness of his plan. In each Mediterranean gulf a chief port would be chosen for the starting point of a railway: Barcelona would thus be connected with Madrid and Lisbon, Marseille with Lyons, Paris, and Havre, Taranto with Venice, Scutari with Bagdad and Bassora, etc. North Africa would be supplied with a railway line running along the Mediterranean coast. Besides, the isthmuses of Panama and Suez would be cut and other canals constructed; the main rivers would be made navigable. The cost of these gigantic enterprises could be covered by the savings resulting from the elimination of military expenditures. The financing of all these projects would be very easy if the governments gave up their warlike policies and joined in a "Mediterranean confederation."[50] Industry would take an immense upswing "on the very day on which a congress would lay the foundations of this confederation."[51] Let us note, however, that Chevalier does not specify at all what he means by "Mediterranean confederation," nor how he imagines its constitution and functioning.

The very drafting of a plan of "Mediterranean" works promises unexpected results. "On the day on which this *Mediterranean* system will be sufficiently elaborated so that its realization can be initiated, peace will return to Europe as by enchantment, and it will return to stay forever, for the state of distrust and armed vigilance in which na-

---

49 Chevalier, *Système de la Méditerranée* (1832), pp. 132, 133.
50 *Ibid.*, p. 148. Cf. also pp. 131 ff.
51 *Ibid.*, p. 148.

tions and cabinets now find themselves in regard to one another flows chiefly from the fact that they do not conceive any peaceful objective of activity."[52]

The Mediterranean system would intimidate the rulers so much that they would no longer dare to provoke wars. It would ensure such a high degree of welfare that Chevalier cannot imagine how "in the midst of so much prosperity a cabinet could be found which, stricken with war fever, should seriously think of tearing the peoples from their fruitful activity in order to fling them into a career of blood and destruction."[53]

How robust the faith of the Saint-Simonians in technological progress must have been to make them expect such revolutionary results from the construction of railways or the carrying into effect of "Mediterranean" work projects!

[52] *Ibid.*, p. 127.
[53] *Ibid.*, p. 146. For further details on the "Mediterranean system," cf. Nicard des Rieux (1912), pp. 79-84.

XIII. IDEALIST SOCIALISM

MARX and Engels habitually opposed their own "materialist" system (in the philosophical sense of the term) to "idealist" socialism. The present chapter is devoted to the most important representatives of the latter (excluding the Saint-Simonians): Robert Owen, Charles Fourier (and his disciples Victor Considérant and André Godin), Constantin Pecqueur, François Vidal, and Louis Blanc.

All these authors do not pay the same amount of attention to the problem of war. Some, such as Owen (1771-1858), Vidal (1812-1872), and Louis Blanc (1811-1882), hardly express an opinion on the subject. Others, such as Fourier (1772-1837), Considérant (1808-1893), and Godin (1817-1888) devote whole chapters to it. Pecqueur (1801-1887) even wrote two special studies on the theme: *De la paix, de son principe et de sa réalisation* (1842) and *Des armées dans leurs rapports avec l'industrie, la morale et la liberté* (1842).

The socialists regard a radical reform of the existing regime of property as a panacea for all the ills of society, of which war is only one manifestation. But the inventors of socialist schemes are far from unanimous on the scope of this reform. Each of them proposes a different plan of economic and social organization.

Owen advocates the abolition of private property, absolute equalitarianism, and remuneration in accordance with the needs and not with the capacity of the individual. Pecqueur, too, is a categorical opponent of private property: the soil, the means of production, and all the sources of social wealth should belong to the State.

Conversely, Fourier envisages for his phalansteries the following distribution of income: four twelfths of the net social produce would be given to the capital employed, five twelfths to labor, and three twelfths to talent. Private property is thus by no means abolished in the phalansterian system: on the contrary, this system tends to generalize it in the form of association. Neither does Louis Blanc think—at least for the near future—of expropriating the capitalists who would collect interest proportionate to their investments in the "social workshop."

Vidal, divided between his sympathy for integral socialism, which to him seems superior to liberal economy, and a desire for immediate practical applications, recommends measures of transition: organization of labor (*organisation du travail*) by the State to the extent that the latter can interfere with matters economic without violating too openly the principle of private property.

1. International Harmony under a Societary System

The socialists who examine the effects of war characterize it as an unprofitable and a socially harmful phenomenon.

According to Pecqueur, every war is contrary to the true prosperity of peoples. It is always a scourge, a miscalculation, and a baleful thing, even for the victorious nation. It is expensive, even to the most successful who exhaust themselves in winning it as much as the weaker ones do in losing it. It is antisocial because incompatible with general welfare. No matter to what historical period one turns, wars have always been waged for the benefit of the privileged few, aristocrats or bourgeois.[1]

Peace, on the contrary, is beneficial to all. "The state of peace," says Considérant, "is much more favorable to the respective interests of the belligerent parties than the prolongation of war could possibly be to the victors themselves."[2]

Louis Blanc stresses human suffering as well as the economic losses entailed by armed strife. "The slaughter of several thousands of men," he notes, "the despair of their mothers and wives, the distress of their children, the de-

[1] Pecqueur, *De la paix*, pp. 39, 434, 57, 80, 55. Cf. also Pecqueur, *Des améliorations matérielles* (1840), p. 218.

[2] Considérant, *Principes du socialisme* (1847), p. 21. Cf. his *Destinée sociale* (1848), vol. I, p. 109.

population of the countryside, the abandonment of agriculture, the paralyzing of industry and commerce, the undue growth of taxes, all this is the balance, not only of defeat, but of victory. To the ignoble cry 'Woe to the vanquished!' history makes this avenging reply: 'Woe to the victors!' "[3]

The permanent threat of war does not even allow the complete enjoyment of the advantages of peace. It leads to a regime of armed peace. "War makes of peace an evil almost as great as war itself."[4]

To this state of things, which they wish to change radically, the socialists oppose the ideal of international brotherhood. "All peoples are brothers,"[5] Considérant asserts, and the same assertion recurs throughout the whole socialist literature. The socialists thus recommend a policy of peace: "The peoples," remarks Vidal, "must establish friendly relations, and exchange peacefully goods and ideas instead of volleys of cannon."[6]

It is not nature but the social order which is making nations warlike. "Reform society," exclaims Louis Blanc, "and you will not have to slander nature!"[7]

Society, and not the individual, is responsible for the state of war which is ravaging the human species. "Remove," says Owen, "responsibility from the individual, who is powerless over society, and shift it to society, which is all-powerful over the individual; the highest destinies of man will be promptly and easily fulfilled: charity, peace, and love will soon be the character of all."[8] In a perfected society, with a suitable pedagogical system, all the misfortunes of mankind would soon cease forever: war, too, would disappear.

[3] Blanc, *Congrès de la paix* (1878), p. 395.

[4] *Ibid.*, p. 396.

[5] Considérant, *La dernière guerre et la paix définitive en Europe* (1850), p. 3. "La Barbarie, c'est la guerre, la force, la conquête." *Ibid.*, p. 6.

[6] Vidal, *Vivre en travaillant!* (1848), p. 209.

[7] Blanc, *Organisation du Travail* (ed. 1850), p. 117.

[8] Owen, *Dialogue sur le système social* (1848), p. 15. Cf. also Owen, *Deuxième Dialogue*, pp. 9-10; *Lectures on an Entire New State*, pp. 153 f.; *The Book of the New Moral World* (1836), pp. 43, 48.

Each socialist sees in the scheme he recommends the definite solution of the problem of war. Fourier assures us that, under a societary system such as he advocates, "unity and perpetual peace will suddenly succeed the furors of a thousand hostile peoples; humanity as a whole will form the family of brothers dreamed of by philosophy."[9]

His pupil, Considérant, shares the same viewpoint. "We announce," he says, "that the immense discoveries of Ch. Fourier lead to the art of associating interests and characters in the Community and in the State—and consequently to the positive means of *establishing social harmony on the globe; of founding peace, work, liberty, in short, happiness, on this earth.*"[10]

Owen is persuaded that, in what he calls "the rational system of society," the warlike spirit would disappear forever to give way to "charity without limit."[11] The forces wasted in wars would be utilized to lift up nations materially and morally. There would be no longer either armies or navies.[12]

According to William Thompson, a disciple of Owen's, a society respecting "the natural laws of distribution" would not know wars of aggression, for if one gets used to living on one's own labor, there is no longer any thought of attacking one's neighbors like a bandit. Under such a regime one would understand that the profit of pillage lasts but a day, and that society has only one permanent source of wealth: labor.[13]

In the opinion of Owen's followers a just distribution would thus ensure peace. The same idea had already been voiced by Charles Hall, an author studied by them with

[9] Fourier, *Théorie de l'unité universelle* (1822), vol. I, p. 173. The societary system will naturally banish "le commerce mensonger," an important source of wars. Cf. Fourier, *Pièges* (1831), p. 59; *Publication des manuscrits,* vol. III, p. 76.

[10] Considérant, *Petit cours de politique* (1847), p. 49.

[11] Owen, *Lectures on the Rational System of a Society* (1841), p. 39. Cf. also Owen, *A Letter Addressed to the Potentates* (1857), p. 4.

[12] Owen, *A Farewell Address* (1850), pp. 9-10.

[13] Thompson, *An Inquiry into the Principles of Distribution of Wealth* (1824), ed. 1850, pp. 170-171.

a good deal of sympathy.[14] In a section of his book, *The Effects of Civilisation on the People in European States* (1805), he deals with the "Cause of the Frequency of Wars." All wars have for their object, says Hall, to increase trade, or to extend territory; they are occasioned by the ambition or irritability of the rich. The latter have frequently recourse to war in order to increase the oppression of their poor compatriots. "Wealth, i.e., inequality of property, therefore, . . . is the cause of almost all wars."[15] If the people, bearing the heavy burden of military conflicts, were to decide for themselves about war or peace, there would be few wars. If property were equally divided, if there were thus no rich people, men, to satisfy their needs, would but rarely leave their parish; each locality would produce everything it really required.[16]

Pecqueur affirms that the most fruitful idea which economic science can instill into men's minds is that of a central administration whose mission would be to direct the economic life of the nation. A representative government must direct the production and distribution of goods. First of all, each nation must organize itself into one immense economic, civilian, and political association. "Then, thanks to the progress of cosmopolitan sentiments, all nations will gradually join together in economy and politics, much as families, parishes, districts, and departments belonging to one and the same nation have already joined together; and the spiritual and material association of mankind will be an accomplished fact."[17]

2. *Productive Armies*

The socialists have little sympathy for the army. In their opinion it is the symbol of unproductivity. Among the

[14] Cf. the introduction of Foxwell to Menger (1899), p. xxxiv. On Hall, cf. Beer (1940), pt. I, pp. 126-132.

[15] Hall, *Effects of Civilisation* (ed. 1850), p. 138. Cf. also pp. 136-137, 133.

[16] *Ibid.*, pp. 137, 136.

[17] Pecqueur, *Théorie nouvelle d'économie sociale et politique* (1842), p. 575. Cf. also pp. 571-574.

"social parasites" Fourier mentions in the first place "the armies of land and sea which divert from labor the most robust youths and the lion's share of the taxes, inclining the young men to depravity by forcing them to sacrifice to a parasitic function the years they should employ preparing themselves for work, all taste for which they lose while in uniform."[18] His aversion to militarism reveals itself in the very appellation he bestows upon it: *Tartarism*.[19] John Gray, who regards even the name of soldier as a disgrace to human nature, would drastically reduce the armies, pending the coming of better times when they will completely disappear. Owen wanted to convince the military themselves of the economic and social noxiousness of their profession and of the necessity of suppressing it.[20]

Conversely, the socialists are partisans of "productive armies." Fourier recommends the substitution, for "destructive armies," of "beneficent" ones (*armées bienfaisantes*) which, formed by "attraction and gallantry," would have for their mission the construction of "superb monuments."[21] He devotes a chapter of his *Théorie de l'unité universelle* to the "industrial armies of the Association," in which he gives a survey of what the harmonious armies (*armées harmoniennes*) and their industrial miracles would be. They would be vast groupings of men who, with their works of reforestation, irrigation, and drainage, would change the face of the globe. Instead of destroying, armies would finally begin to produce. It is needless to add that their cost would be much below that which war entails: in addition to the saving of men slaughtered, cities burned, and fields devastated, one would save the expenditure of armaments and, moreover, enjoy the gain reaped from the work. "Never," concludes Fourier, "was a generation more surfeited with the fumes called the laurels of victory, than is

---

[18] Fourier, *Théorie de l'unité universelle*, vol. III, p. 175.

[19] Fourier, *Le nouveau monde industriel et sociétaire* (1829), p. 420.

[20] Gray, *A Lecture on Human Happiness* (1825), p. 23; *Social System* (1831), pp. 171-172. Owen, *To the Members* (1830), pp. 43-44; *Owen's Millennial Gazette*, May 1, 1857.

[21] *Théorie des quatre mouvements* (1808), pp. 265-266. Cf. also p. 263.

ours. Our century should therefore be disposed to give thought to laurels more useful than those of slaughter, namely to industrial trophies."[22]

Considérant describes the industrial armies such as Fourier's phalansterian system would employ, in the following words: "One of the greatest consequences of the new social order will be the substitution, for destructive armies, of pacific and industrial ones of different degrees, which will be put to work to reforest mountains denuded by our improvident society; to reclaim deserts, supplying them with water and gradually covering them with loam, in order to restore them to life and fruitfulness; to drain swamps; to construct bridges and to regulate, by dikes and embankments, the course of rivers large and small; to dig irrigation and navigation canals; to build roads and railways between the principal points of the continents; to cut isthmuses such as those of Suez and Panama; in a word, to carry out, as if by magic, vast projects of general utility requiring legions of workers, which will have for their result the improvement, embellishment, and utilization of the entire surface of the terrestrial domain, of which mankind is the perpetual usufructuary."[23]

Vidal and Weitling, both influenced by Fourier, likewise advocate the establishment of industrial armies.[24]

In contrast to numerous socialists, Pecqueur is interested not only in the future, ideal and far off, which will perhaps not need military armies properly speaking. He is also seriously preoccupied with the necessity of national defense in the present-day world, and he consequently endeavors to reconcile the socialist ideal with military duty. He comes out in favor of a transformation of the idle and onerous armies into active and hard working ones, contributing to material prosperity as much as to national security. One should withhold from production, he notes, only that part

[22] Fourier, *Théorie de l'unité universelle*, vol. III, pp. 563-564.

[23] Considérant, *Exposition abrégée du système phalanstérien* (1846), p. 50.

[24] Vidal, *Vivre en travaillant!*, p. 209; Weitling, *Die Menschheit wie sie ist und wie sie sein sollte* (ed. 1845), pp. 28-29.

of the male population which must be kept with the colors permanently for the safeguard of national security. The whole remaining part should be returned to social life, to productive labor, and to liberty.[24a]

3. Projects of Peace Organization

The French socialists have conceived manifold projects of European and world organization. It is not our intention to examine them here in detail. This work has already been done by M. Puech in his interesting study *La tradition socialiste en France et la Société des Nations*. What matters to us is to review these projects briefly in order to determine the importance their authors attribute to the economic factor.

We disregard the writers dealing with international organization merely in the form of a utopia, such as Cabet, for example, or who, like Louis Blanc, discuss it only cursorily. Let us note, however, as a matter of curiosity, that Cabet advocates "general disarmament, the brotherhood of peoples, freedom of the import and export trades, and the abolition of tariff duties."[25] He also recommends "a confederation [of peoples] and an annual federal congress to discuss the common interests of the confederates."[26] In a brief passage, Louis Blanc expresses himself in favor of the establishment of a "federal high court";[27] but he gives no detail permitting us to specify his thought.

On the contrary, we shall dwell on the socialists who, preoccupied by the problem of war, have not failed to state how they imagined the political unification of peoples or the international organization of peace: Fourier, Considérant, Godin, Pecqueur, and Vidal.

Curiously enough, in spite of his aversion to war, Fourier develops a project for the unification of mankind based on the conquest of the entire world by a genial and enlight-

---

[24a] Pecqueur, *De la paix*, p. 223; *Des armées*, p. 237. For more details, cf. Marcy, 1934, pp. 159-162.

[25] Cabet, *Voyage en Icarie* (1845), pt. II, chap. v, p. 357.

[26] *Ibid.*   [27] Blanc, *Congrès de la paix*, p. 394.

ened despot. He announces, in 1803, that Europe is approaching a catastrophe which is bound to cause a frightful war but which will end in perpetual peace. A plan of pacification like that of the Abbé de Saint-Pierre is to Fourier's mind, however, out of the question. His vision is altogether different. Russia, Austria, and France, after beating Prussia, will form a continental triumvirate. Austria will be eliminated by her two copartners, who will end up by fighting each other. The victorious triumvir—and France must do all she can to become that power—will rule Europe and dictate her condition to the rest of the world.

"The sovereign of Europe will impose tribute on the entire globe and will establish *temporary* peace on earth. It remains to be seen by what means he will be able to perpetuate this peace. Before explaining them, I observe that philosophers, short-sighted people that they are, have not yet foreseen the principle of *temporary* peace. This principle is the formation of the Triumvirate, leading to the ultimate shock and the unity of the continent."[28]

There can be no tranquillity on the globe before a general conquest has united all peoples under a central government. Such a conquest, its military character notwithstanding, would be justified by its end: to save the world. "Ever since the art of navigation furnished us with the means of overrunning the earth, there has been no more wholesome passion than a boundless ambition of conquest; for if one of the monarchs only succeeds in the conquest of two thirds of Europe, he may compel the other third to join his banner and immediately effect the Federal Union of the Globe and universal pacification."[29]

There are no preoccupations of an economic order in Fourier's meditations on the "Federal Union of the Globe." Nowhere does he seem interested in looking for the economic basis on which nations should form an international organization.

[28] Fourier, *Triumvirat continental* (1803), p. 458. As for the explanation promised by Fourier, we have not found it in his works.
[29] Fourier, *Théorie des quatre mouvements* (1808), p. 323.

Fourier, a solitary dreamer, not having found a genial despot to establish the universal monarchy by conquest, recommends still another means of world pacification: the "phalansterian" system. He is persuaded that, once introduced, this system would assure "constant peace" to men.[30] Let them dissolve their States, let them group themselves in harmonious phalanges (*phalanges d'harmonie*), scattered over the whole earth and containing each about 1,500 persons; let them all submit to the omniarch residing in Constantinople, the "seat of the Congress of Spherical Unity,"[31] and peace will come about all by itself, easily and immediately.

Considérant, the best known of Fourier's disciples, demands that governments give up bellicose policies in order to begin (to use his expression) to direct labor and peace.[32] He sums up as follows his viewpoint on the close relation between the social order advocated by the Fourierists and the establishment of peace:

"There can be no tranquillity, security, peace, or stable order in France and in Europe so long as the workers and all industrious people have not conquered material well-being and moral dignity;

"There can be no general well-being without a tremendous growth in national wealth;

"There can be no well-being, liberty, or dignity without a guarantee for all of a reasonable *minimum* [of means of subsistence];

"There can be no *guarantee* of a *minimum* without *attractive labor*."[33]

However, independently of this realization of peace by

---

[30] Fourier, *Théorie de l'Unité universelle*, vol. II, p. 53.

[31] *Ibid.*, p. 353. Cf. also *ibid.*, p. 376, and Fourier, *Harmonie universelle* (1803), p. 53. For further details on the phalansterian system, cf. Bourgin's fine book, *Fourier* (1905).

[32] Considérant, *La paix et la guerre* (1839), p. 42. Cf. also his *De la politique nouvelle* (1843), pp. 30-33.

[33] Considérant, *Le socialisme devant le vieux monde* (1848), pp. 54-55. Cf. also his *Bases de la politique positive* (1847), p. 189.

a complete social transformation, Considérant envisages still another route leading to world pacification and involving no change in the social structure.

The unity of peoples, which is the supreme goal of humanity, might be obtained by their free association. To attain this aim, he suggests "the transformation of present-day occasional congresses, chiefly diplomatic, into a regular European institution."[34] The foundation of such an institution seems to him realizable because of the economic advantages which the nations would derive from it.

The European States will create not only a permanent "Congress" but also a *unitary law* and even a unitary *administration*."[35] The European Congress will have an authority superior to that of the participating nations. On the day when the United States of America will send their representative to this Congress, the latter will doff the qualification "European" and will take the name of "World Congress" or that of "Congress of Spherical Unity."[36] In the realization of this vision the role attributed by Considérant to France is primordial.

The transformation of the sporadic congresses into a regular European institution seems to him to lie in the near future. "This sovereign institution will be the work of the nineteenth century," he says in 1847.[37] The disappointments, to which his previsions were doomed by the events, did not discourage him. His optimism was not affected. His *Prédictions sur la guerre*, published in 1870, are an eloquent testimony of it: the Franco-German conflict is there regarded as the "last war." It will not prevent the final establishment of the Republic of the United States of the Occident, Europe, and America.

The permanent Congress advocated by Considérant would not restrict its action to territorial and political regulations. Industry, commerce, and the arts and sciences

---

34 Considérant, *De la politique en général* (1840), p. 103.
35 *Ibid.*, p. 30.   36 *Ibid.*, p. 98.
37 Considérant, *Principes du socialisme* (1847), p. 67.

as well as coins, weights, and measures would furnish their share of subjects "to deal with and to unify."[38]

Economic collaboration will be of particular importance. Thanks to the development of their industrial activity, nations are no longer under a necessity of forming coalitions to fight in order to conquer each other; they should rather ally themselves for the purpose of exchanging their goods and of multiplying their productive forces, their means of well-being, of freedom, and of social perfectibility. Tariff barriers must be suppressed, freedom of trade alone being favorable to the peoples. Finally, "industrial armies" would take the place of the destructive ones.[39]

Though Considérant's project differs from Fourier's "continental triumvirate" in that it is based on free association and not on conquest, the two have one feature in common: they presuppose no modification of the social structure, which, since both authors are socialists, is certainly strange. Considérant even sees in the protection of property one of the essential aims of the "General Congress, the common unitary authority."[40]

The idea of a permanent congress of European States, formulated by Considérant, is taken up again and further developed by another Fourierist, Godin, the founder of the famous *familistère* of Guise. The evils of war, he observes, make peace essential to human welfare. The abolition of war therefore occupies first place in his program of social reforms. "Peace," he says, "is the first of the social questions."[41] Without peace, all social reform will be powerless to assume a truly durable character.

The inauguration of the republican form of government

---

[38] Considérant, *De la politique en général*, p. 32.

[39] *Ibid.*, pp. 76 f. For further details, cf. Dommanget (1929), pp. 152 f.

[40] Considérant, *De la politique en général*, p. 31. Let us note in passing that at the time when they formulated their projects of peace, Fourier and Considérant (as well as Godin, Pecqueur, and Vital, whose plans will be analyzed below) already are full-grown socialists.

[41] Godin, *Le Gouvernement* (1883), p. 296: "La paix est la première des questions sociales." Cf. also his *La politique* (1875), pp. 154-158; *La République* (1889), pp. 564-572.

among all European nations would easily lead them to a federal union. Does this mean that no attempt at a federation of peoples and a peace organization must be made before the conversion of the whole of Europe to the republican system? No, one must proceed without delay to the formation of a permanent congress of European States which should prepare for the abolition of war and the organization of peace, European disarmament, international arbitration, and a confederation for the enforcement of the arbitral decisions.[42]

The European federal union should create economic conditions favorable to the prosperity of the participating nations. "Consequently," says Godin, "the confederation institutes, among the nations forming the union, absolute freedom of trade and traffic because it is convinced that customs, by saddling consumer goods with a tax to be borne by the peoples, raise the price of daily necessities and constitute a cause of poverty and misery for the workers. Customs have, besides, the serious inconvenience of giving rise to dissensions, disagreements, and conflicts between nations because they have no other motive than the spirit of greed and monopoly, which are wholly opposed to justice and equity."[43]

In the work of Pecqueur, the founder of State collectivism, as in those of Fourier and Considérant, one can distinguish two conceptions of universal peace: according to one of these, world peace would be the natural product of a recasting of the social system; according to the other it would flow from a political reorganization of mankind.

The "Republic of God" as imagined by Pecqueur is by definition peaceful: it is nothing but a "religious union for the immediate practice of universal equality and fraternity."[44] In such a "republic"—it is needless to say—inter-

---

[42] Godin, *Le Gouvernement*, pp. 283-345; *Solutions sociales* (1871), pp. 188-193.
[43] Godin, *Le Gouvernement*, p. 343.
[44] Subtitle of Pecqueur's *République de Dieu* (1844).

national peace would come about by itself. A society organized in conformity with the religious and social system of Pecqueur would naturally not know military conflicts. However, Pecqueur, independently of his own system, conceives yet another possibility, purely secular and political, of establishing a regime of peace.[45] He asserts, indeed, that social progress makes realizable "a European merger, a federation of the nations of this continent under the moral and political unity of a general congress,"[46] and that social evolution is tending toward a "union analogous to that of the United States of America."[47]

The Congress would pursue, in principle, a free-trade policy. Without its consent the federated nations could not impose tariff duties. They would be absolutely forbidden to wage trade wars with each other by means of trade regulations, prohibitions, and restrictions. If, instead of recognizing commercial freedom, they should reciprocally refuse the free exchange of their products, the Congress would have the right to intervene and the power to enforce its decision.

It would have for its chief mission to equilibrate the general economic interests. Each contracting nation would be obliged to participate proportionately and in common in the colonizations, clearings, work projects of international character, and vast enterprises aiming at the exten-

---

[45] Let us note here the like attitude of a nonsocialist economist, inspired by Christianity: Le Play (1806-1882). "To tell the truth . . . ," he says, "war is neither the first nor the chief cause of the evils besetting mankind: it is merely the manifestation of more intimate and profound disorders. Just as a disease is the ordinary consequence of the bad passions of the individual, so war is the punishment for the vice of nations." (Le Play, 1864, chap. 40, sect. 4, vol. II, pp. 205-206.) War results from the fact that nations fail to observe the Decalogue (Le Play, 1875, vol. I, pp. 311-314). Peace can therefore not be definitely established so long as men do not conform to the ten commandments. But, apart from this religious precept, Le Play (1881, pp. 257-258, 198-203) also formulates, though very briefly, a project of a "European Union" of continental States, whose essential aim should be the abolition of war and a regime of armed peace.

[46] Pecqueur, Économie sociale (1839), vol. II, p. 401.

[47] Ibid., pp. 401-402.

sion and advancement of civilization. Subjects of one nation would enjoy the right of citizenship in all others.

Each nation would preserve its sovereignty in everything
not absolutely opposed to the existence of an international
authority and international justice. Only the Congress
would have the right to declare war, to conclude peace, to
make treaties of alliance and commerce with nonsignatory
States, to establish tariff duties and to take measures of re-
prisal against them, to decree the levying of an army, to fix
the contingent each nation has to furnish for it, to raise
loans, and, under a collective guarantee, to issue paper
money acceptable as legal tender throughout the confederation.[48]

"The *European* association, even a *universal* association,
is not a dream which must for ever remain senseless."[49]
What is dreamy about it is to wish to proclaim it too early
or according to too rigid a scheme. It must be prepared
with much patience. Pecqueur describes the direct and
indirect means which should pave the way for this association, one of the most important of which is the development of foreign commerce.

"Every policy tending toward peace must therefore endeavor to establish relations between all the peoples of the
world, to multiply commercial intercourse so as to link
and *intertwine* all individuals, all peoples, and all interests, in a vast net of transactions and affairs, one which
creates solidarity between them, and of events stirring not
only Europe but the entire world."[50]

Curiously enough, it is in customs unions such as the
German *Zollverein* that the socialist Pecqueur sees one of
the most effective means of preparing for peace.

"One of the measures carrying with it most chances of
peace is the formation of trade alliances or customs unions
on the bases and in the spirit of the German [customs]
association. There is nothing more decisive both for the

[48] Pecqueur, *De la paix*, pp. 390-394.
[49] Pecqueur, *Économie sociale*, vol. II, p. 402.
[50] Cf. Pecqueur, *De la paix*, p. 185.

prosperity of all peoples and the advancement of the peaceful destinies of the world."[51]

The world union will be realizable only among nations which have attained the same level of economic development. To put themselves on an equal footing industrially, weaker nations should in Pecqueur's opinion adopt temporary protection.[52] He thus advocates the same economic nationalism as List.

A determined cosmopolite, according to whom there is no justice possible so long as men will "remain fenced in as [separate] nations,"[53] he speaks as a nationalist as soon as he makes a practical approach to the question of an international organization. He explains this contradiction by saying that he prefers to make concessions to the spirit of the times rather than be unable to reform anything at all. "Perhaps, too," remarks one of his commentators, "he does belong to that line of French socialists who, while endeavoring to establish the reign of peace among nations, have always kept a weather eye on the interests of their country and have always desired to defend them."[54]

Like Pecqueur, Vidal sees in regional customs unions the best practical means of driving nations toward larger and larger international associations.

He notes, in 1846, that for as many as thirty years civilized nations have ceased to play the ruinous and bloody game of battles, and that military war is on the point of disappearing. But war properly speaking has been superseded by industrial and trade war. Today one is fighting over markets as fiercely as one did formerly over provinces. And such a war is, unfortunately, no less regrettable than military conflicts.

Nations begin, however, to feel instinctively that they cannot get on without one another, that they must ex-

[51] *Ibid.*, p. 189.
[52] Pecqueur, *Économie sociale*, vol. II, pp. 414-415, 419-423.
[53] Pecqueur, *République de Dieu*, p. 201.
[54] Marcy, *Constantin Pecqueur* (1934), p. 153.

change their products, and that they are necessarily bound together. They are tending to establish closer and closer relations. By digging canals, constructing railway lines and thus shortening time and space, they are all the while drawing nearer and nearer to one another. "A few years more, and an immense revolution will have been accomplished peacefully in the world."[55]

Nations will finally understand better the close solidarity which necessarily unites them and will then find commercial treaties insufficient. "One will speak," says Vidal, "of union and association, of political union and industrial association; one will follow the example given by Prussia to Northern Germany; then one will go even further and at last try to realize positively economic order and peace. The various countries of Europe will have become, as it were, provinces of one empire; all will be united, confederated; but each will keep its language, its customs, its laws, and its national institutions, until the time is ripe for the definitive constitution of a vaster and more intimate unity, a general unity, the universal unity. That day will mark the triumph of the true social economy."[56]

Let us say in addition, before bringing this chapter to a close, that most socialists see in the political liberty of peoples one of the essential conditions for a lasting peace. As long as, says Leroux, the human race is divided into "tyrants and slaves," war will be the inevitable consequence. According to Pecqueur, the European tribunal will be formed on the day on which the majorities will have the decisive word to say. European confederation and perpetual peace—such are, in the words of Considérant, the immediate goals of democracy. The democratization of Europe, Godin thinks, would necessarily bring with it the federal union of peoples. And finally in the opinion of Louis Blanc one must not count upon the realization of the generous thoughts which animate the friends of peace

[55] Vidal, *De la répartition des richesses* (1846), p. 3.
[56] *Ibid.*, p. 4.

so long as the peoples are not their own masters, since kings and emperors need war.[57]

From this rapid survey of peace plans outlined by the socialists it clearly follows that, independently of their specifically socialist projects, they recommend a federal organization of the world conceivable even within the frame of liberal economy. The federalist idea of Considérant, Godin, Pecqueur, and Vidal—we naturally pass over Fourier's project of a world monarchy—presupposes no economic or social upheaval. At first sight this is astonishing, for it is characteristic of socialism to consider itself the true remedy for all social ills, of which war is evidently one of many manifestations. But the socialists we have just reviewed consider war an evil so patent to almost everybody that they do not regard as utopian the possibility of eliminating it even in the framework of contemporary society. They would no doubt have preferred to see the socialist order established simultaneously with the foundation of a federal union of peoples. They would no doubt also have preferred to see socialism inaugurate world peace. But they conceive the latter without the former. The problem of war being in their view easier to solve than that of social justice, they do not hesitate to propose the formation of a universal federation of nations even before the latter become socialist. Resolutely hostile to war, they seem to have thought that an attempt should be made to solve the problem by some means to which the ruling classes would have infinitely less reason to be opposed than to the partial or total abolition of private property. Such an attitude, which is very probable in the case of the authors discussed in this chapter, would reveal a depth and independence of mind all the more remarkable because they were regarded by their contemporaries as mediocre doctrinaires and mere spinners of theories.

[57] Leroux, *Réfutation* (1841), p. 43; Pecqueur, *Économie sociale* (1839), vol. II, p. 364; Considérant, *La dernière guerre* (1850), p. 4; Godin, *Le Gouvernement* (1871), p. 307; Blanc, *Congrès de la paix* (1878), p. 399.

XIV. MARX AND ENGELS

THE founders of materialist socialism—Marx[1] and Engels[2]—do not examine, explicitly and systematically, the problem of war. One finds in their works numerous pages on wars and, by collecting them, one could easily make a heavy volume; but one would look in vain for a theoretical inquiry into the problem of war and peace. This fact deserves being pointed out all the more because these two writers have thrown into relief the interdependence of the economic and war. They have also evinced, notably Engels, considerable interest in strategy. It is astonishing that Marx and Engels, sociologists and economists though they were, have not been tempted to give a theoretical and comprehensive view of the problem. What can be the reason for this omission?

It seems to us that the very structure of the Marxist doctrine explains this curious neglect. The theoretical construction of Marxism is such that it lends itself particularly to the explanation or the filling of its gaps. Indeed, its

[1] Son of a lawyer of Jewish origin, Karl Marx (1818-1883) studied law, philosophy, and history at Bonn and Berlin. Having reached the conclusion that the economic determines the whole of social life, he began, in 1844, while in Paris, to devote himself to the study of political economy. After his expulsion from France (1845), he pursued his economic studies in Belgium, from where he was expelled in 1848. He took part in the revolutionary movement of the Rhineland and at Cologne edited the *Neue Rheinische Zeitung* (1848-1849). Expelled once more, he took refuge in Paris. Driven from there, he settled in London, where he led the hard life of a political exile until his death. He played a prominent part in the foundation and direction of the International Workers' Association. Cf. Mehring, 1923. Our study has been facilitated by L. Kaufmann's interesting dissertation (1932).

[2] Son of a businessman and a businessman himself, Friedrich Engels (1820-1895) left Germany in 1842, to fill, at Manchester, a position in an enterprise of which his father was a shareholder (1842-1844 and 1850-1869). He met Marx, first, in 1842, and then again in 1844, when the two became life-long friends. He spent the years from 1845 to 1850 in France, Germany, and Belgium, organizing there the revolutionary movement. After the failure of the revolution of 1848-1849, he returned to England. In 1869 he retired from business, to devote himself entirely to literary and revolutionary activity. He played an important role in the Workers' International. Cf. Mayer, 1934; Drahn, 1915.

partisans can always point out that the element omitted is *implicitly* contained in the fundamental postulate of Marxism: historical materialism. Such might have been, we think, the reply of Marx and Engels to the question posed. Such might be even now the answer of their disciples.

In the history of socialism the names of Marx and Engels are linked together so closely and so justly that it does not seem very important to distinguish the contribution of each to the common work. The elaboration of the system must doubtless be credited to Marx. It is to him exclusively that his friend Engels[3]—with an admirable, though perhaps excessive, modesty—ascribes the discovery of the materialist interpretation of history and the theory of surplus-value. From our particular point of view, however, Engels presents as much interest as Marx, if not more, for he is a passionate student of military art and has written more on war than the author of *Das Kapital*. After his death, Engels's military writings were collected in a number of special publications (*Notes on War*, 1923; *Militär-politische Schriften*, 1930; *Der deutsch-französische Krieg*, 1931).

The bibliographical sources of this chapter are numerous: the works of Marx and Engels which appeared during their lifetime, their posthumous publications, and their correspondence. The ten volumes published thus far of the monumental edition of their *Complete Works*—the whole is to comprise forty-two—make available important materials which in many cases had never been published before.

Among Marx's writings of particular importance for our study we must cite, apart from several articles printed in the political press, his *Discours sur la question du libre échange* (1848), his *Randglossen zum Programm der deutschen Arbeiterpartei* (1875), and the *Manifest der kommunistischen Partei* (1848), which he published with Engels. In *Das*

[3] *Anti-Dühring*, p. 13; *Manifest der kommunistischen Partei* (preface, 1883); *Ludwig Feuerbach*, pp. 36-37.

Kapital he mentions war several times, but these references —which can be easily found in the index of the edition prepared by Kautsky—have no special interest for our work.

Several of Engels's works deserve particular attention. Let us mention in the first place: *Umrisse zu einer Kritik der Nationalökonomie* (1844), *Herrn Eugen Dührings Umwältzung der Wissenschaft* (1878), and *Kann Europa abrüsten?* (1893). Many observations on the problems under discussion are found also in his speeches made at Elberfeld (1845), as well as in his articles on Panslavism (1849) and on England (1852). His preface (1888) to Borkheim's brochure is of very great historical interest.

Marxist doctrine has been so violently controverted by its opponents and so variously interpreted by its followers that it is not superfluous to state its meaning more explicitly. By Marxist doctrine (or Marxism) we mean the theoretical system developed exclusively by Marx and Engels. We shall then intentionally omit all interpretations or application's[4] of Marxism, however interesting they may be, in order to restrict ourselves wholly to the thought of the founders of the doctrine as expressed in their writings.

Nor shall we examine the various theories of imperialism, developed by several of the disciples of Marx and Engels, such as Hilferding (*Finanzkapital*, 1910), Rosa Luxemburg (*Die Akkumulation des Kapitals*, 1913), Lenin (*Imperialism the highest stage of Capitalism*, 1917). They all date from the twentieth century. Their study and analysis (which can be easily found elsewhere)[5] would go beyond the chronological limits of this book. Suffice it to state that neither Marx nor Engels has formulated any theory of economic imperialism, according to which the capitalist system, at a certain stage of its development, inevitably produces war.

1. War in the Light of Historical Materialism

In the preface to his *Critique of Political Economy* (1859)

4 As, for example, those of Loria and Cicotti (cf. Bibliography).
5 Cf. Hashagen, 1919; Hovde, 1928; Winslow, 1931; Robbins, 1939.

Marx briefly sketches the principle of historical material-ism. Of this classic outline, so frequently quoted, it is suf-ficient to reproduce here the opening passage.

"In the social production which men carry on, they en-ter into definite relations that are indispensable and inde-pendent of their will; these relations of production corre-spond to a definite stage of development of their material powers of production. The sum total of these relations of production constitutes the economic structure of society—the real foundation, on which rise legal and political super-structures and to which correspond definite forms of social consciousness. The mode of production in material life determines the general character of the social, political, and spiritual processes of life."

War, a social and political phenomenon, by its very es-sence belongs to the superstructure spoken of by Marx. From this it follows that, like any other social phenome-non, it is conditioned and determined by the mode of pro-duction in material life. Now, with the exception of primi-tive Communism this mode of production is antagonistic in all societies which have existed heretofore. It inevitably produces class struggle in the interior of societies and pro-vokes armed conflicts between States or rather between their ruling classes. The class struggle thus is, as it were, the national expression of this antagonistic mode of pro-duction, while foreign war is its international manifesta-tion.

Still, if the class struggle is an essential element of Marx-ist doctrine, this cannot be said of foreign war. Marxism cannot, without collapsing, give up its thesis of the perma-nency of the class struggle in a capitalist society. It is in-conceivable without the axiom of the class struggle. On the contrary, it might admit the *possibility* of suppressing wars in a capitalist world. Indeed, the existence of a capitalist *world* State, that is to say, a State which is by definition immune from foreign wars, would in no way upset the Marxist interpretation of the world. In other words, so far as Marxism is concerned, there is no incompatibility in the establishment of peace in a capitalist system. Within the frame of the doctrine it is also possible to imagine a federation of capitalist States eliminating the danger of war. If Marx and Engels envisage neither the possibility of a world State nor that of a federation of States, nor any other form of international or inter-State organization of peace within the set-up of class society, the reason is not that these constructions are contradictory, in principle, to historical materialism, but solely, it seems, that the two thinkers saw no practical possibility of their realization. It is thus purely practical considerations which determined their attitude. A theoretical controversy on the subject: Is a class society incompatible with a supernational organization of peace? is, to our knowledge, absent from their writings.

Economic conditions not only provoke war but closely determine its conduct. This Engels demonstrates by several examples. Nothing, he affirms, is more dependent on these conditions than the army and navy. Armament, military organization, tactics and strategy depend above all on the degree of development of production and communications. What has produced, in this field, revolutionary effects is not the "free creations of the mind" of genial captains, but the invention of better arms and changes in military equipment. The influence of generals of genius is limited, even under the most favorable conditions, to the adaptation of the fighting methods to new arms and new combatants.[6]

Marx shares this viewpoint. In his letter to Engels, of July 7, 1866, we read: "Is there anywhere where our theory that the *organisation of labour is determined by the means of production* is more brilliantly confirmed than in the human slaughter industry? It would really be worth while for you to write something about it (I have not the necessary knowledge) which I could insert under your name as an appendix to my book [Marx here probably refers to his *Capital*]."[7]

[6] Engels, *Anti-Dühring*, pp. 173-176.
[7] Marx-Engels, *Briefwechsel*, vol. III, p. 345 (English translation in Marx and Engels, *Correspondence 1846-95*, p. 209).

The influence of economic transformations on military art is not limited to the past. They will determine also in the future the art of warfare. According to Engels it is clear that the emancipation of the proletariat will express itself also in the military field: it will create a new strategy. One can even now foresee the material bases of this new type of warfare. Thus, for example, production will be so increased that it will permit a larger number of men (15 to 20 per cent of the total population) to participate in the fighting. Technical progress will facilitate a greater strategic mobility.[8]

Engels's work abounds in forecasts of a military nature. Those concerning the future evolution of the art of war are too hasty. Thus Engels believes that military art reached its apogee at the time of the Franco-Prussian war of 1870-1871. Weapons have attained such a degree of perfection that further progress, which would have any revolutionizing influence, is no longer possible. With guns which can hit a battalion at any range at which it can be distinguished, and with rifles equally effective for hitting individual men, rifles whose loading takes less time than aiming, all further improvements are more or less unimportant for field warfare. The era of development is therefore essentially closed in this direction.[9]

On the other hand, Engels's previsions on the future world war have proven astonishingly exact.

In the militarism of his time he sees one of the factors

[8] Engels, *Die Möglichkeiten* (written in 1851), pp. 300-302.

[9] "Mit dem deutsch-französischen Krieg ist ein Wendepunkt eingetreten von ganz andrer Bedeutung als alle frühern. Erstens sind die Waffen so vervollkommnet, dass ein neuer Fortschritt von irgend welchem umwälzenden Einfluss nicht mehr möglich ist. Wenn man Kanonen hat, mit denen man ein Bataillon treffen kann, soweit das Auge es unterscheidet, und Gewehre, die für einen einzelnen Mann als Zielpunkt dasselbe leisten, und bei denen das Laden weniger Zeit raubt als das Zielen, so sind alle weitern Fortschritte für den Feldkrieg mehr oder weniger gleichgültig. Die Aera der Entwicklung ist nach dieser Seite hin also im Wesentlichen abgeschlossen." Engels, *Anti-Dühring*, pp. 176-177.

likely to undermine Europe. In our time, he observes,[10] wars in most cases paralyze political and social progress.

In 1888 he foresees a world war lasting from three to four years and of a heretofore unimaginable violence. In a passage which deserves reproduction in extenso, he draws a gloomy picture, but one which in certain respects was prophetically true, of what this universal conflagration, in which "Prussia-Germany" was to participate, would be like.

"Henceforth," Engels says, "no war is possible for Prussia-Germany except a world war and a world war indeed of an extension and violence hitherto undreamt of. Eight to ten millions of soldiers will mutually massacre one another and in doing so devour the whole of Europe until they have stripped it barer than any swarm of locusts has ever done. The devastations of the Thirty Years' War compressed into three or four years, and spread over the whole Continent; famine, pestilence, general demoralization both of the armies and of the mass of the people produced by acute distress; hopeless confusion of our artificial machinery in trade, industry, and credit, ending in general bankruptcy; collapse of the old states and their traditional state wisdom to such an extent that crowns will roll by dozens on the pavement and there will be nobody to pick them up; absolute impossibility of foreseeing how it will all end and who will come out of the struggle as victor; only one result absolutely certain: general exhaustion and the establishment of the conditions for the ultimate victory of the working class."[11]

10 At the conference of the General Council of the International Working Men's Association held in London, at the beginning of 1871 (cited according to Mayer [1934], vol. II, p. 205).

11 "Und endlich ist kein andrer Krieg für Preussen-Deutschland mehr möglich, als ein Weltkrieg, und zwar ein Weltkrieg von einer bisher nie geahnten Ausdehnung und Heftigkeit. Acht bis zehn Millionen Soldaten werden sich unter einander abwürgen und dabei ganz Europa so kahl fressen, wie noch nie ein Heuschreckenschwarm. Die Verwüstungen des dreissigjährigen Krieges zusammengedrängt in drei bis vier Jahre und über den ganzen Kontinent verbreitet; Hungersnoth, Seuchen, allgemeine, durch akute Noth hervorgerufene Verwilderung der Heere wie der Volks-

A European war, writes Engels on January 7, 1888, to his friend Sorge, would result in a formidable increase of chauvinism. If it were to be fought to the bitter end, without ending in a social upheaval, Europe would be more exhausted than she has been for two centuries.[12]

Now, Engels often feared that this war might not end in a social revolution. His correspondence is full of apprehensions on that score. We content ourselves with quoting two examples. A universal war, he writes on December 16, 1879, to his friend Bebel, "would be our greatest misfortune: it might throw back the [socialist] movement by twenty years."[13] In a letter addressed to the same, under date of December 22, 1882, Engels observes: "I should regard a European war as a misfortune. This time it would become dreadfully serious, inflame chauvinism everywhere and for years to come, since every nation would fight for its existence."[14]

He was nevertheless convinced that a world war, no matter what its immediate effects might be, would by its final consequences lead to the victory of communism.

Militarism, which is dominating and devouring Europe, carries in itself the seeds of its own destruction. It becomes more and more costly and hastens the financial collapse of States. On the other hand, compulsory military service makes the whole people familiar with the use of arms.

massen; rettungslose Verwirrung unsres künstlichen Getriebs in Handel, Industrie und Kredit, endend im allgemeinen Bankerott; Zusammenbruch der alten Staaten und ihrer traditionellen Staatsweisheit, derart, dass die Kronen zu Dutzenden über das Strassenpflaster rollen und Niemand sich findet, der sie aufhebt; absolute Unmöglichkeit, vorherzusehn, wie das alles enden und wer als Sieger aus dem Kampf hervorgehen wird; nur ein Resultat absolut sicher: die allgemeine Erschöpfung und die Herstellung der Bedingungen des schliesslichen Siegs der Arbeiterklasse." Engels, *Einleitung* (1888) to S. Borkheim's *Zur Erinnerung*, p. 7 (English trans. in Marx and Engels, *Correspondence 1846-95*, pp. 456-457).

[12] *Briefe an . . . F. A. Sorge* (1906), pp. 288-289. Such a war would end moreover with the hegemony of American industry. *Ibid.*

[13] Unpublished correspondence preserved in the Archives of the German Social-Democratic Party, cited according to Mayer (1934), vol. II, p. 463.

[14] *Ibid.* Cf. also *ibid.*, p. 533. "Since 1879 Engels voices misgivings to any war." Kautsky (1937), p. 250.

The working classes thus gain an opportunity of opposing by arms the capitalist system. At the proper moment they will not hesitate to make use of a favorable opportunity to seize the helm. Having laid hold of it, they will put an end to standing armies and to militarism. The latter unleashes forces which doom it to death: it will thus be burst asunder "from within," according to Engels's formula. Like any other historical phenomenon, militarism will collapse by the dialectic of its own evolution.[15]

2. *Hostility toward Free Trade*

While the liberal economists deduce their pacifism from the doctrine of *laissez faire, laissez passer,* Marx and Engels feel only contempt—one might even say disgust—for liberal economy and its theoreticians. By giving to their science the name of *vulgar economy* or *bourgeois political economy,* they show this openly. No doubt, they do respect the great classics such as Quesnay, Smith, Ricardo, and a few others. But, with a few exceptions, liberal political economy of the nineteenth century is in their eyes only an expression of the decay of the ruling classes, whose scientific representatives, fearful of uncovering the contradictions of the capitalist system, merely express platitudes suitable to the interests of the dominant classes. That is why Marx and Engels deny to nineteenth century economic science the character of objectivity.

According to them, the more we approach the present, the more the decline of this science becomes evident; its representatives are more and more losing the feeling of intellectual honesty. To keep their science up to date, these economists pile up sophism upon sophism. For this reason, observes Engels,[16] Ricardo is more guilty than Smith, and MacCulloch and John Stuart Mill are more guilty than Ricardo.

In the preface to the second edition of *Das Kapital,* Marx observes that political economy, particularly since

15 Engels, *Anti-Dühring,* pp. 177, 181.
16 *Umrisse zu einer Kritik der Nationalökonomie* (1844), p. 381.

1830, has been transforming itself into a vulgar economy. The latter is trying to deny the real economic contradictions and all class antagonism. In the person of Bastiat it achieves an apology of the established economic order, combined with plagiarism and ignorance.[17]

The laws formulated by the bourgeois economists, notwithstanding their assertions to the contrary, have nothing absolute about them. To give but one example, the entire contemporary political economy and the laws of wages would come to an end if the workers, instead of letting themselves be bought and sold, were resolved to act, in the determination of the value of labor, not only as owners of their labor power but also as *men* possessed of will.[18]

The schools of political economy merely reflect the class interests they represent. "Just as the *economists* are the scientific representatives of the bourgeois class, so the *socialists* and the *communists* are the theoreticians of the proletarian class."[19] However, while the former are prevented by the oppressive character of the interests of the bourgeoisie from proclaiming objective truth, the latter are quite capable of doing so, for the interests of the proletariat tally with those of all mankind.

The conceptions of the liberal economists on competition and international free trade, according to Marx and Engels, are altogether erroneous. For the liberals, competition is a condition indispensable to economic progress. Marxism takes a different view: competition, it asserts, favors economic progress only at a certain stage of social evolution, a stage already left behind by contemporary society. From a factor of progress that it once was, competition has now become a barrier which henceforth prevents the growth of production and of social wealth.

Engels observes that Adam Smith's liberal system unquestionably constitutes progress over the past. But this system has outlived its usefulness. At present it can be

17 Marx, *Theorien über den Mehrwert*, vol. III, pp. 573-574.
18 Engels, *Die Lage der arbeitenden Klasse* (1845), pp. 208-209.
19 Marx, *Misère de la philosophie* (1847), p. 191.

qualified only with the words hypocrisy, inconsistency, and immorality. Marx also denounces "the hypocritical character common to all free-trade sermons."[20]

"In the present state of society," he asks himself, "what *is* free trade? It is the freedom of capital. When you have overthrown the few national barriers which still restrict the progress of capital, you will merely have given it complete freedom of action. So long as you let the relation of wage-labor to capital exist, no matter how favorable the conditions under which the exchange of commodities takes place, there will always be a class which will exploit and a class which will be exploited. It is really difficult to understand the claim of the free-traders who imagine that the most advantageous use of capital will eliminate the antagonism between industrial capitalists and wage-workers. On the contrary, the only result will be that the antagonism between these two classes will stand out still more clearly."[21]

Competition is the most perfect expression of the war of all against all which dominates bourgeois society. It is the manifestation of the merciless struggle of individuals against individuals, of classes against classes, and of nations against nations. It is profoundly immoral. Under this economic regime each desires a monopoly for himself. Each wishes to obtain as much as possible. The general interest and the individual interest are thus diametrically opposed.[22]

Free trade, which is so much advocated by the liberals, in reality amounts to "unscrupulous freedom of commerce" (*gewissenlose Handelsfreiheit*) and to "free huckstering" (*der freie Schacher*).[23] Marx and Engels do not expect from it the solution of the social problem. One of the numerous manifestations of this problem, for example, pauperism, this sore of modern society, diminishes or increases inde-

[20] Marx, *Discours* (1848), p. 443. Cf. Engels, *Umrisse*, p. 381.
[21] Marx, *Discours sur la question du libre échange*, pp. 445-446.
[22] Cf. Engels, *Die Lage der arbeitenden Klasse* (1845), p. 77; *Zwei Reden* (1845), p. 387; *Umrisse* (1844), p. 393.
[23] Marx and Engels, *Manifest der Kommunistischen Partei*, pp. 528, 540.

pendently of free trade or protectionism.[24] How can one
see, then, in commercial freedom a remedy against social
suffering? It is at bottom merely a means for assuring to
the bourgeoisie the unlimited power of capital over labor.
It is nothing but "the liberty of capital to crush the worker."[25]

In Marx's opinion the impoverishment of the working
classes is on the increase in capitalist economy. "In the
same proportion as wealth is created," he says, "misery is
produced, too."[26] The wages of the worker correspond to
the minimum of existence and are not a function of free
trade or tariffs. Whatever the liberals' phraseology, the
more intelligent among them fully realize that wages will
not rise as a result of liberal reforms.

According to the political circumstances, the working
classes may have an interest in supporting either the liberals or the protectionists. In Germany, for instance, it is
in the workers' interest to back protectionism. The latter
is indispensable for the German bourgeoisie to increase its
strength in the interior, to destroy what remains of feudalism, and to assume political power. Once the social terrain
has been prepared in this manner and cleaned of all its
archaic forms, it will lend itself marvelously to the final
struggle of the proletariat against the bourgeoisie.[27] It is
thus to the advantage of the working classes to support protective tariffs whenever the latter constitute, for the national bourgeoisie, "weapons against feudalism and absolute government."[28]

"But in general," Marx concludes, "the protective system in our times is conservative, while the free-trade system is destructive. The latter breaks up old nationalities
and carries to extremes the antagonism between bourgeoisie and proletariat. In a word, the system of commer-

24 Cf. Marx, *Pauperismus und Freihandel* (1852), p. 29.
25 Marx, *Discours*, p. 446. Cf. also Marx, *Das Parlament*, p. 53.
26 Marx, *Misère de la philosophie*, pp. 189-190.
27 Engels, *Schutzzoll und Freihandelssystem* (1847), pp. 431-432.
28 Marx, *Discours sur la question du libre échange* (1848), p. 447.

cial freedom hastens the coming of the social revolution."[29]
It is in this revolutionary sense alone that Marx votes in
favor of free trade.

There remains the task of analyzing the thought of
Marx and Engels on free trade and protection as instruments of peace or war.

The first text furnishing information on the subject is
the editor's note to a protectionist article printed in the
Rheinische Zeitung on November 22, 1842. This note is
anonymous, and the Marxist scholar Ryazanoff attributes
it to Marx. We here reproduce the text in extenso.

"Commerce and industry must be *protected*, but the
point at issue is whether *protective tariffs* do really protect
commerce and *industry*. We rather consider such a system
as the *organization of* a *state of war* in time of peace, a state
of war which, first directed against foreign countries, must
in its execution necessarily turn against its own country.
But since an *individual* country, however much it may admit the principle of free trade, is dependent upon the condition of the world, this question can be decided only by
a congress of nations, but not by an individual cabinet."[30]

This note seems to show that Marx, its presumed author,
prefers *in principle* free trade to protectionism. In his eyes
the latter is a warlike implement no less dangerous to the
fatherland than to foreign countries. None the less, whatever the benefits of free trade, the latter is not realizable
by a single State. Marx thus refers to a "congress of nations" as the only institution susceptible of introducing

---

[29] *Ibid.*

[30] "Handel und Gewerbe sollen *beschützt* werden, aber eben das ist der
streitige Punkt, ob *Schutzzölle Handel* und *Gewerbe* wahrhaft beschützen?
Wir betrachten vielmehr ein solches System als *Organisation des Kriegszustandes* im Frieden, eines Kriegszustandes, der, zunächst gegen fremde
Länder gerichtet, in seiner Ausführung sich notwendig gegen das eigene
Land kehrt. Allerdings ist aber ein *einzelnes* Land, so sehr es das Prinzip
der Handelsfreiheit anerkennen mag, durch den Weltzustand überhaupt
bedingt, und kann daher diese Frage nur von einem Völkerkongress, aber
nicht von einem einzelnen Kabinett entschieden werden." Marx, *Ueber
Schutzzölle*, pp. 308-309.

and of extending freedom of commerce. But, after hardly touching upon this possible solution, he abandons it without ever reverting to it. He draws from it no immediate or remote conclusion. The problem of international organization does not preoccupy him at that time, nor will it do so in the future.

One is tempted to deduce from the note in question that, seeing in protectionism a factor of war, Marx views free trade as an element of peace. This seems the more plausible to us because a trace of this conception is found in a later writing, this time above Marx's unquestioned signature. In the *Manifesto of the Communist Party* one reads in effect that free trade is tending, with other factors, gradually to efface national differences and antagonisms.[31] On this point Marx's philosophy and that of the liberal school are in agreement. However great the abyss separating them, both admit the pacifying influence of free trade. Marx, it is true, does not say anything about the degree or intensity of this influence. Neither does he specify that, all other conditions being equal, freedom of trade diminishes the risk of war. But it seems difficult to interpret differently the fragment of the *Manifesto* to which we have just referred.

Marx recognizes that free trade gradually effaces international antagonisms. But this admission does not modify in any way his attitude, in principle hostile to economic liberalism. Whether or not the latter generates peaceful tendencies seems to him of little importance. It is evident that it is not the pacifism or bellicism of any particular current which would enlist his sympathies for it. He combats free trade from a totally different point of view: he blames it for being, in its very substance, only the representative, and a hypocritical one, of the bourgeoisie.

[31] *Manifest der Kommunistischen Partei*, p. 543 (we reproduce this passage, in its context, below. Cf. p. 271. On the "cosmopolitanism of the commodity owner" as a product of the universalization of the markets and of the currency, cf. Marx, *Zur Kritik der politischen Oekonomie* (1859), ed. 1897, pp. 155-156 (English trans., pp. 207-208).

To assert, as is done by the partisans of free trade, that the latter begets a feeling of brotherhood among the various classes of one and the same nation is, according to Marx, altogether erroneous. The "brotherhood" which free trade would establish between the various nations of the earth would be no less illusory. "To call cosmopolitan exploitation universal brotherhood is an idea which could be engendered only in the brain of the bourgeoisie. All the destructive phenomena which free competition gives rise to within one country are reproduced in more gigantic proportions on the world market. We need not pause any longer over the sophisms uttered on this subject by the free traders."[32]

The latter habitually see concord everywhere. They claim, for example, that free trade would lead to an international division of labor beneficial to all nations, because it would allot to each country the production which is most in harmony with its natural advantages. But they forget the existence of international monopolies which exercise a contrary influence. There are, in our times, some branches of industry assuring to the nations which most largely exploit them the command of the world market. Such nations thus enjoy a monopoly which permits them to grow fat at the expense of others. If the free traders cannot understand this phenomenon, one need not wonder, "since these same gentlemen also refuse to understand how within one country one class can enrich itself at the expense of another."[33]

The attitude of Engels toward free trade is in principle the same as that of Marx. He admits that commercial freedom reduces the number of wars. This does not prevent him, however, from launching out into a vehement diatribe against the free traders whom he blames as much for their hypocrisy as for their moral baseness.

Is it true, as asserted by Adam Smith, that trade humanizes international relations? In certain respects it does so, observes Engels. Indeed, there is nothing absolutely im-

[32] Marx, *Discours*, p. 446.   [33] *Ibid.*, p. 447.

264

moral in the world. Trade, too, by certain of its aspects constitutes an homage to morality and humanity. But what homage! The highway robbery of the Middle Ages has been humanized: it disappeared to give way to mercantilism. In its turn, mercantilism, too, was gradually humanized. Needless to say that it is in the interest of the trader to live on good terms with the seller from whom he buys cheap, and with the buyer, to whom he sells dear. Thus a nation harboring hostility toward its purveyors and customers acts foolishly. The friendlier these trade relations are, the more profitable they are to both parties of the transaction. Such is the humanization introduced by trade; and this hypocritical manner of abusing morality for immoral ends constitutes the pride of the free-trade system. Engels continues thus:

"Have we not torn down the barbarism of monopolies? cry the hypocrites, have we not carried civilization into remote continents? Have we not established the brotherhood of peoples and reduced the number of wars? Yes, all this you have done, but *how* did you do it! You destroyed the small monopolies in order to give an all the more free and unlimited rein to the one great basic monopoly, property; you civilized the ends of the earth in order to win new fields for the display of your base greed; you established the brotherhood of peoples, but it is a brotherhood of thieves, and you reduced the number of wars, in order to make all the fatter profits in peace, in order to carry to extremes the enmity of individuals, the dishonest and the infamous war of competition! Where did you do anything out of pure humanity, from a consciousness of the futility of the opposition between the general and the individual interest? Where have you been moral without being self-interested, without harboring immoral and egoistical motives in the back of your mind?"[34]

[34] Engels, *Umrisse*, p. 384. (". . . haben wir nicht die Völker verbrüdert und die Kriege vermindert?—Ja . . . ihr habt die Völker verbrüdert, aber zu einer Brüderschaft von Dieben, und die Kriege vermindert, um im Frieden desto mehr zu verdienen, um die Feindschaft der einzelnen, den ehrlosen Krieg der Konkurrenz, auf die höchste Spitze zu treiben!—Wo

This acrid criticism of free trade proves how much economic liberalism was repugnant to Engels. But it in no wise modifies the fact that he ascribes to free trade a tendency to pacify, in the strict sense of the term, international relations. On this point he agrees—as does Marx—with the free traders themselves.

A passage in his correspondence attests that he saw in protectionism a factor making for war. In a letter to his Russian friend Danielson, of October 29, 1891, Engels, referring to a special case—the wheat market crisis in Russia—briefly indicates how protectionism produces a warlike attitude. When the home market, protected by tariffs, becomes insufficient, those who are hit, "naïve folks" according to Engels's expression, imagine that nothing is more natural than to enlarge it by a successful war.[35]

3. Antipacifism

An essentially dynamic and revolutionary doctrine such as that of Marx and Engels cannot be pacifist in the traditional sense of the word. Aiming at a social upheaval, both national and international by force, it is irreconcilable with pacifism. While the latter condemns violence, Marx and Engels consider it as a factor indispensable to progress.

According to them, nothing in history is accomplished without violence and brutality.[36] They have therefore no reason to be opposed to armed strife as such. First, they approve its use within the State. Secondly, they approve of it as between States in every case where a foreign war favors the interests of the proletariat. Whether war is aggressive or defensive is of little importance. The decisive point is that, directly or indirectly, it be useful to the working classes.

Pacifism, if it is not an expression of pure hypocrisy, is

habt ihr etwas aus reiner Humanität, aus dem Bewusstsein der Nichtigkeit des Gegensatzes zwischen dem allgemeinen und individuellen Interesse getan?") Lassalle (1863, p. 485) is no less indignant at the immorality of the Manchester School than Engels.

[35] *Briefe von Marx und Engels an Danielson*, p. 54.

[36] Engels, *Der demokratische Panslavismus* (1849), p. 255.

only a manifestation of intellectual confusion. The pacifist ideas born during the revolution of 1848—international brotherhood, a European federal republic, and perpetual peace—according to Engels attest only the limitless perplexity and the complete inactivity of the spokesmen of the period. Painful experience teaches that the true brotherhood of peoples will come about neither by simple words nor by vain desires: it can only be the work of profound revolutions and bloody strife. Engels combats and ridicules the theory of a general brotherhood of peoples, a theory which, without taking into consideration the degree of development of each of them, is content with "fraternizing at random" (*verbrüdern ins Blaue hinein*). He approves of conquest when it brings civilization to the conquered country, as happened, for example, in the occupation of California by the United States.[37]

Marx, too, is hostile to liberal pacifism and opposed to its penetration among the working classes. In his critique of the Program of Gotha he writes:

"And to what does the German Workers' Party reduce its internationalism? To the consciousness that the result of its efforts will be '*the international brotherhood of peoples*'—a phrase borrowed from the bourgeois League of Peace and Freedom, [and] which is intended to pass as equivalent to the international brotherhood of the working classes in the joint struggle against the ruling classes and their governments. . . .

"In fact, the international consciousness expressed in the program stands *even infinitely below* that of the Free Trade Party. The latter, too, asserts that the result of its efforts will be 'the international brotherhood of peoples.' But it also *does* something to make trade international and by no means contents itself with the consciousness—that all peoples are carrying on trade at home."[38]

The apostle of liberal pacifism, Cobden, is severely judged by Marx. He regards him as a false prophet, whose

[37] *Ibid.*, pp. 246-247, 250.
[38] Marx, *Randglossen* (1875), p. 569. (English trans., p. 13.)

gospel of peace, devoid of all philosophical bearing, merely replaces the feudal method of warfare by a commercial method: capital takes the place of guns.[39]

If the Manchester School wants peace, it does so in order to be able to wage industrial war, both abroad and at home. It wants the hegemony, in the world market, of the English bourgeoisie, whose bales of cotton will be the only weapons. It also wants the supremacy of the bourgeoisie in England, so that this class may govern the State and secure public office for itself, after shoving aside the aristocracy, an element useless in modern production, and reducing to slavery the proletariat, a simple tool in this production.[40]

In 1852, when Louis Napoleon's coup d'état had given rise, in England, to the fear of a French invasion, Engels wrote an article in which he foresees the failure of pacifism. He thinks that the fraud of pacifist congresses and peace societies will some day come to an end. The English bourgeoisie will come to understand that pacifism hurts it and is prejudicial to its own interests as well as to those of England as a whole, for it leaves the country disarmed. Though an alliance of the entire Continent would not suffice to beat England, her carelessness in the field of national defense presents a great danger to her. Now, one of the factors which has contributed to this regrettable state of things is pacifism à la Cobden.[41]

This brief outline shows the fundamental difference between revolutionary Marxism and liberal pacifism. While the latter is desirous of preserving, without any use of violence, the *status quo*, the former endeavors to attain peace by means of a social revolution. Both aim at universal peace, but by different means: the one by free trade, the other by socialism.

[39] Marx, *Die Todesstrafe* (1853), p. 84.
[40] Marx, *Parlamentarisches*, pp. 280-281.
[41] Engels, *England* (1852), pp. 458-460.

4. *Peace and Socialist Society*

To establish a lasting peace, it is necessary, in the view of Marx and Engels, to consider first a profound transformation of the economic and social regime. A permanent peace, they assure us, presupposes the building of a new society. One is thus led to ask oneself what idea they have formed of this society which they think the only one susceptible of realizing both social justice and international peace.

Yet, on approaching the texts, one observes the aversion of Marx and Engels to clarifying their vision of that future society. It is on this point that they part company, quite voluntarily of course, with the "utopians." They deem it idle to draw a more or less detailed picture of a social regime whose forms will become clear only as time goes on and whose constitution will be the work of experience alone. Contrary to the "utopians," they do not wish to "invent" a new regime, but at the most indicate some essential features of the future commonwealth, and this only to the extent to which it appears to them already constituted *in nuce* in contemporary society.

Neither Marx nor Engels has ever expressed himself with any precision on the economic regime of the future. On this point only rather vague remarks are found in their works: the destruction of capitalism and the seizure of power by the proletariat seems to them of far greater importance than the contemplation of detailed forms of future economy. They insist, however, on the political means for bringing about the social transformation. As chief instrument of the workers' policy, which must aim, above all, at the social revolution, they recommend the class struggle. They deduce, as it were, mathematically the necessity of this revolution. "Just as certainly as we are able to formulate on the basis of given mathematical principles, a new theorem, just as certainly we can deduce from the existing economic conditions and from the principles of political

economy a coming social revolution."[42] The very foundations of Marxist economy, the theories of surplus value, of
the accumulation of capital, and of progressive proletariza-
tion—an examination of which would go beyond the scope
of the present volume—furnish in their opinion the best
proof of the solidity of this deduction.

Once emancipated, that is, after having seized power,
the proletariat will gradually efface all class differences and
consequently, according to Marxist terminology, the State
itself. Not only will the bourgeois State be destroyed, but
the State as such will die away as a result of the socialization of the means of production.[43]

At a certain stage of economic evolution the State is a
necessity. This is no longer the case when the productive
forces attain a higher degree of development. The world
is now approaching rapidly a phase in the development of
production at which the existence of classes has not only
ceased to be a necessity, but is becoming a positive hin-
drance to production.

"The classes," says Engels, "will fall as inevitably as they
once arose. The state inevitably falls with them. The society which organizes production anew, on the basis of free
and equal association of the producers, will put the whole
state machinery where it will then belong—into the museum of antiquities, next to the spinning wheel and the
bronze ax."[44]

By banishing economic competition and anarchy the
new collectivist regime will guarantee well-being and liberty to the individual. It will remove all sources of social
discontent and will render social strife impossible. Communism will do away with the opposition between the
individual and society and will substitute social peace for
social war.[45] "The old bourgeois society with its classes
and class conflicts will be replaced by an association in

[42] Engels, *Zwei Reden* (1845), p. 388.
[43] Engels, *Anti-Dühring*, p. 302.
[44] Engels, *Der Ursprung der Familie* (1884), p. 182 (English trans.,
p. 158).
[45] Cf. Engels, *Zwei Reden*, p. 374.

which the free development of each is the condition for the free development of all."[46]

What form will this new social order assume? To this question we find a summary answer, half a page in length, in one of Engels's manuscripts, which remained unpublished for more than half a century: the new society will abolish private property and competition. It will socialize all means of production and introduce a planned economy. It will replace competition by association. It will utilize all the instruments of production and distribute all products by common agreement (*nach gemeinsamer Uebereinkunft*). The new society will thus be the so-called community of goods (*die sogenannte Gütergemeinschaft*).[47]

This society will know neither social classes nor exploitation of man by man. It will therefore know neither internal social strife nor external political conflicts. To suppress wars definitely, it must of necessity extend over the entire globe. A universal classless society means permanent peace.

To bring into being this state of things is the historical mission assigned by Marx and Engels to the working classes.

"Inasmuch as the proletariat must first win political power, must raise itself up to the position of a national class and constitute itself as the nation, it is, so far, still national, though by no means in the bourgeois sense of the word.

"National differences and antagonisms between peoples are already disappearing more and more, owing to the development of the bourgeoisie, to freedom of commerce, to a world market, to the uniformity of industrial production and to the corresponding conditions of life.

"The rule of the proletariat will efface these differences and antagonisms even more. United action, at least of the

[46] Marx and Engels, *Manifest der Kommunistischen Partei*, p. 546.

[47] Engels, *Grundsätze des Kommunismus* (1847), p. 511. Among the measures which are to lead contemporary society toward the new one, Marx and Engels recommend the following: "Universal and equal obligation to work, organization of industrial armies, especially for agriculture." *Manifest der Kommunistischen Partei*, p. 545.

civilized countries, is one of the first conditions requisite for the emancipation of the workers.

"In proportion as the exploitation of one individual by another is abolished, the exploitation of one nation by another will come to an end.

"The ending of class opposition within the nations will put an end to the hostile attitude of nations toward one another."[48]

Having eliminated the sources of war, the communist regime will have no need of standing armies. While contemporary society is obliged to maintain this unproductive institution, the most costly of all, the communist regime will easily get on without it.

Why, asks Engels, should this regime have need of a standing army? To preserve order in the interior? Useless worry, since no one would have an interest in troubling it. The fear of revolution is only the result of class antagonism: one cannot conceive of it in a society based on harmony of interests. For a war of aggression? The question does not even arise. Communist society will never commit an aggression, knowing very well that it is an unprofitable enterprise. For defensive war? Neither for this purpose will a standing army be required, for one can train without it the citizens in the handling of the arms indispensable for the defense of the country. One must also consider that in the case of a defensive war—which, besides, is possible only against an anticommunist society—each member of the community will have a *true* fatherland and a *true* home to defend. He will therefore fight with a tenacity and a courage that will overcome the aggressor. If one recalls the miracles performed, between 1797 and 1799, by the French revolutionary armies, though they were fighting only for an *illusory fatherland*, one can realize the power that would be shown by an army defending a *real father-*

---

[48] *Ibid.*, p. 543. The second paragraph in the German original reads as follows: "Die nationalen Absonderungen und Gegensätze der Völker verschwinden mehr und mehr schon mit der Entwicklung der Bourgeoisie, mit der Handelsfreiheit, dem Weltmarkt, der Gleichförmigkeit der industriellen Produktion und der ihr entsprechenden Lebensverhältnisse."

land. In short, these incalculable masses which armies divert from creative work will be turned back by communism to production. They will produce not only what is necessary for their own maintenance but even a surplus of products which will be stored in public warehouses.[49]

5. Can Europe Disarm?

Engels's pronounced antipacifist attitude did not prevent him from drawing up, toward the end of his life, a disarmament project. He developed it on the occasion of a discussion of the military budget by the Reichstag, in a series of articles published, in March 1893, in the Berlin *Vorwärts* and reprinted under the title *Kann Europa abrüsten?* (*Can Europe disarm?*).

These twenty-five years, he states, the whole of Europe has been arming to an unheard-of degree. Each State endeavors to outstrip the military might of the others. Germany, France, and Russia exhaust themselves in excessive armament efforts. The German government has just demanded of the people such a display of forces that even the Reichstag, however complacent, recoils in fright. In these circumstances, Engels asks, is it not outright stupidity to speak of disarmament?

Still, the plain people of all countries, those who furnish the bulk of the soldiers and pay most of the taxes, are clamoring for disarmament. Furthermore, the military demands have been so great that strength begins to give out everywhere: here recruits are lacking, there it is money that is wanting; in a third country both together are missing. Is there no other way out of this deadlock except a war of destruction such as the world had never seen before?

"I affirm," says Engels, "that disarmament and hence the guarantee of peace, is possible, nay realizable with relative ease, and Germany, more than any other civilized State, has the power and the mission to carry it through."[50]

The system of standing armies has been pushed to such

49 Engels, *Zwei Reden*, pp. 375-376.
50 Engels, *Kann Europa abrüsten?*, p. 5.

extremes that it will finally either ruin the nations economically or degenerate into a war of universal destruction. These fatal consequences can be avoided only by a transformation of standing armies into militias based on the general arming of the people. This transformation could be carried out immediately, for the contemporary States are in a position to adopt the militia system without thereby compromising their national security. From the purely military point of view there is no obstacle to the abolition of standing armies. Their conservation is dictated less by military than by political reasons. They are in fact destined to protect the State less against its external enemies than against the enemy in the interior.

A gradual reduction of military service as a result of some international agreement, the central point of his project, is, according to Engels, the simplest and quickest means of preparing the transition from standing armies to militias. The terms of such an agreement would naturally vary with the character of the contracting parties and with the political situation. The latter, at the time of his writing (1893), seems to him particularly favorable for the conclusion of such an understanding. To begin with, he proposes to reduce military service to two years and notes that it may perhaps be possible, a few years later, to fix upon a training period of much shorter duration.

Engels is convinced that the reduction of service time would in no way interfere with the military value of the army. To increase still more the physical worth of the future soldiers, he advocates the introduction, in the schools, of a preliminary military training for all boys. By making this training a *conditio sine qua non* of his project, Engels believes he can expressly exclude all confusion between militias as conceived by him and those already in existence, notably in Switzerland.[51]

An international agreement aiming at a reduction of the length of military service seems feasible to Engels. Germany should propose it to Austria, to Italy, and to France.

51 *Ibid.*, preface.

The two former powers, in view of their multiple internal difficulties, both economic and political, would be happy to sign it. As for France, her adherence is not certain. But Germany runs no risk in proposing to her such an agreement. If she accepts, all will be well. If she refuses, the moral benefit will redound to the credit of Germany who will thus have shown her will to peace. If, however, France should refuse her signature, the project would be doomed to failure, for Germany will not reduce military service unless her western neighbor does. As for Russia, her attitude does not matter. She is so poorly developed economically and so decomposed socially that, whatever the number of her soldiers and the length of their service, she could not present any danger to Germany.[52]

6. Marxist Theory and War

Whatever the differences between Marx and Engels on the one side and the liberals such as Say or Bastiat on the other, it is worth noting that both admit the functioning of a certain economic automatism supposed to lead to peace. The former call this automatism "socialism," the latter give it the name of "free trade." The former think that peace will be realized as a result of the socialization of the means of production, the latter that it will follow from the adoption of the *laissez faire, laissez aller* policy. Both, in spite of the differences separating them, see only the economic aspect of the problem of war and neglect or ignore all others. Both believe unnecessary a powerful international organization of peace, endowed with coercive executory force. It is true that toward the end of his life Engels sketches a project of international collaboration destined to bar the way to a militarism running wild. But this project is limited, as we have already seen, to disarmament and includes no plan of an international and permanent organization of peace.

The Marxist theory does not seem to us to furnish as evident and complete an explanation of war as its authors

[52] *Ibid.*, pp. 26-29.

fancy. It reduces the causes of war, in the last analysis, to the economic. No doubt, economic causes do play a decisive part in certain cases. But Marxism has by no means proved that the primary source of all wars must be sought in the economic. If it asserts this, it is an abstract assertion true in some cases, false in others, susceptible of satisfying certain monistic minds, but much less satisfactory to those who attach as much importance to the agreement of theories with the facts as they do to the theories themselves. In our opinion there is no objective reason for admitting that all wars, at all epochs, have been due exclusively and in the last analysis to economic factors. To strengthen the plausibility of such a view, the Marxist theory should have illustrated it conclusively by a large number of monographic studies dealing at least with the principal wars of world history. We very much doubt that such studies, based on first-hand sources, would support this conclusion.

The Marxist theory sees in the economic the ultimate source of all armed international conflicts. Such a conception might be countered by other theories which likewise endeavor to explain wars by one single principle, whether biological, racial, religious, mystical, sexual, or other. Every one of these exclusive interpretations is false because one-sided. Furthermore, one fails to see the slightest logical necessity for thus explaining all wars by one and the same order of causes. Why should one reduce a social phenomenon as complex as war to a single formula? The desire to explain war or, for that matter, any other complex social phenomenon by one single factor seems to us contrary to the spirit of science. On that score, monism prevents the advancement of the social sciences.

Since it is not proved that the ultimate causes of all wars are of an economic order, it is impossible to admit that a transformation of the economic regime would be sufficient to assure lasting peace. The noneconomic causes of wars might still be active in a socialist society. The latter might therefore still know wars quite as much as does a class society. The problem of war and peace would then come up also in the international community of socialist States. A modification of the economic system, however profound, is of itself inadequate to guarantee peace.

Let us suppose, however, with Marx and Engels that every war is ultimately provoked by economic causes and has for its aim the economic exploitation of the conquered for the benefit of the ruling class of the victorious State. Would it follow from this that war would necessarily disappear between societies (States) in which private property had been abolished and the means of production socialized?

We shall ignore the case of a socialist society in which a new ruling class or social stratum of the bureaucratic type might come to the fore, a class or stratum having its own special interests opposed to those of the mass of the people. For it is obvious that such a class or social stratum might foment wars in its own exclusive interest, in quite the same manner as is done now (according to the Marxists) by the ruling classes.

Let us imagine, then, a classless society (State). Now, one can perfectly well conceive that such a society as a whole constitutes itself as a class exploiting and oppressing some foreign country. Let us suppose, for example, that the working class of a colonial empire seizes political power. It establishes the dictatorship of the proletariat and, after a period of transition, the mother country passes from this stage to that of complete socialism. Is it not possible, indeed even probable, that such a socialist society, as a whole, will continue to exploit the colonial peoples which it has inherited from the capitalist regime? What assures us that this nation would give back to the colonial peoples their liberty without being forced thereto by a rebellion?

The colonial peoples are used here only as an example. We can apply the same reasoning to the economic exploitation of a relatively undeveloped socialist nation by another socialist society more developed and more powerful. If economic exploitation is based on the dependence of the weaker upon the stronger, it is, or may be, in the international field, a phenomenon transcending classes, that is to say, it may exist even among societies which are not divided into classes.

Conflicts between socialist national units may, in certain respects, be provoked even more easily than between capitalist nations. For in the latter the class interests diverge, oppose, and sometimes neutralize one another, thus being able to prevent war in certain cases. Conversely, the homogeneity of the material interests within a socialist society evidently excludes such a neutralization of warlike forces and may thus facilitate the passing from peace to war.

To refute these objections, one cannot just assert that socialist society will know neither nations (in the ethnical sense of the term) nor States. The disappearance of nations, if it should ever come to pass, seems to us so remote that we see no point in discussing such an eventuality in the present book.[53] As for the disappearance or the dying away of the State—by which term Marxism means a sovereign political unit divided into classes—it does not exclude, as we have already observed, the exploitation of one nation by another. "The State" (broken up into classes) has not a monopoly in oppressing other nations. "Socialist society," too, could do this under cover of some more or less refined dialectic.

To say that with the establishment of a socialist economy in the entire world all division into national units or into States will disappear by itself is a gratuitous assertion. In accordance with the aims pursued by them, socialist States will or will not merge into a superior political unit. If such a unit favors the policy followed by a given socialist State, this State will join; otherwise it will not do so and will remain neutral or will even fight the unit. If a socialist State oppresses and exploits certain foreign countries, it will not associate with a socialist federation based on economic equality and political liberty. If on the other hand

[53] And even supposing this racial and cultural leveling, the splitting up of mankind into States, and hence war, will still be possible.

a socialist State aspires to universal peace, economic justice, and political freedom, it will not hesitate to form a federation with other States pursuing the same objective. The decision of each socialist State can therefore not be predicted: it will be a function of its policy. In short, the transformation of the capitalistic society into a socialistic one does not mean the inevitable establishment of international peace, even if this transformation were to comprise all nations in the world.

CONCLUSIONS AND FINAL
OBSERVATIONS

THE reader will have found, we believe, in this somewhat lengthy study, if not a complete picture, at least an exact sketch of nineteenth century economic doctrines on war. At the close of the book we may be permitted to formulate briefly a few general conclusions as well as to make some final observations which appear to us to be of some interest.

I. The main economic currents of the nineteenth century, liberalism, economic nationalism, and socialism adopt different attitudes toward war.

1. For the liberals war is a phenomenon economically and socially harmful. In their view it is one of the greatest misfortunes that can befall a nation. Those provoking it are guilty of the most execrable of crimes. War is not only immoral but also stupid: it is in effect merely the natural state of men ignorant of the laws of political economy. Inevitable and perhaps useful in the past, war has now become only calamitous and useless; it is an element purely destructive of national wealth and prosperity.

The liberals do not think that war is produced by unsurmountable international contradictions. It is due rather to national interests ill understood. Indeed, liberals never tire of repeating that it is only an infinitesimal part of society that really profits from war. And it is this minority which provokes military conflicts in its own private and exclusive interest. But the nation as such never derives any profit from them. For the nation as a whole war is always an unprofitable business, the more so because the losses it involves are becoming more serious as time goes on. Liberal economy thus teaches that peoples have an obvious interest in living at peace.

In this respect the interests of all social classes are essentially identical. True, war strikes them in different ways. Depending upon the circumstances, it is sometimes one and sometimes another class which suffers most. But none of them escapes completely from the sacrifices imposed by military conflict. Often the working masses are most affected, but neither are the wealthy classes of society spared —capitalists, landowners, rentiers, etc.

War is doubly ruinous if one takes into consideration not only the direct losses resulting from it but also what it prevents from being produced. Furthermore, one does not realize the sum total of these losses until one includes the immense cost of an armed peace. Depopulation, disturbance of the economic equilibrium, destruction of capital, reduction of international commerce, increase of taxation, an ever growing public debt, diminution of the national income, and general impoverishment; such are, according to the liberals, the most important economic consequences of war. Nor do they forget the ensuing spiritual decline and the moral sufferings which, however important, cannot be translated into economic terms.

In liberal opinion it is sufficient to compare this state of things with the advantages of free trade, to be convinced that peace is preferable to war and commerce to spoliation. While war destroys wealth, free trade creates ideal conditions for the enrichment of peoples. It permits them to specialize in the production of the goods and services for which they have most natural or acquired aptitudes. It enables them to sell their products at the highest prices and to buy what they require as cheaply as possible. By favoring international concord, it contributes not only to the material prosperity of nations but also to the intellectual and moral progress of mankind as a whole. Of all known economic systems it is therefore, according to the liberal school, the most favorable to each nation as well as to the human race in its entirety.

The final victory of free trade will not be deferred indefinitely: it will triumph in the end. Now, if we are to believe the liberals, the establishment of commercial freedom will bring about one of the most profound revolutions in history. Free trade will assure to all men the maximum possible of material well-being, which will in fact know no other limits than the natural resources of the globe and the creative work of man. What is more, the influence of free trade will not be restricted to the economic field: freedom of international commerce will also considerably increase the external security of nations.

The role assigned by liberals, in this matter, to political economy is most significant. This science must deal with war because peace is an essential element of public prosperity. Political economy, let us recall, is regarded by the liberals as the science *par excellence* of peace. The diffusion of economic knowledge thus tends, in their eyes, to prevent wars. Though hostile to militarism, they make it clear that their attitude is opposed neither to an enlightened patriotism nor to the principle of nationalities.

Opposition to bellicism is an integral part of liberal theory. The liberals are not satisfied with denouncing war of aggression as a crime against the economic laws properly understood. They do not limit themselves to pointing out the economic senselessness of war. With the exception of Malthus they also assert that they have found in free trade the best possible solution of the problem of war: some assume, implicitly or explicitly, that freedom of commerce will eliminate all or nearly all wars (Say, Dunoyer, Cobden, Bastiat); others, more moderate, that it will substantially reduce the risk of war (Ricardo, James Mill, MacCulloch, John Stuart Mill, Chevalier, Baudrillart, Molinari). And whatever their differences of view, they all take it for granted that, if war is truly inevitable, free trade, by enriching the nations, prepares them better for it than does the protective system, which impoverishes them all.

They think that peace really requires no organization. To suppress war, it is not necessary to form any international (or supernational) organization endowed with coercive force. Free trade by itself suffices to vouchsafe a lasting peace or, should this ideal be unrealizable, at least to pacify international relations to the extent human nature permits. What matters is thus not the creation of an international organism susceptible of compelling the nations to live at peace. To make peace enduring, it is sufficient to establish an economic order that will strengthen spontaneously the peaceful ties uniting the nations. Now, of all imaginable economic systems free trade alone, in the liberal view, is able to foster spontaneously the pacific spirit and peace.

The only important member of the liberal school who does not trust completely in this conception of a spontaneous peace is Gustave de Molinari. He advocates in effect a sort of international organization of peace which would have at its disposal, if need be, a military force necessary and adequate to vanquish a possible aggressor.

Some few liberals recommend an international court but —with the exception of Émile de Laveleye[1]—they either do not admit the necessity of its being supported by an executory force (James Mill), or they do not explicitly demand such a force (John Stuart Mill and Cliffe Leslie[2]).

It is rather interesting to compare the attitude of the liberals toward the State with their attitude toward a supernational (or super-State) peace organization. The view they take of the State is positive, that is, they admit its *raison d'être*, and they do so in spite of their opposition to State intervention in matters economic. On the other hand, with a few exceptions, they are, as we know, opposed or hostile to a supernational organization.

This opposition is astonishing, for one fails to understand what warrants their belief that international order can be maintained without any sort of supernational organization endowed with coercive force. Has free trade this power? Can it compel States, by their sole economic interest, to observe international law and to avoid war? Can it do so in the absence of an international organism provided with coercive force?

If such is the case, as certain liberals appear to think, one may ask oneself why they do not also attribute to free

[1] A liberal follower of the historical method.
[2] Another liberal follower of the historical method.

trade the power of guaranteeing of itself the internal order of each nation. In other words, why do they not credit free trade with the faculty of replacing the State as the guardian of public order in the interior? It is but logical to pose this question, for it does not seem very reasonable to admit, as they do, that free trade can guarantee international order without being able, of itself, to assure public order within a nation. Such is none the less their point of view. On the one hand they assert that the State is necessary for the maintenance of public order within; on the other, they deny the necessity of a coercive organism to guarantee international order. Is there not a contradiction in such a conception of the social world? This contradiction is indeed most obvious and deserved being pointed out.

2. The protectionists take a view of war different from that of the liberals. Unlike the latter, they do not think that war is produced by national interests ill understood. On the contrary, in their eyes it is an inevitable manifestation of the struggle of nations to obtain real, and not chimerical, advantages.

They contradict the liberal thesis which considers war as an unprofitable enterprise for the nation. While the liberals affirm that war is a phenomenon economically harmful to all nations, the protectionists draw a distinction between the victors and the conquered. For the former it may well be profitable. It assures them not only territorial acquisitions, new markets (which would otherwise be closed to them), commercial preponderance, and industrial supremacy, but also—and this is even more important—contributes to the industrialization of the country, that is, it favors the development of what List calls the productive forces of the nation.

According to the protectionists, a victorious war may therefore be of advantage to the entire nation and not only to some thin strata of its population. Consequently, it is not always a bad calculation. It is unprofitable only when uselessly provoked and badly conducted. If then an adequately prepared nation cannot peacefully realize certain of its economic aspirations, it may do so by means of a war of aggression.

Since war can assure to nations real economic advantages, the protectionists do not think it probable that it can vanish forever. It appears to them as a phenomenon bound to last even into a far distant future. Quite true, some of them do foresee the possibility of a durable peace, but they conceive it only in a future so remote that they themselves regard it as almost chimerical.

The protectionists view history as an inevitable struggle between nations, where force is one of the chief factors deciding on their political independence, their grandeur, or their decline. The world at the present time is given to war, and everything points to its remaining so within human foresight. To disarm in such a world would be sheer madness. The peoples who would do so would not obtain peace: they would merely permit those nations which keep their military force intact to attack them all the more brutally. If there still is a factor that may from time to time prevent war, it is not the absence of military force but, on the contrary, the existence of powerful armies ready to repulse the aggressor. Their *raison d'être* is therefore beyond dispute. They fill a necessary and hence useful function in contemporary society. It would thus be wrong to begrudge the army the funds it needs to become a powerful instrument of defense or aggression. It would be equally erroneous to consider military life as wholly sterile and not to discern in it certain elements quite useful to society.

In short, the protectionists do not hesitate to justify militarism on economic grounds. They endeavor to show the utility of military preparations, the advantages of standing armies, the necessity of a navy, and the economic senselessness of disarmament.

In liberalism they see a phenomenon economically dangerous for many nations. Freedom of commerce, they think, is advantageous only to those countries which for any reason have the opportunity of enjoying an industrial and commercial supremacy. It is favorable only to highly industrialized nations whose trade has reached an advanced degree of development. It has advantages only for countries whose industry is already so well developed that it has truly no need of being protected or encouraged artificially. Contrariwise, "young" countries have an interest in pursuing an economic policy different from that recommended by the liberals. Agricultural countries having the resources necessary for their industrialization, as well as countries which already are effectively in this process, need to be economically encouraged and protected. Economic encouragement and tariff protection, which are frequently necessary for the very birth of certain industries, tend to increase the pace of a nation's industrialization.

In favoring industrialization, the State must not necessarily be satisfied with purely economic measures. It may accelerate it also by other means such as territorial expansion and wars of conquest. The latter may help a nation to increase its industrial potential by the acquisition of fresh resources and new markets. In the protectionist view, there is a reciprocal action between the economic and war: industrialization facilitates the conduct of war, and military victories increase the possibilities of industrialization and of economic prosperity. This point of view recalls that of the mercantilists: wealth increases power, and power augments wealth. Let us add, however, that, in spite of this resemblance between mercantilism and protectionism, the latter, contrary to the former,[3] generally takes care not to idealize war too overtly.

According to the protectionists, liberalism jeopardizes the security of economically poorly developed nations. National defense is not efficacious if the country does not possess a sufficiently developed industry. The strategic importance of industry even increases continually with the progress of military and naval technique. The military superiority of industrial over agricultural or half-industrialized nations is patent and unquestionable. Now, the policy of *laissez-faire*, the protectionists assert, prevents the indus-

[3] Cf. Silberner, 1939, pt. I: *Le bellicisme des mercantilistes.*

trialization of relatively undeveloped countries and thus imperils their defense. It tends to prolong indefinitely their military inferiority.

It would evidently be erroneous to believe that the protectionists are opposed to liberalism solely for military reasons. They consider protectionism as an economic system calculated to raise the social level of a nation. They advocate it then quite as much on military as on social grounds. However, though they see in this system more than a means necessary to defend the nation, there is not the slightest doubt that this necessity alone would in their eyes justify the legitimacy of protectionism.

The latter is a national current. One might say, of course, that liberalism is not antinational either: it, too, desires national grandeur and attempts to enhance it. It does not deny that the power of a nation largely depends on economic factors. Nevertheless, it recommends no specifically national economic policy. On the contrary, it asserts that from the economic viewpoint nothing favors national power more than the absence of all economic intervention by the State, that nothing increases it more than the free interplay of economic forces. It considers the entire world, and not the nation, as an economic unit. In its economic reasonings it therefore disregards the existence of political frontiers. It follows more or less faithfully Turgot's old precept: Whoever fails to forget that there are States politically separated from one another will never understand any problem of economic science.

On the contrary, protectionism never loses sight of the division of mankind into nations. It regards the State as an economic entity. It blames liberalism for ignoring that the policy of *laissez-faire* is beneficial only for economically advanced and politically unified countries. It rejects the liberal doctrine which considers the entire world as a single market and as a single workshop. Such a conception, it affirms, while compatible with the interests of nations enjoying an industrial monopoly, is altogether contrary to the interests of all others. In concentrating their thought on the economic problems of the nation, in regarding the latter as an economic unit distinct from all others, in advocating the superposing of political frontiers by economic barriers, protectionism favors the unification and the consolidation of the nation. In this sense it is an essentially national movement.

3. The socialists express themselves on the effects of war in terms which frequently recall those used by the liberals. War, they observe, entails not only moral suffering but material loss. Both from the moral and the economic point of view it is, at present, an antisocial phenomenon, a manifestation of modern barbarism: it seriously impedes the material and spiritual progress of peoples. It brutalizes and impoverishes them at the same time. It is incompatible with a lasting progress of material welfare. It benefits some individuals and certain privileged classes, but for the peoples, whether they are victors or vanquished, it is a money-losing enterprise. Even Marxism, which does not condemn in principle all wars of aggression, points out the more and more disastrous character of contemporary military conflicts.

What is true of war is equally true of armed peace. The armament race prevents the complete utilization of the economic advantages of peace. The socialists are therefore hostile to militarism.

As for the manner of establishing peace, they arrive, as is to be expected, at a conclusion different from that of the liberals. The latter (resembling in this point the protectionists) do not think that there is a relation of cause and effect between a social order based on private property and armed conflict among nations. Their analysis of war and militarism thus involves no fundamental criticism of the contemporary social order.

Contrariwise, most socialists consider war the consequence of a vicious social order, erected on a rotten basis, namely the institution of private property. The danger of war can thus not be eliminated definitely without a previous suppression of the social system which produces it. To annihilate war, it is therefore necessary to eliminate private property completely or at least to restrict it drastically.

Let us note, however, that certain socialists envisage the possibility of establishing peace without a radical transformation of the social order. Thus Considérant, Godin, Pecqueur, and Vidal propose to create a European (or world) federation even within the frame of liberal society.

All socialists are convinced that the introduction of the socialist regime would definitely abolish war. The socialist community, free from private property and competition, from exploitation and corruption, would not have the slightest reason for bellicism. It would devote itself entirely to the growth of material production and to the moral uplift of its members. It could not think of attacking its neighbors. It would therefore have no need of standing armies: its military organization, should it be needed at all, would be limited to national militias of a purely defensive character. In short, socialist society would free the world from the curse of militarism. And it would do so of itself, without the aid of a supernational organism to guarantee peace.

II. What is the contribution of nineteenth century economists to our knowledge and to the eventual solution of the problem of war? Let us review, from this point of view, the three economic currents of which they form a part.

1. The nineteenth century liberals, continuing the work of their predecessors,[4] have shown that in principle war is not worth its cost. They are wrong in asserting too categorically that in no case could war henceforth be economically beneficial to the victorious country. In a juncture of exceptional circumstances it may well be so. Still, with a few exceptions, the liberal thesis is correct: modern war is an unprofitable enterprise even for the victorious nation. This thesis evidently takes for granted that the victor observes certain elementary rules of modern international

---

[4] Such as Crucé, Quesnay and his school (Mercier de la Rivière, Dupont de Nemours, Baudeau, Le Trosne) in France; North, Vanderlint, Hume, Tucker, and Adam Smith in England. Cf. Silberner, 1939.

law, more particularly respect for the private property of conquered populations. But if he does not observe them, if he violates them brutally, may a successful war not be economically advantageous to him? We should not hesitate to give an affirmative answer. The liberals, however, persuaded of the continuity of social progress, do not even pose this question. They would no more have dreamed of examining it than they would have asked themselves, for example, if slavery applied on a universal scale would be economically profitable to the conqueror of the globe. If this problem does not worry them, the reason is that they could not foresee the return to barbarism of certain civilized peoples and the threat resulting from this to all others.

If it is erroneous to admit, as a number of liberals do, that the establishment of commercial freedom would lead to permanent peace, it is impossible not to acknowledge that certain tendencies of free trade favor peace. To what extent they strengthen other pacific tendencies and thwart the forces making for war naturally depends on each particular situation that is being examined. By abolishing economic barriers between States, by permitting a free movement of goods and capital, by favoring migration, and by suppressing all sorts of obstacles impeding international communications, free trade seems to bring nations closer together and to diminish the danger of war. The liberals (or, at all events, many of them) doubtless exaggerated the strength of this peaceful influence. But they were right in pointing out the phenomenon itself and to insist on its importance for the economic and social evolution of mankind.

The liberals prove that nations may secure far greater economic advantages by peaceful labor than by war and spoliation. From this they conclude that the advancement of economic science and the diffusion of its teachings among the masses will finally suppress wars or considerably reduce their number and duration. This excessive optimism is due to the exaggerated importance they attribute to the role played by the economic factor in the life of nations.

A conception such as that of the liberals, which constructs the whole edifice of pacifism upon one single factor, is indefensible and even harmful. It is indefensible because the facts do not seem to confirm the validity of historical economism. It is harmful, for in concentrating the attention upon one single element of social life, it loses sight of the totality of social factors and prevents the finding of a true solution of the problem of war. But reduced to its just proportion, the liberal thesis furnishes a solid basis for pacifism: it shows that from the economic point of view nations do not need war to enrich themselves, that they all may raise their material condition by free trade and peace as they could not by war.

2. Starting from the principle according to which free trade and peace offer ideal conditions for the material progress of mankind, the liberal school neglects the problem of national defense. In examining this problem, it is indeed not sufficient to show the superiority of peace over war and to prove that free trade favors most both the peaceful cohabitation of peoples and the growth of their wealth. One must still pose another essential question: can each nation pursue, in a world in which lasting peace has not yet been established, a free-trade policy without thereby compromising the external security of the State? The liberals answer it affirmatively, but without proof. They endeavor to show that free trade is the best economic system even from the military point of view. However, one of the most intelligent protectionists, List, has shown, it seems to us, that in a warlike world nations relatively undeveloped economically run a risk of falling victims to industrial powers, if they do not protect their infant industries. In some cases one may even feel compelled to protect permanently the branches of economic life absolutely indispensable to the external security of the State.

Quite true, protectionism frequently abuses the argument of national defense. It often makes use of this argument merely in order to increase the profits of those economic groups whose interests it represents. Nevertheless, this abuse does not invalidate the principle itself which stresses the necessity of protection for the sake of national defense.

3. The assertion of the socialists that war is only a product of bad economic organization of society and that it will necessarily disappear in a socialist community is more than doubtful. It is none the less true that there is a certain interdependence between the economic organization of society and bellicism. An economic order which assures power to a class that is by definition warlike is evidently making for war. In a society where the mass of the people are living in wretched poverty or in an intolerable misery, whatever their causes, bellicism, too, will find a congenial breeding ground. Poverty is certainly not sufficient to explain bellicism completely, though it is unquestionably one of the factors favoring it. Misery is not the only cause of bellicism and, consequently, its elimination alone does not suffice to abolish war. It has not been proved that the abolition of social misery is a *sufficient* condition for the establishment of peace. Yet everything seems to indicate that this abolition is one of the *necessary* conditions for the suppression of war.

By their criticism of the contemporary economic order the socialists have doubtless contributed to the elucidation of this social aspect of the problem of war. Whatever one's view on socialism, one must accept as true the following assertion of several of its adherents: to establish peace, it is necessary to suppress poverty or social misery. That this suppression depends upon the progress of economic justice, on which the socialists have discoursed so much, is undeniable.

III. The conditions permitting the realization of a lasting peace have for centuries engaged the attention of thinkers. In an historical study of great interest, *The Quest of Peace* (1940), Professor William E. Rappard examines also this problem. "Lasting peace," he says, "is possible between separate political units in any one of four hypotheses: (1) if there be no contact whatever between them and any of their citizens; (2) if they cooperate freely and fraternally; (3) if they be all subjected to the supreme rule of one of them; and finally (4) if they, of their own volition, all accept a common law to which they once and for all consent to sacrifice a share of their independence."[5]

The first and third hypotheses hardly deserve to be mentioned. Their realization, even if it were conceivable in the contemporary world, would entail such a great loss of human civilization and of human freedom that we do not care to consider them. The second hypothesis is nothing but the condition in which mankind lives in a peaceful period between two wars. "In order to be lasting, such a peace, which we may call a peace of cooperation, supposes that all States be either satisfied with their international status, or able to improve it by peaceful methods, or unwilling or powerless to alter it by force. If the past and especially if the recent past has any lesson to teach, it is that such conditions are always precarious and never obtain for long."[6]

The fourth and last hypothesis is that of a "peace of federation." It has never been realized over the entire globe, but it does exist in certain of its regions, namely in the United States of America and in the Swiss Confederation.[7]

Extended over the whole world, a federal union would assure universal peace without destroying human freedom. A "peace of federation," we think, is both the only one possible and the only one desirable within the frame of modern civilization.[8]

Admitting, as we do here, that a lasting peace can be assured only by a federal union of all nations, or at least of the principal powers, the nineteenth century economists furnish, we think, some important lessons which such a federation should consider carefully.

[5] Rappard, *op. cit.*, p. 497.   [6] *Ibid.*
[7] *Ibid.*, p. 498.

[8] It would be superfluous to develop here this point of view, the federalist idea having been set forth in a large number of publications in recent years.

1. The economic relations between the members of the federation should be as unhampered as possible. The more one approaches complete free trade among nations, the more easily will one be able to utilize the natural resources of each country and the peculiar aptitudes of its inhabitants. By thus increasing the well-being of nations, by linking their economic interests, and by increasing their interdependence one will intensify the factors which, when acting in a propitious environment, favor international concord.

Commercial freedom among the members of the federation will thus contribute to the coherence of the organization. In the interior of the federation it will act as a centripetal force. The federated nations will have a twofold interest in following a policy of free trade: first because it will greatly benefit them materially, and second because, by tightening the material bonds uniting them, it will constitute a counterpoise against the centrifugal forces that might spring up within the federal union.

2. A universal federation cannot be durable when its members are not satisfied with their participation in it. It is not incumbent upon political economy to enumerate all the conditions which must be met in order to satisfy the members of the federation. It does fall within its purview, however, to point out the economic conditions indispensable to this end. Now, among these conditions there is one which seems to us fundamental: the industrialization of agricultural or semi-industrial countries. Without their industrialization it seems impossible to content them economically within the federation.

As long as industrial civilization is considered, rightly or wrongly, superior to agrarian civilization, it is unthinkable that they would be satisfied as members of a federation likely to prolong or to perpetuate their inferior status. A world federation which did not favor their industrialization would be in advance condemned to death.

List's theory of productive forces shows that a temporary protection may be profitable in the long run even from the purely economic point of view. If an industry, encouraged at the start, after a reasonable transition period acquires such great productivity that it compensates for the material losses incurred by the nation during this period, the protection granted it is justified. In the long run an intelligent encouragement of industrialization would thus be advantageous to those members of the federation which are not far advanced economically. To the extent that such encouragement develops the potentially productive forces, it would be beneficial, in the last analysis, not only to these but to all other members of the federation as well.

This industrialization will require the application of some protectionism by agricultural and semi-industrial nations who are members of the federation. But this protectionism should be limited to tariff duties really indispensable to the industrial education of the country, to use an expression of List, and should not be used as a means artificially to swell the profits of a few private individuals. Thus restricted, protectionism would be an instrument for industrializing economically backward countries and would permit them to attain a degree of industrial civilization compatible with their natural resources and their special aptitudes.

Should certain members of the federation feel that permanent protection is indispensable to them for the maintenance of their industries, it would still pay the federation to allow them to follow a protectionist policy. The result would doubtless be a certain material loss for the free-trade members of the federation. But this loss, which they could bear without undue difficulties, would be a sort of insurance premium against war. It would be the price they would pay to protect themselves against the danger of war that would threaten them if States with protectionist tendencies should prefer to leave the federation rather than find themselves compelled to follow a free-trade policy. It would not be excessive as compared with the benefits of peace and would in all probability be more than compensated for by the latter. Moreover, in a peaceful world it is rather unlikely that the citizens of a nation applying protectionism should want to endure for too long a time the inconveniences resulting therefrom. Everything seems to point to the probability that in the long run free trade would triumph over protectionism within a world federation.

List understood very well that peace is unrealizable without a federation of peoples. But he made of free trade, without any necessity, one of the prerequisites for the establishment of such a federation. Indeed, one fails to understand why the principal world powers should endeavor to attain the same industrial level *before* federalizing, if the federal union were to grant to each of its members the right to industrialize itself and would even favor such industrialization. Why should it be impossible to form a federation and at the same time leave the way open for each member to develop its industries? To propose, as does List, the inverse course, means in practice rendering a federal union of nations impossible. He would probably have recognized this himself, had he been truly attached to the idea of a world federation. Such, however, as we have shown, does not seem to have been the case. List has none the less the merit of having untiringly shown that peace and free trade cannot be realized outside a world federation of peoples.

3. The socialists have written a good deal on the relations between the economic order and the policy of peace. They too hastily identified socialism with peace. Still, whatever one's attitude toward them, it would be difficult to deny the validity of the fundamental idea which guides them all, namely, the impossibility of a lasting peace among societies disregarding economic justice.

It does not fall within the scope of this book to define this justice. Its idea varies, naturally, according to time and place. Yet it is not too difficult to discern what the masses in any given society consider a minimum of economic justice. Now, whenever this minimum is not granted them, warlike tendencies will find a favorable breeding ground.

Economic justice of itself, contrary to the tenets of the socialists, is of course far from guaranteeing world peace. But without it peaceful cohabitation among nations seems unrealizable. A federation of nations which ignored this truth would fall into ruin rather quickly. It can be lasting only on condition that it observes economic justice in the relations among the participating nations as well as in the interior of each of them.

War is a "problem" only for those who regard it as a harmful and partly or wholly eliminable phenomenon.[9] All schools reviewed in this book, with the exception of the historical one, consider it as such. They study this problem and endeavor to solve it. Each of them believes it has found the true solution, the true remedy against war in the economic and social system it endorses: the liberal school in free trade, the national school in temporary protection, and the socialist schools in a transformation of the social order.

Each of them, if one leaves out of account certain exceptionally clear-sighted ones among their partisans, seems to be ignorant of the fact that this problem is too complex to admit of a unilateral solution. Quite true, each of them has contributed to our knowledge of the problem of war. But none of them has found, or could have found, the complete solution, which naturally goes beyond the limits of the economic.

Too many economists had an excessive confidence in their own systems. Their research would doubtless have gained in depth if they had let themselves be guided by the principle so well formulated by Antoine-Augustin Cournot in his *Revue sommaire des doctrines économiques* (1877): "The systems have their fanatics: science never has any, science which uses up systems and gradually supplants them in what in the long run admits of a scientific construction."[10]

[9] Cf. Wright, *A Study of War* (1942), p. 3.
[10] Page 339.

297

The problem of war is, as pointed out above, too complex to be solved by a single system or even by a single discipline. Baudrillart was right in recalling it to those economists who, proud of their science, seemed to overlook the limits which the nature of things assigns to economics as to any other science. The existence of these limits, however, should not discourage political economy from shedding light on the problem of war nor should it dispense economics from contributing its own part to the solution of this problem. That it has effectively contributed this part we believe we have shown in the present work. This contribution is not as large as certain nineteenth century economists thought, but it is without doubt great enough to deserve the attention of all those who tackle one of the most difficult problems presented by history to man and mankind: the problem of war.

BIBLIOGRAPHY

Note on the Bibliography

No publication has, to our knowledge, examined the problem dealt with in the present volume. E. V. Robinson's article, "War and Economics in History and in Theory," published in *Political Science Quarterly*, xv (1900), pp. 581-622, devotes little attention to the history of economic theory relating to war.

Our bibliography includes all publications referred to in the text of this work.

It is divided into two parts: the first, rather lengthy, contains the primary sources; the second, kept short intentionally, the auxiliary sources.* In part one of our bibliography we generally indicate, after the title, the date of the first edition, followed (in parentheses) by that of the edition to which we had recourse. Whenever the year of the first edition could not be determined, the date following the title is that of the edition used.

Citations in the Text

In order not to increase the bulk of the footnotes we do not quote the title of the works cited accessorily but only the author and date of publication, which will permit the reader to find the title in question in this bibliographical annex.

Biographical Notes

Our biographical notes, of a quite summary character, are destined to orient the readers who are not specialists. These notes have been extracted, without indication of the sources,

---

* Publications analyzing certain economic consequences of war which are not examined in this book, for instance, the effects of military conflicts on the price movements, are not listed in our bibliography. For this reason we omit, for example, the books of Thomas Tooke which study this problem (*Thoughts and Details on the High and Low Prices of the Thirty Years from 1793 to 1822*, 2nd ed., London, 1824, pp. 145-222; *A History of Prices . . . 1793-1856*, London, 1838-1857, 6 vols., especially vol. 1, pp. 86-117). Neither shall we enumerate the manuals written for the use of quartermasters general rather than of economists, as for instance the work of Cancrin (Graf Georg), *Ueber die Militärökonomie im Frieden und Krieg und ihr Wechselverhältnis zu den Operationen.* St. Petersburg, 1820-1823, 3 vols.

from the *Nouveau Dictionnaire d'Economie politique* (Paris, 1891-1892, 2 vols.; *Supplément*, 1897), Palgrave's *Dictionary of Political Economy* (London, 1925-1926, 3 vols.), the *Encyclopaedia of the Social Sciences* (New York, 1930-1935, 15 vols.), and several other encyclopedias and dictionaries.

Abbreviations

CCE   *Cobden Club Essays*, Second Series, 1871-1872, 2nd ed., London, 1872.

CPE   *Collection des principaux économistes*, Paris.

JDE   *Journal des Economistes*, Paris.

JNS   *Jahrbücher für Nationalökonomie und Statistik*, Jena.

JPE   *Journal of Political Economy*, Chicago.

MEGA   Karl Marx und Friedrich Engels, *Historisch-kritische Gesamtausgabe. Werke, Schriften, Briefe.* I. Abteilung, 6 vols.; III. Abteilung, 4 vols., Berlin, 1927-1932.

NMS   *Neudrucke Marxistischer Seltenheiten*, Leipzig.

RHES   *Revue d'histoire économique et sociale*, Paris.

SJG   *Schmollers Jahrbuch für Gesetzgebung, Verwaltung und Volkswirtschaft*, Berlin.

PRIMARY SOURCES

ANGELL, NORMAN. The Great Illusion. London, 1910.

ARND, KARL. Die Volkswirtschaft begründet auf unwandelbare Naturgesetze. Neue Ausgabe. Frankfort on the Main, 1868.

ASHLEY, WILLIAM. The Tariff Problem, 1903 (ed. London, 1920).

BAGEHOT, WALTER. Physics and Politics, 1872 (ed. London, 1900).

———. Count Your Enemies and Economise Your Expenditure, 1862. (*The Works and Life of Walter Bagehot*, IV, 1915.)

BASTIAT, FRÉDÉRIC. Cobden et la Ligue, 1845 (vol. III of *Oeuvres complètes de Frédéric Bastiat*. Paris, 1854-1864. 7 vols.).

———. Sophismes économiques, 1845-1848. (*Ibid.*, IV.)

———. Le libre échange, 1846-1848. (*Ibid.*, II.)

———. Capital et Rente, 1849. (*Ibid.*, V.)

———. Paix et liberté ou le budget républicain, 1849. (*Ibid.*, V.)

———. Ce qu'on voit et ce qu'on ne voit pas, 1850. (*Ibid.*, v.)

———. Gratuité du crédit, 1849-1850. (*Ibid.*, v.)

———. Harmonies économiques, 1850. (3rd ed., *ibid.*, vi.)

———. Correspondance. (*Ibid.*, i.)

Baudrillart, Henri. Manuel d'économie politique. Paris, 1857.

———. Études de philosophie morale et d'économie politique. Paris, 1858. 2 vols.

———. Philosophie de l'économie politique. Des Rapports de l'économie politique et de la morale, 1860 (2nd ed. Paris, 1883).

———. Cf. Congress 1866, pp. 715-722 (speech of Baudrillart).

Béranger, Charles. Religion Saint-Simonienne. La guerre détruit tout commerce et toute industrie. Paris [1832].

Biard, Gustave. Aperçu des vues morales et industrielles des Saint-Simoniens. Blois [1832].

Bibliothèque de la Paix, publiée par les soins de la Ligue Internationale, et Permanente de la Paix. Neuvième livraison.—Deuxième assemblée générale. 24 juin 1869. Discours de MM. Michel Chevalier, Fréd. Passy, etc. 2nd ed. Paris, n.d.

Blanc, Louis. L'organisation du travail, 1839 (9th ed. revised. Paris, 1850).

———. Congrès de la paix. Lettre à M. Crémer, président du Congrès [de l'Association ouvrière des Amis de la Paix], du 25 août 1878. (In: Louis Blanc *Questions d'aujourd'hui et de demain.* 5th series, Paris, 1884.)

Blanqui, Adolphe. Précis élémentaire d'économie politique. Paris, 1842.

Bloch, Jean de. The Future of War in its Technical, Economic, and Political Relations. New York, 1899.

Boccardo, Gerolamo. Trattato teoretico-pratico di economia politica, 1853 (6th ed. Turin, 1879).

———. Dizionario della Economia politica e del Commercio. Turin, 1858-1863. 4 vols.

Bolles, Albert S. Chapters in Political Economy. New York, 1874.

Briefe . . . an F. A. Sorge, 1906. Cf. Marx and Engels.

Cabet, Etienne. Voyage en Icarie. Paris, 1845.

Cairnes, John Elliot. Our Defences: A National or a Standing Army? 1871. (In his *Political Essays*, New York, 1873.)

————. Some Leading Principles of Political Economy. New York, 1874.

CANARD, NICOLAS-FRÉD. Principes d'économie politique. Paris, an X (1801).

CARBALLO Y WANGÜEMERT, BENIGNO. Curso de Economía Política. Madrid, 1855-1856. 2 vols.

CAREY, HENRY CHARLES. The Past, the Present, the Future. Philadelphia, 1848.

————. Principles of Political Economy. Philadelphia, 1837-1840. 3 vols.

————. Principles of Social Science. Philadelphia, 1858. 3 vols.

CATTANEO, CARLO. Dell'economia nazionale di Federico List, 1843 (*Opere edite ed inedite di Carlo Cattaneo*, v, Florence, 1888).

————. Dell'Insurrezione di Milano nel 1848. Lugano, 1849.

CAUWÈS, PAUL. Cours d'économie politique, 1878 (3rd ed. Paris, 1893. 4 vols.).

CHALMERS, THOMAS. On Political Economy. Glasgow, 1832.

CHAPTAL, COMTE CHARLES. De l'industrie françoise. Paris, 1819. 2 vols.

CHERBULIEZ, ANTOINE-ELISÉE. Essai sur les conditions de l'alliance fédérative en général et sur le nouveau projet d'Acte fédéral. Geneva, 1833.

————. Congrès de la Paix, JDE, xxx (1851).

————. Précis de la science économique. Paris, 1862. 2 vols.

————. Le droit international et la paix perpétuelle, *Bibliothèque universelle et la Revue suisse*, XXXIII (1868).

CHEVALIER, MICHEL. Organisation industrielle de l'armée. (In: *Religion saint-simonienne. Politique industrielle et système de la Méditerranée*. Paris, 1832, pp. 7-14.)

————. Politique d'association. (*Ibid.*, pp. 29-39.)

————. Système de la Méditerranée. (*Ibid.*, pp. 103-150.)

————. Aux hommes politiques (In: *Religion saint-simonienne. A tous*. Paris, 1832, pp. 7-22.).

————. La paix est aujourd'hui la condition de l'émancipation des peuples, *Le Globe*, January 20, 1832.

————. Cours d'économie politique. Deuxième année. Paris, 1844.

————. Lettres sur l'organisation du travail. Bruxelles, 1848.

————. Examen du système commercial connu sous le nom de système protecteur. Paris, 1852.

———. Cours d'économie politique, 1842. (2nd ed. Paris, 1855-1858. 2 vols.)

———. Exposition Universelle de 1867 à Paris. Rapports du Jury International. Vol. I: Introduction par M. Chevalier. Paris, 1868.

Cobden, Richard. Speeches on Peace . . . delivered during 1849. London, s.d.

———. Political Writings. London and New York, 1867. 2 vols.

———. Speeches on Questions of Public Policy. London, 1870. 2 vols.

Colmeiro, Manuel. Principios de Economía Política, 1859. (2nd ed., Madrid, 1865.)

Comte, Auguste. Considérations sur le pouvoir spirituel (2nd article), *Le Producteur*, II (1826).

———. Cours de philosophie positive, 1830-1842 (3rd ed. Paris, 1869. 6 vols.).

———. Système de politique positive. Paris, 1851-1854. 4 vols.

Congress 1848 = Congrès des Amis de la Paix Universelle, réuni à Bruxelles en 1848. Séances des 20, 21 et 22 sept. Bruxelles, 1849.

Congress 1849 — Congrès des Amis de la Paix Universelle, réuni à Paris en 1849. Compte-rendu . . . précédé d'une note historique sur le mouvement en faveur de la Paix, par Joseph Garnier. Paris, 1850.

Congress 1866 = Annales de l'Association Internationale pour le Progrès des Sciences sociales, 4e Session. Congrès de Berne. Bruxelles, 1866.

Considérant, Victor. La paix ou la guerre, 1839. (2nd ed. Paris, 1839.)

———. De la politique en général et du rôle de la France en Europe. Paris, 1840.

———. De la politique nouvelle convenant aux intérêts actuels de la société, 1843 (2nd ed. Paris, 1843).

———. Exposition abrégée du système phalanstérien de Fourier, 1845. (3rd ed., 4e tirage. Paris, 1846.)

———. Principes du socialisme, manifeste de la démocratie au XIXe siècle. Paris, 1847.

———. Petit cours de politique et d'économie sociale, 1844. (2nd ed., 4e tirage. Paris, 1847.)

———. Bases de la politique positive; manifeste de l'école sociétaire, 1841. (2nd ed. Paris, 1847.) [Anonymous.]

——. Le socialisme devant le vieux monde. Paris, 1848.

——. Destinée sociale, 1834-1838. (2nd ed. Paris, 1848-1849. 2 vols.)

——. La dernière guerre et la paix définitive en Europe. Paris, 1850. 13 pp.

——. Prédictions sur la guerre. La France imposant la paix à l'Europe. Paris, 1870. 4 pp.

CONSTANT, BENJAMIN. De l'esprit de conquête, 1813 (*Oeuvres politiques de Benjamin Constant*. Paris, 1874).

COOPER, THOMAS. Lectures on the Elements of Political Economy, 1826. (2nd ed. Columbia, South Carolina, 1831.)

COURCELLE SENEUIL, JEAN GUSTAVE. Traité théorique et pratique d'économie politique. Paris, 1858. 2 vols.

——. 2nd ed. Paris, 1867. 2 vols.

——. 3rd ed. Paris, 1891. 2 vols.

COURNOT, ANTOINE-AUGUSTIN. Principes de la théorie des richesses. Paris, 1863.

——. Considérations sur la marche des idées. Paris, 1872. 2 vols.

——. Revue sommaire des doctrines économiques. Paris, 1877.

CUNNINGHAM, WILLIAM. Nationalism and Cosmopolitanism in Economics. (*British Association. Report of the 61st meeting*. London, 1892, pp. 723-734.)

——. English Imperialism, *Atlantic Monthly*, LXXXIV (1899).

——. Prospects of Universal Peace, *Atlantic Monthly, ibid.*

——. An Essay on Western Civilisation in Its Economic Aspects (Mediaeval and Modern Times). Cambridge, 1900.

——. The Rise and Decline of the Free Trade Movement. London, 1904.

——. The Case against Free Trade, with a Preface by Joseph Chamberlain. London, 1911.

——. The Economic Basis of Universal Peace—Cosmopolitan or International? (*British Association. Report of the 82d Meeting*. London, 1913, pp. 545-546.) [Abridged text.] Complete text in: *Economic Review*, XXIII (1913).

——. The Progress of Capitalism in England. London, 1916.

DAMETH, H. Introduction à l'étude de l'économie politique, 1865 (2nd ed. Paris, 1878).

DELAPORTE, L. De l'application de l'armée aux travaux et de la nouvelle organisation de l'armée, *Le Globe*, March 3, 1832.

DOCTRINE DE SAINT-SIMON. Exposition. Première année. 1829.

3e éd. revue et augmentée, 1831 (*Collection des économistes et des réformateurs sociaux de la France,* XIII, Paris, 1924).

DOCTRINE SAINT-SIMONIENNE. Exposition. Paris, 1854.

DUEHRING, EUGEN. Kritische Grundlegung der Volkswirthschaftslehre. Berlin, 1866.

DUNOYER, CHARLES. Du système de l'équilibre des puissances européennes, 1817 (in vol. III of the *Oeuvres de Charles Dunoyer.* Paris [1886-1887], 3 vols.).

———. Politique tirée des doctrines économiques, 1818. (*Ibid.,* III.)

———. Notice historique sur l'industrialisme, 1827. (*Ibid.,* III.)

———. De la liberté du travail, 1845. (*Ibid.,* I-II.)

———. De la liberté du commerce international, 1847-1848. (*Ibid.,* III.)

DUPONT-WHITE, CHARLES BROOK. Le libre échange, *La liberté de penser, revue démocratique,* VIII (1851).

———. L'Individu et l'État, 1857. (3rd ed. Paris, 1865.)

———. Les Banques et la Guerre, *Le Correspondant,* LXIX (1866). [In this study, dealing with money and banking, war is hardly mentioned.]

DUPUIT, J. La liberté commerciale, son principe et ses conséquences. Paris, 1861.

DUTENS, JOSEPH. Philosophie de l'économie politique. Paris, 1835. 2 vols.

ENFANTIN, P. Des banquiers cosmopolites, *Le Producteur,* II (1826).

———. Considérations sur l'organisation féodale et l'organisation industrielle. Comment *l'esprit d'association* se substitue graduellement dans les rapports sociaux à *l'esprit de conquête, Le Producteur,* III (1826).

———. Économie politique et politique. Articles extraits du Globe. 2nd ed. Paris, 1832.

———. Correspondance philosophique et religieuse, 1843-1845. Paris, 1847.

ENGELS, FRIEDRICH. Umrisse zu einer Kritik der Nationalökonomie, 1844. (MEGA, I. Abt., vol. II.)

———. Die Lage der arbeitenden Klasse in England, 1845. (*Ibid.,* IV.)

———. Zwei Reden in Elberfeld, 1845. (*Ibid.,* IV.)

———. Grundsätze des Kommunismus [written in 1847; published in 1914]. (*Ibid.,* VI.)

——. Schutzzoll oder Freihandelsystem, 1847. (In vol. II *Aus dem Nachlass von K. Marx und F. Engels 1841-50*, ed. Mehring, Berlin, 1923. 3 vols.)

——. Der demokratische Panslavismus, 1849. (*Ibid.*, III.)

——. England [written in 1852]. *Die Gesellschaft*, 1928, II.

——. Die Möglichkeiten und Voraussetzungen eines Krieges der Heiligen Allianz gegen Frankreich im Jahre 1852, *Die neue Zeit*, 33rd year, I (1915).

——. Herrn Eugen Dührings Umwältzung der Wissenschaft [=Anti-Dühring], 1878. (Stuttgart, 1901.)

——. Der Ursprung der Familie, des Privateigenthums und des Staats, 1884. (12th ed. Stuttgart, 1908.) English trans.: The Origin of Family. New York [1942].

——. Einleitung zu Sig. Borkheim's: Zur Erinnerung für die deutschen Mordspatrioten, 1806-1807. (*Sozialdemokratische Bibliothek*, XXIV, Zürich, 1888.)

——. Ludwig Feuerbach, 1888. (3rd ed. Stuttgart, 1903.)

——. Kann Europa abrüsten? Separatabdruck aus dem *Vorwärts*, 1893. (NMS, IV, Leipzig, 1929.)

——. Notes on War. Sixty articles reprinted from the *Pall Mall Gazette*, 1870-1871. Edited by Friedrich Adler. Vienna, 1923.

——. Militärpolitische Schriften. Berlin, 1930. (*Elementarbücher des Kommunismus*, I.)

——. Der deutsch-französische Krieg 1870-1871. Kriegsgeschichtliche Schriften. Vienna-Berlin, 1931. (*Marxistische Bibliothek*, XX.)

FAWCETT, HENRY. Manual of Political Economy, 1863. (7th ed. London, 1888.)

——. Free Trade and Protection, 1878 (4th ed. London, 1881).

FERRARA, FRANCESCO. Biblioteca dell'Economista. Prima serie, VII, Turin, 1855. *Introduzione*.

——. Oeuvres économiques choisies. Paris, 1938.

FERRIER, FR.-L.-A. Du gouvernement considéré dans ses rapports avec le commerce. Paris, 1805.

FICHTE, JOHANN GOTTLIEB. Der geschlossene Handelsstaat, 1800 (*Fichte's Sämmtliche Werke*, III, Berlin, 1845).

FLÓREZ ESTRADA, ALVARO. Curso de Economía Política, 1828. (5th ed., Madrid, 1840. 2 vols.)

FOURIER, CHARLES. Triumvirat continental et paix perpétuelle sous trente ans, 1803 (In vol. I of *Oeuvres complètes de Charles Fourier*, 2nd ed. Paris, 1841-1845. 6 vols.).

———. Théorie des quatre mouvements et des destinées générales, 1808. (*Ibid.*, I.)

———. Théorie de l'unité universelle [original title: Traité de l'association domestique agricole, 1822]. (*Ibid.*, II-V.)

———. Le nouveau monde industriel et sociétaire, 1829. (*Ibid.*, VI.)

———. Pièges et charlatanisme des deux sectes Saint-Simon et Owen. Paris, 1831.

———. Publication des manuscrits de Charles Fourier. Paris, Librairie Phalanstérienne, 1851-1858. 4 vols.

———. Harmonie universelle, 1803. (In: Publication des manuscrits de Charles Fourier, vol. I, pp. 52-53.)

GANILH, CHARLES. Des systèmes d'économie politique. Paris, 1809. 2 vols.

———. La théorie de l'économie politique. Paris, 1815. 2 vols.

GARNIER, JOSEPH. Éléments de l'économie politique, 1846 (2nd ed. Paris, 1848).

———. Note historique. Cf. CONGRESS 1849.

———. Réponse à la lettre de M. Cherbuliez, JDE, XXX (1851).

GENTZ, FRIEDRICH VON. Sendschreiben an Friedrich Wilhelm III, 1797 (*Schriften von Friedrich von Gentz*, ed. Schlesier, II, Mannheim, 1838).

GEORGE, HENRY. Protection or Free Trade, 1886 (New York, 1891).

GIOJA MELCHIORRE. Nuovo prospetto delle scienze economiche. Milan, 1815-1817. 6 vols.

GODIN, ANDRÉ J.-B. Solutions sociales. Paris, 1871.

———. La politique du travail et la politique des privilèges. Paris, 1875.

———. Le gouvernement. Paris, 1883.

———. La République du travail et la réforme parlementaire. Paris, 1889.

GRAY, JOHN. A Lecture on Human Happiness, 1825 (Reprint, London, 1931).

———. The Social System. Edinburgh, 1831.

GUÉPIN, ANGE. Traité d'économie sociale. Paris, 1833.

GUYOT, YVES. La jalousie commerciale et les relations internationales. (*Publication de la ligue du libre-échange*, no. VII, Paris, 1911.)

HALL, CHARLES. The Effects of Civilization on the People in European States, 1805. (Reprint, London, 1850.)

HALLER, CARL LUDWIG VON. Restauration der Staats-Wissenschaften, vol. III, 1819. (2nd ed. Winterthur, 1821.)

HAMÉLIUS, É. Philosophie d'économie politique. Paris, 1891.

HAMILTON, ALEXANDER. Report on Manufactures, 1791. (In: *Papers on Public Credit, Commerce and Finance* by Alexander Hamilton. New York, 1934.)

HANDELS- UND MACHTPOLITIK. Reden und Aufsätze, hgg. von Gustav Schmoller, Max Sering, Adolph Wagner. Stuttgart, 1900. 2 vols.

HILDEBRAND, BRUNO. Die Nationalökonomie der Gegenwart und Zukunft. vol. I [the only one published]. Frankfort on the Main, 1848.

———. Naturalwirthschaft, Geldwirthschaft und Creditwirthschaft, JNS, II (1864).

HUFELAND, GOTTLIEB. Neue Grundlegung der Staatswirthschaftskunst, I, Vienna, 1815.

JAKOB, LUDWIG HEINRICH. Grundsätze der National-Oekonomie oder Nationalwirthschaftslehre, 1805. (3rd ed. Vienna, 1814.)

KAUTZ, JULIUS. Die geschichtliche Entwicklung der National-Oekonomik, I. Vienna, 1860.

KNIES, KARL. Die politische Oekonomie vom Standpunkte der geschichtlichen Methode. Braunschweig, 1853.

———. Die Dienstleistung des Soldaten und die Mängel der Conscriptionspraxis. Eine volkswirtschaftlich-finanzielle Erörterung. Freiburg in Breisgau, 1860.

———. Das moderne Kriegswesen. Ein Vortrag. Berlin, 1867.

———. Geld und Kredit. Berlin, 1873-1879. 2 vols. in 3.

LASSALLE, FERDINAND. Die indirekte Steuer, 1863. (Ferdinand Lassalle, *Gesammelte Reden und Schriften*, II, Berlin, 1919.)

LAVELEYE, ÉMILE DE. Études historiques et critiques sur les principes et les conséquences de la liberté du commerce international. Paris and Brussels, 1857.

———. On the Causes of War, and the Means of Reducing Their Number, CCE, 1872.

———. Des causes actuelles de guerre en Europe et de l'arbitrage. Paris and Brussels, 1873.

———. Les tendances nouvelles de l'économie politique en Angleterre: Cliffe Leslie, *Revue des Deux Mondes*, XLIV (1881).

———. Éléments d'économie politique. Paris, 1882.

———. Le Gouvernement dans la Démocratie, 1891. 2nd ed., 1892. 2 vols.

LE PLAY, FRÉDÉRIC. La constitution de l'Angleterre. Tours, 1875. 2 vols.

———. La réforme sociale en France, 1864. (5th ed., Tours, 1874. 3 vols.)

———. L'organisation du travail selon la coutume des ateliers et la loi du décalogue, 1870. (6th ed., Tours, 1893.)

———. La constitution essentielle de l'humanité. Tours, 1881.

LEROUX, PIERRE. De l'Union européenne, 1827 (In: *Oeuvres de Pierre Leroux*, I, Paris, 1850).

———. Réfutation de l'éclectisme. Nouvelle edition. Paris, 1841.

LEROY-BEAULIEU, PAUL. Les guerres contemporaines (1853-1866); recherches statistiques sur les pertes d'hommes et de capitaux. 2nd ed. Paris [1869].

———. Traité théorique et pratique d'économie politique, 1895. (2nd ed. Paris, 1896. 4 vols.)

LESLIE, THOMAS EDWARD CLIFFE. The Question of the Age— Is It Peace? 1860 (in his *Essays in Political and Moral Philosophy*, Dublin, 1879).

———. The Future of Europe Foretold in History, 1860. (*Ibid.*)

———. The Military Systems of Europe in 1867, 1867. (*Ibid.*)

LEVASSEUR, ÉMILE. La population française. Paris, 1889-1892. 3 vols.

LIPS, ALEXANDER. Der allgemeine Friede, oder wie heisst die Basis, über welche allein ein dauernder Weltfriede gegründet werden kann? Erlangen, 1814.

LIST, FRIEDRICH. Die Staatskunde, 1818 (in vol. I, part 2 of his *Werke: Schriften, Reden, Briefe*. Berlin, 1927-1935, 10 vols. in 12).

———. Briefe über den ökonomischen Zustand Deutschlands, 1819. (*Ibid.*)

. Denkschrift, die Handels- und Gewerbsverhältnisse Deutschlands betreffend, 1820. (*Ibid.*)

———. Outlines of American Political Economy, 1827. (*Ibid.*, II.)

———. Idées sur les réformes économiques, commerciales et financières, applicables à la France, 1831. (*Ibid.*, v.)

———. Ueber ein allgemeines Eisenbahnsystem in Frankreich, 1832. (*Ibid.*, III, pt. 2.)

———. Arbeit, 1834. (*Ibid.*, v.)

——. Deutschlands Eisenbahnsystem in militärischer Beziehung, 1834-1836. (*Ibid.*, III, pt. 1.)

——. Le Système Naturel d'Économie Politique [written in 1837]. (*Ibid.*, IV.)

——. L'économie politique devant le tribunal de l'histoire, 1839. (*Ibid.*, V.)

——. Die Freiheit und die Beschränkungen des auswärtigen Handels, 1839. (*Ibid.*)

——. Ueber das Wesen und den Wert einer nationalen Gewerbsproduktivkraft, 1840. (*Ibid.*)

——. Dr. Bowring und der Deutsche Zollverein, 2nd part, 1841. (*Ibid.*)

——. Das Nationale System der Politischen Oekonomie, 1841. (*Ibid.*, VI.)

The National System of Political Economy, translated by Sampson S. Lloyd. New York, 1904.

——. Die Ackerverfassung, die Zwergwirtschaft und die Auswanderung, 1842. (*Werke*, V.)

——. Die gegenwärtige Lage der Industrie im Zollverein, 1843. (*Ibid.*)

——. Unsere Gegner, 1843. (*Ibid.*, VI.)

——. Die grosse Gewerbsrevolution, 1843. (*Ibid.*, VII.)

——. Bülow-Cummerow und die deutsche Nationalökonomie, 1843. (*Ibid.*)

——. Unsere Fortschritte, 1844. (*Ibid.*)

——. Belgien und der Zollverein, 1844. (*Ibid.*)

——. Die politisch-ökonomische Nationaleinheit der Deutschen, 1845-1846. (*Ibid.*)

——. Ueber den Wert und die Bedingungen einer Allianz zwischen Grossbritannien und Deutschland, 1846. (*Ibid.*)

——. Tagebücher und Briefe, 1812-1846. (*Ibid.*, VIII.)

——. Letzte Abrechnung mit den englischen Freihandelspredigern, 1846. (*Ibid.*, IX.)

——. Cobden als Nachfolger von Quesnay, 1846. (*Ibid.*)

——. Die Times und das deutsche Schutzsystem, *Zollvereinsblatt*, IV (1846), no. 44, pp. 691-694.

LUEDER, AUG. FERD. Ueber Nationalindustrie und Staatswirthschaft. Berlin, 1800-1804. 3 vols.

MacCULLOCH, JOHN RAMSAY. A Discourse on the Rise, Progress, Peculiar Objects, and Importance of Political Economy. Edinburgh, 1824.

——. Principles of Political Economy, 1825. (4th ed. Edinburgh, 1849.)

MADRAZO, SANTIAGO DIEGO. Lecciones de Economía Política. Madrid, 1874-1875. 2 vols.

MALTHUS, THOMAS ROBERT. First Essay on Population, 1798 (reprint, London, 1926).

——. An Essay on the Principle of Population. 6th ed. London, 1826. 2 vols.

——. Observations on the Effects of the Corn Laws, 1814. (A Reprint of Economic Tracts, ed. J. H. Hollander. Baltimore, 1932.)

——. The Grounds of an Opinion on the Policy of Restricting the Importation of Foreign Corn. London, 1815.

——. Principles of Political Economy, 1820 (ed., Boston, 1821).

MARSHALL, ALFRED. Industry and Trade. London, 1923.

MARTELLO, TULLIO. L'economia politica antimalthusiana e il socialismo. Venice, 1894.

MARX, KARL. Ueber Schutzzölle, *Rheinische Zeitung*, Nov. 22, 1842. (MEGA, I. Abteilung, vol. I, part I.) [Anonymous text attributed by Ryazanoff to Marx. Cf. *ibid.*, page LVIII.]

——. Misère de la philosophie, 1847. (MEGA, I. Abteilung, vol. VI.)

——. Discours sur la question du libre-échange, 1848. (*Ibid.*)

——. Pauperismus und Freihandel, *New York Tribune*, Nov. 1, 1852. (In vol. I of *Gesammelte Schriften von K. Marx und F. Engels 1852-62*, ed. Ryazanoff. Stuttgart, 1917. 2 vols.)

——. Das Parlament, *New York Tribune*, Dec. 28, 1852. (*Ibid.*)

——. Die Todesstrafe.—Herrn Cobdens Pamphlet, *New York Tribune*, Feb. 18, 1853. (*Ibid.*)

——. Parlamentarisches, *Neue Oder Zeitung*, June 12, 1855. (*Ibid.*, II.)

——. Zur Kritik der politischen Oekonomie, 1859. (Stuttgart, 1897.) English trans.: A Contribution to the Critique of Political Economy. New York, 1904.

——. Das Kapital, 1867-1894 (ed., Kautsky, Berlin, 1914-1929. 3 vols. in 4).

——. Randglossen zum Programm der deutschen Arbeiterpartei [written in 1875], *Die neue Zeit*, 9th year, I (1891).

English trans.: Critique of the Gotha Programme. New York, 1938.

———. Theorien über den Mehrwert, ed., Kautsky, Stuttgart, 1905-1910. 4 vols.

MARX and ENGELS. Manifest der Kommunistischen Partei, 1848. (MEGA, I. Abteilung, vol. VI.)

———. Briefe und Auszüge aus Briefen von J. Ph. Becker, J. Dietzgen, F. Engels, K. Marx u. A. and F. A. Sorge und Andere. Stuttgart, 1906.

———. Briefwechsel zwischen Karl Marx und Friedrich Engels. (MEGA, III. Abteilung, 4 vols.)

———. Die Briefe von Karl Marx und Friedrich Engels an Danielson (Nikolai-on). (NMS, III, Leipzig, 1929.)

———. Correspondence 1846-1895. A Selection with Commentary and Notes. New York [1934].

MILL, JAMES. Commerce Defended. An Answer to the Arguments by which Mr. Spence, Mr. Cobbett and Others Have Attempted to Prove That Commerce Is Not a Source of National Wealth, 1807. (2nd ed. London, 1808.)

———. The History of British India in Six Volumes, 1821 (3rd ed. London, 1826).

———. Elements of Political Economy, 1821. (2nd ed. London, 1824.)

———. "Colony," *Supplement to the . . . Encyclopaedia Britannica*, III. Edinburgh, 1824.

———. "Government" (*ibid.*, IV).

———. "Nations (Law of)" (*ibid.*, VI).

MILL, JOHN STUART. Principles of Political Economy, 1848 (ed., New York, 1929).

———. A Few Words on Non-Intervention, 1859. (In his *Dissertations and Discussions*, III, London, 1867.)

———. Autobiography. London, 1873.

———. Considerations on Representative Government. London, 1861.

———. Correspondance inédite avec Gustave d'Eichthal (1828-1842)— (1864-1871). Translated by E. d'Eichthal. Paris, 1898.

MINGHETTI, MARCO. Des rapports de l'économie publique avec la morale et le droit. Translated from the Italian, Paris, 1863.

MOLINARI, GUSTAVE DE. Études économiques. Paris, 1846.

———. "Nations," in vol. II of the *Dictionnaire de l'Économie Politique*, by Ch. Coquelin and Guillaumin, 1852-1854. 2 vols.

———. "Paix—Guerre," *ibid.*

———. L'Abbé de Saint-Pierre. Paris, 1857.

———. Projet d'Association pour l'établissement d'une Ligue des neutres, 1887. Reprinted in: La morale économique. Paris, 1888, pp. 431-438.

———. Comment se résoudra la question sociale. Paris, 1896.

———. Grandeur et décadence de la guerre. Paris, 1898.

———. Esquisse de l'organisation politique et économique de la société future. Paris, 1899.

———. Les problèmes du XXe siècle. Paris, 1901.

———. Questions économiques à l'ordre du jour. Paris, 1906.

———. Économie de l'Histoire. Théorie de l'évolution. Paris, 1908.

———. Ultima verba, mon dernier ouvrage. Paris, 1911.

MORENO VILLENA, PEDRO. Tratado de Economía Política o Filosofía del Trabajo. 6th ed. Madrid, 1896.

MÜLLER, ADAM HEINRICH. Die Elemente der Staatskunst. Berlin, 1809. 3 vols.

OLÓZAGA Y BUSTAMENTE, JOSÉ MARIA DE. Tratado de Economía Política. Madrid, 1888-1889. 2 vols.

OWEN, ROBERT. Lectures on an Entire New State of Society. London, s.d. [1820?]

———. To the Members of the Learned, Naval, and Military Professions. [In: *The Addresses of Robert Owen (as published in the London Journals)* . . . London, 1830.]

———. The Book of the New Moral World. London, 1836.

———. Lectures on the Rational System of Society. London, 1841.

———. Dialogue sur le système social. Paris, 1848.

———. Deuxième dialogue sur le système social. Paris, 1848.

———. A Farewell Address Delivered to the Scientific Institution. London, 1850.

———. Robert Owen's Millennial Gazette. May 1, 1857. Congress of the Advanced Minds of the World. S.d.n.l.

———. A Letter Addressed to the Potentates of the Earth in Whom the Happiness and Misery of Human Race Are Now Invested. [November 24, 1857.] S.d.n.l.

PARETO, VILFREDO. Cours d'économie politique. Lausanne, 1896-1897. 2 vols.

———. La liberté économique et les événements d'Italie. Lausanne, 1898.

PASSY, FRÉDÉRIC. Leçons d'économie politique faites à Montpellier par Frédéric Passy recueillies par E. Bertin et P. Glaize. Montpellier, 1861.

———. La liberté commerciale. (In: *Association Polytechnique. Cours d'Économie industrielle, recueilli par E. Thénevin.* 4th series. Paris, 1866, pp. 151-257.)

———. Ce que coûte la paix armée. Paris, 1871.

———. La barbarie moderne. Paris, 1871.

———. Le libre-échange et la paix, *Revue Bleue*, XLVIII (1891).

———. La question de la paix, *Le Monde Économique*, January 13 and 20, 1894.

———. Les armements de l'avenir. Paris, 1895.

———. Les causes économiques des guerres, *La Grande Revue*, June 15, 1905.

———. Pour la paix, notes et documents. Paris, 1909.

———. Préface à Androcles, Anathème à la Guerre! Recueil d'extraits d'auteurs . . . suivi de statistiques. 2nd ed. Paris, 1890.

———. Préface à Bernard Serrigny, Les conséquences économiques et sociales de la prochaine guerre. Paris, 1909.

PATTEN, SIMON N. The Economic Basis of Protection. Philadelphia, 1890.

PECQUEUR, CONSTANTIN. Économie sociale. Paris, 1839. 2 vols.

———. Des améliorations matérielles. Paris, 1840.

———. De la Paix, de son principe et de sa réalisation. Paris, 1842.

———. Des armées dans leurs rapports avec l'industrie, la morale et la liberté. Paris, 1842.

———. Théorie nouvelle d'économie sociale et politique. Paris, 1842.

———. De la République de Dieu; Union religieuse pour la pratique immédiate de l'égalité et de la fraternité universelles. Paris, 1844.

PRINCE-SMITH, JOHN. Ueber Handelsfeindseligkeit, 1843. (In: vol. II of his *Gesammelte Schriften.* Berlin, 1877-1880. 3 vols.)

———. Petition um Schutz gegen Beschränkung des Verkehrs, 1848. (*Ibid.*)

———. Ueber die weltpolitische Bedeutung der Handelsfreiheit, 1860. (*Ibid.*, III.)

———. Der Staat und der Volkshaushalt, 1873. (*Ibid.*, I.)

PROUDHON, P.-J. La guerre et la paix. Paris, 1861.

——. Correspondance de P.-J. Proudhon. Paris, 1875. 14 vols.

RAU, KARL HEINRICH. Karl Heinrichs Rau's Lehrbuch der Finanzwissenschaft. Sechste Ausgabe . . . neu bearbeitet von Ad. Wagner. Erste Abteilung. Leipzig, 1872.

RAYMOND, DANIEL. The Elements of Political Economy in Two Parts, 1820. (2nd ed. Baltimore, 1823. 2 vols.)

RELIGION SAINT SIMONIENNE. L'ARMÉE GUERRIÈRE ET L'ARMÉE PACIFIQUE. [Paris, 1832.]

RICARDO, DAVID. An Essay on the Influence of a Low Price of Corn on the Profits of Stock, 1815. (In his *Works*, ed., MacCulloch. London, 1871.)

——. Proposals for an Economical and Secure Currency, 1816. (*Ibid.*)

——. Principles of Political Economy, 1817. (3rd ed. 1821. *Ibid.*)

——. Essay on the Funding System, 1820. (*Ibid.*)

——. On Protection to Agriculture, 1822. (*Ibid.*)

——. Observations on Parliamentary Reform [posthumous article]. (*Ibid.*)

——. Letters of David Ricardo to Th. R. Malthus 1810-1823. Oxford, 1887.

——. Letters of David Ricardo to H. Trower and Others 1811-1823. Oxford, 1899.

——. Ricardo in: Hansard, Parliamentary Debates, XLI (1819-1820), p. 1208.

——. Un manuscrit inédit . . . sur le problème monétaire. Cf. Silberner, 1940.

ROCHETTE, PAUL. Du désarmement de la France, *Le Globe*, Feb. 13, 1832.

ROGERS, JAMES EDWIN THOROLD. The Free Trade Policy of the Liberal Party. A speech delivered at Pendleton, Sept. 1868. Manchester, s.d.

——. The Colonial Question, CCF., 1872.

——. Cobden and Modern Political Opinion. London, 1873.

——. A Manual of Political Economy. 3rd ed. Oxford, 1876.

——. The Economic Interpretation of History. London, 1888.

ROMAGNOSI, G. D. Sulle Colonie. (In his *Opere*, x, Florence, 1835.)

ROSCHER, WILHELM. Grundriss zu Vorlesungen über die Staatswirtschaft. Göttingen, 1843.

——. Zur Geschichte der englischen Volkswirtschaftslehre. Leipzig, 1851.

———. Ansichten der Volkswirtschaft. Leipzig, 1861.

———. Geschichte der National-Oekonomik in Deutschland. Munich, 1874.

———. System der Volkswirtschaft:

Vol. I: Grundlagen der Nationalökonomie, 1854 (15th ed. Stuttgart, 1880).

Vol. III: Nationalökonomik des Handels und des Gewerbefleisses, 1881 (5th ed. Stuttgart, 1887).

Vol. IV, 1-2: System der Finanzwissenschaft, 1886 (5th ed. Stuttgart, 1901).

———. Politik. Stuttgart, 1892.

ROSSI, PELLEGRINO. Cours d'économie politique, 1840-1851. (5th ed. Paris, 1884. 4 vols.)

ROTTECK, CARL VON. Ueber stehende Heere und Nationalmiliz, 1816. (In his *Sammlung kleinerer Schriften*, II, Stuttgart, 1829.)

ROUEN, PIERRE-ISIDORE. Société commanditaire de l'industrie, (2nd article), *Le Producteur*, I (1825).

ROUX, VITAL. De l'influence du gouvernement sur la prospérité du commerce. Paris, 1801.

SAINT-CHAMANS, VICOMTE DE. Traité d'économie publique. Paris, 1852. 3 vols.

SAINT SIMON, COMTE HENRI DE. De la réorganisation de la société européenne, 1814. (BIBLIOTHÈQUE ROMANTIQUE, no. 10, Paris [1925].)

———. L'Industrie ou discussions politiques, 1817. Vol. I, 2e partie: Politique, par A. Thierry, fils adoptif de Henri Saint-Simon. (In: *Oeuvres de Saint-Simon et d'Enfantin*, XVIII, Paris, 1868.) Vol. II. (*Ibid.*, XIX, Paris, 1869.)

———. Lettres de Henri Saint-Simon à un Américain [1817?]. (*Ibid.*, XVIII.)

———. Le parti national ou industriel comparé au parti antinational, 1819. (*Ibid.*, XIX.)

———. L'Organisateur, 1819-1820. (*Ibid.*, XX, 1869.)

SARTORIUS, GEORG. Von den Elementen des Nationalreichtums und von der Staatswirtschaft nach A. Smith. Göttingen, 1806.

SAY, JEAN-BAPTISTE. Traité d'économie politique. Paris, an XI, 1803. 2 vols.

———. 2nd ed. Paris, 1814. 2 vols.

———. 6th ed. Paris, 1841 (Guillaumin).

———. Épitome des principes fondamentaux de l'économie politique, 1814. [Contained in the 6th ed. of Say's *Traité*.]

———. Olbie ou Essai sur les moyens de réformer les moeurs d'une nation, an VIII. (In his *Oeuvres diverses*, CPE, XII, 1848.)

———. De l'Angleterre et des Anglais, 1815. (*Ibid.*)

———. Catéchisme d'économie politique, 1815. (3rd ed. 1826, *ibid.*)

———. Petit volume, 1817. (3rd ed. 1839, *ibid.*)

———. Erreurs où peuvent tomber les bons auteurs qui ne savent pas l'économie politique. (*Ibid.*)

———. Cours complet d'économie politique pratique, 1828-1829. (6th ed. Brussels, 1843.)

SCHAEFFLE (Alb. E. F.), Kapitalismus und Socialismus. Tübingen, 1870.

———. Das gesellschaftliche System der menschlichen Wirtschaft. Tübingen, 1873. 2 vols.

———. Pas de guerre! La prochaine guerre au point de vue de chiffres. Paris, 1887.

———. Der nächste Krieg in Zahlen, *Zeitschrift für die gesammten Staatswissenschaften*, XLIII (1887).

———. Die Friedenskonferenz im Haag. Beiträge zu einer sozialwissenschaftlichen Theorie des Krieges, *ibid.*, LV (1899).

———. Zur sozialwissenschaftlichen Theorie des Krieges. Erster Artikel [the only one published]. Auseinandersetzung mit den Abrüstungsfreunden. *Ibid.*, LVI (1900).

———. Deutsche Kern- und Zeitfragen. Berlin, 1894.

———. Die Steuern. Allgemeiner Teil. Leipzig, 1895.

———. Bau und Leben des socialen Körpers 1875-1878. (2nd ed., Tübingen, 1896. 2 vols.)

———. Aus meinem Leben. Berlin, 1905. 2 vols.

———. Abriss der Soziologie. Tübingen, 1906.

SCHMOLLER, GUSTAV. Der moderne Verkehr im Verhältnis zum wirtschaftlichen, socialen und sittlichen Fortschritt, 1873. (In: Gustav Schmoller, *Zur Social- und Gewerbepolitik der Gegenwart*. Leipzig, 1890.)

———. Die sociale Frage und der Preussische Staat, 1874. (*Ibid.*)

———. Das Merkantilsystem in seiner historischen Bedeutung, 1884. (In: Gustav Schmoller, *Umrisse und Untersuchungen*. Leipzig, 1898.)

——. Zur Litteraturgeschichte der Staats- und Sozialwissenschaften. Leipzig, 1888.

——. Grundriss der allgemeinen Volkswirtschaftslehre, 1900. (Leipzig, 1923. 2 vols.)

——. Die Wandlungen in der europäischen Handelspolitik des 19. Jahrhunderts, SJG, xxiv (1900).

——. Die wirtschaftliche Zukunft Deutschlands und die Flottenvorlage. (In: HANDELS- UND MACHTPOLITIK. Stuttgart, I, 1900.)

SENIOR, NASSAU WILLIAM. Three Lectures on the Transmission of the Precious Metals from Country to Country and the Mercantile Theory of Wealth, 1828 (*London School of Economics, Series of Reprints of Scarce Tracts in Economic and Political Science*, no. 3, London, s.d.).

——. An Outline of the Science of Political Economy, 1836 (*The Library of Economics*, sect. I, vol. I, London, 1938).

——. The Law of Nations, 1843. (In vol. I of his *Historical and Philosophical Essays*. London, 1865.)

SISMONDI, J.-C.-L. SIMONDE DE. De la richesse commerciale. Geneva, 1803. 2 vols.

——. Nouveaux principes d'économie politique, 1819. (2nd ed. Paris, 1827, 2 vols.)

——. Études sur l'économie politique. Paris, 1837-1838. 2 vols.

SMITH, ADAM. An Inquiry into the Nature and Causes of the Wealth of Nations, 1776 (The Modern Library, New York, 1937).

SOMBART, WERNER. Krieg und Kapitalismus. Munich, 1913.

SPENCER, HERBERT. The Principles of Sociology, 1876-1896 (New York, 1898-1899. 3 vols.).

STEIN, LORENZ VON. System der Staatswissenschaft. Stuttgart, 1852. 2 vols.

——. Die Grundlagen und Aufgaben des künftigen Friedens. Vienna, 1856.

——. Volkswirtschaftliche Studien über stehende Heere, *Oesterreichische Militärische Zeitschrift*, 2nd year, II, no. 7, pp. 130-143 (Vienna, 1861).

——. Die Lehre vom Heerwesen. Als Theil der Staatswissenschaft. Stuttgart, 1872.

STORCH, HENRI. Cours d'économie politique, 1815 (ed., J.-B. Say. Paris, 1823. 4 vols.).

THOMPSON, WILLIAM. An Inquiry into the Principles of the

Distribution of Wealth Most Conducive to Human Happiness, 1824 (New ed., London, 1850).

TORRENS, ROBERT. An Essay on the External Corn Trade. London, 1815.

TOYNBEE, ARNOLD. The Ideal Relation of Church and State, 1879. (In his *Lectures on the Industrial Revolution.* London, 1937.)

TURGOT, A.-R. J. Oeuvres, ed. Schelle, Paris, 1913-1923. 5 vols.

VAUBAN. Projet d'une dixme royale, 1707 (CPE, I, 1843).

VIDAL, FRANÇOIS. De la répartition des richesses. Paris, 1846.

———. Vivre en travaillant! Projets, voies et moyens de réformes sociales. Paris, 1848.

VILLIAUMÉ, N. L'esprit de la guerre. Paris, 1861.

———. Nouveau traité d'économie politique 1857. (2nd ed. Paris, 1864. 2 vols.)

WAGNER, ADOLF. Elsass und Lothringen und ihre Wiedergewinnung für Deutschland, 1870. (3rd ed., Leipzig, 1870.)

———. Die Veränderungen der Karte von Europa. Berlin, 1871.

———. Allgemeine und theoretische Volkswirtschaftslehre. Erster Theil. Grundlegung, 1876. (2nd ed., Leipzig, 1879.)

———. Finanzwissenschaft. 3rd ed., vol. I, Leipzig, 1883.

———. Cf. RAU, 1872.

———. Die Flottenverstärkung und unsere Finanzen. (In: HANDELS- UND MACHTPOLITIK, II, Stuttgart, 1900.

———. Agrar- und Industriestaat, 1901. (2nd ed., Jena, 1902.)

WALRAS, LÉON. Études d'économie politique appliquée (Théorie de la production de la richesse sociale). Lausanne, 1898.

———. "La paix par la justice sociale et le libre-échange," *Questions pratiques de législation ouvrière et d'économie sociale,* Sept.-Oct., 1907.

WAYLAND, FRANCIS. The Elements of Political Economy. New York, 1837.

WEITLING, WILHELM. Die Menschheit wie sie ist und wie sie sein sollte, 1838 (2nd ed. Berne, 1845).

WHATELY, RICHARD. Introductory Lectures on Political Economy, 1832 (3rd ed. London, 1847).

WIRTH, MAX. Grundzüge der Nationalökonomie, vol. II, 1859. (2nd ed., Cologne, 1861.)

WOLOWSKI, L. Études d'économie politique et de statistique. Paris, 1848.

AUXILIARY SOURCES

ALLIX, EDGAR. Jean-Baptiste Say et les origines de l'industrialisme, *Revue d'Économie Politique*, 24th year (1910).

———. . . . . Charles Dunoyer, *Revue d'Histoire des Doctrines Économiques et Sociales*, 4th year (1911).

BAHR, FRIEDRICH. Die politischen Anschauungen Friedrich Lists . . . Eibau, Sa. [1929]. Dissertation—Univ. of Leipzig.

BAIN, ALEXANDER. James Mill, A Biography. London, 1882.

BASTABLE, CHARLES F. art., "Leslie," *Supplément au Nouveau Dictionnaire d'Économie Politique de Léon Say*. Paris, 1897.

BEER, (M.). A History of British Socialism. One volume edition. London, 1940.

BIDET, FRANÇOIS. Frédéric Bastiat. L'homme, l'économiste. Paris, 1906. Dissertation—Univ. of Montpellier.

BONAR, JAMES. Malthus and His Work, 2nd ed. London, 1924.

———. "German School of Political Economy," Palgrave's Dictionary of Political Economy, II (London, 1923).

BOURGIN, HUBERT. Fourier. Paris, 1905.

BOUSQUET, G. H. Vilfredo Pareto, sa vie et son oeuvre. Paris, 1928.

BOUVIER-AJAM, MAURICE. Frédéric List, sa vie, son oeuvre, son influence. Paris, 1938. Dissertation—Université de Paris.

BRINKMANN, CARL. Gustav Schmoller und die Volkswirtschaftslehre. Stuttgart, 1937.

CASTELOT, E. Introduction to Rogers, Interprétation économique de l'histoire. Paris, 1892.

CHARLÉTY, SÉBASTIEN. Histoire du saint-simonisme. Paris, 1931.

CICOTTI, ETTORE. La pace e la guerra nell'antica Atene, *Rivista Italiana di Sociologia*, 1st year (1897).

———. La guerra e la pace nel mondo antico. Turin, 1901.

COSSA, LUIGI. Histoire des doctrines économiques. French transl. Paris, 1899.

DAWSON, WILLIAM H. Richard Cobden and Foreign Policy. London, 1926.

DOMMANGET, MAURICE. Victor Considérant, sa vie, son oeuvre. Paris, 1929.

DRAHN, ERNST. Friedrich Engels als Kriegswissenschaftler. Gantzsch b. Leipzig, 1915.

DUPRAT, JEANNE. La conception proudhonnienne des facteurs

économiques de la guerre et de la paix, *Revue Internationale de Sociologie*, 37th year (1929).

———. Le paupérisme, facteur de bellicisme d'après Proudhon, *Annales de l'Institut International de Sociologie*, vol. xvi: Sociologie de la guerre et de la paix. Paris, 1932.

EARLE, EDWARD M. "Adam Smith, Alexander Hamilton and Friedrich List: The Economic Foundations of Military Power," in *Makers of Modern Strategy*, Princeton, 1943. pp. 117-154.

ESPINAS, A. Histoire des doctrines économiques. Paris, s.d.

GIDE, CHARLES and RIST, CHARLES. Histoire des doctrines économiques depuis les physiocrates jusqu'à nos jours. 3rd ed. Paris, 1920.

GOBLET D'ALVIELLA, A. J. . . . Laveleye, sa vie et son oeuvre, *Annuaire de l'Académie Royale de Belgique*, 1895.

GUYOT, YVES. L'oeuvre de Levasseur, JDE, XXXI (1911).

———. Gustave de Molinari, JDE, XXXIII (1912).

HALÉVY, ELIE. La doctrine économique de Saint-Simon et des saint-simoniens. Reprint from *Revue du Mois*, 1907-1908.

HAMILTON, ROBERT. An Inquiry Concerning . . . the National Debt of Great-Britain and Ireland. 3rd ed., Edinburgh, 1818.

HASHAGEN, J. Marxismus und Imperialismus, JNS, CXIII (1919).

HIRST, FRANCIS W. Free Trade and Other Fundamental Doctrines of the Manchester School. London, 1903.

HOLLANDER, JACOB H. David Ricardo. Baltimore, 1910.

HOVDE, B. J. Socialistic Theories of Imperialism Prior to the Great War, JPE, XXXVI (1928).

INGRAM, JOHN KELLS. A History of Political Economy. New and enlarged edition. London, 1923.

ISAMBERT, GASTON. Les idées socialistes en France de 1815 à 1848. Paris, 1905.

KAUFMANN, LOTTE. Die Einstellung von Karl Marx und Friedrich Engels zu Krieg und Frieden. Würzburg, 1932. Dissertation—Univ. of Berlin.

KAUTSKY, KARL. Sozialisten und Krieg. Ein Beitrag zur Ideengeschichte des Sozialismus von den Hussiten bis zum Völkerbund. Prague, 1937.

LABRACHERIE, PIERRE. Michel Chevalier et ses idées économiques. Paris, 1929. Dissertation—Univ. of Paris.

LAGORGETTE, JEAN. Le rôle de la guerre. Paris, 1906. Dissertation—Univ. of Dijon.

LENZ, FRIEDRICH. Friedrich List, der Mann und das Werk. Munich and Berlin, 1936.

LORIA, ACHILLE. La teoria economica della costituzione politica. Turin, 1886. Cf. pp. 90-94.

———. Les bases économiques de la constitution sociale. Paris, 1893. Cf. pp. 282-318.

MARCY, G. Constantin Pecqueur, fondateur du collectivisme d'État. Paris, 1934. Dissertation—Univ. of Lille.

MAYER, GUSTAV. Friedrich Engels. Eine Biographie. The Hague, 1934. 2 vols.

MEHRING, FRANZ. Karl Marx. Geschichte seines Lebens. 4th ed. Leipzig, 1923.

MENGER, ANTON. The Right to the Whole Produce of Labour. Translated by M. E. Tanner. With an Introduction by H. S. Foxwell. London, 1899.

MOLTKE, COMTE DE. Lettre à M. Bluntschli [December 11, 1880], *Revue de Droit International et de Législation Comparée*, XIII (1881).

MORLEY, JOHN. The Life of Richard Cobden. London, 1881, 2 vols.

NEILL, CHARLES P. Daniel Raymond. Baltimore, 1897.

NICARD DES RIEUX, SAMUEL. Michel Chevalier, saint-simonien. Limoges, 1912. Dissertation—Univ. of Poitiers.

NOTZ, WILLIAM. F. List in Amerika, *Weltwirtschaftliches Archiv*, XXII (1925).

PICARD, ROGER. Un saint-simonien démocrate: Le Docteur Ange Guépin, RHES, XIII (1925).

PIROU, GAÉTAN. Les doctrines économiques en France depuis 1870. Paris, 1925.

PUECH, J.-L. Proudhon et la guerre. (In: Proudhon et notre temps, [par:] Augé-Laribé and others. Paris, 1920.)

———. La tradition socialiste en France et la Société des Nations. Paris [1921].

RAPPARD, WILLIAM-E. The Common Menace of Economic and Military Armaments, being the *Richard Cobden Lecture* for 1936. London, 1936.

———. The Quest for Peace Since the World War. Cambridge, Mass., 1940.

———. Antoine-Elisée Cherbuliez et la propriété privée. Zurich, 1941.

ROBBINS, LIONEL. The Economic Causes of War. London, 1939.

RUYER, R. L'humanité de l'avenir d'après Cournot. Paris, 1930.

SCHUMACHER, AUGUST. Frédéric Bastiat's Staatsfinanz-Grundsätze. Basel, 1929. Dissertation—Univ. of Fribourg.

SCHUMACHER, HERMANN. "The Historical School," *Encyclopaedia of the Social Sciences*, v (New York, 1931).

SCOTT, W. R. William Cunningham. (In: *Proceedings of the British Academy*, 1919-1920.)

SEVIN, LUDWIG. Die Listsche Idee einer deutsch-englischen Allianz, SJG, XXXIV (1910).

SILBERNER, EDMUND. L'oeuvre économique d'Antoine-Elisée Cherbuliez. Geneva, 1935. Dissertation—Univ. of Geneva.

———. La guerre dans la pensée économique du 16e au 18e siècle. Préface par William-E. Rappard. (Études sur l'histoire des théories économiques, VII.) Paris, 1939.
    An English translation of the preface and of the conclusions appeared in *Annals of Collective Economy*, January-April, 1940, pp. 21-30.

———. Un manuscrit inédit de David Ricardo sur le problème monétaire. Extrait de la RHES, XXV (1940), nos. 3-4†.

SOMMER, ARTHUR. Friedrich Lists System der politischen Oekonomie. Jena, 1927.

———. F. List, Werke, VI (1930), pp. 497 ff.: Kommentar.

TEILHAC, ERNEST. L'oeuvre économique de Jean-Baptiste Say. Paris, 1927. Dissertation—Univ. of Bordeaux.

THOMAS, P.-FÉLIX. Pierre Leroux, sa vie, son oeuvre, sa doctrine. Paris, 1904.

VILLEY, DANIEL. La vie, l'oeuvre et la doctrine de Charles Brook Dupont-White, vol. I, Caen, 1936. Dissertation—Univ. of Caen.

† Because of the German occupation of France, this number of the RHES has not yet been distributed to the public. We have however succeeded in obtaining a small number of reprints, which have been placed at the disposal of some large libraries (Library of Congress, British Museum, New York Public Library, Bibliothèque Nationale Suisse, Bern, etc.). Professor Attilio Cabiati has devoted to the work a special study, *Riflessioni su un manoscritto inedito*. (Estratto dal Giornale degli Economisti, Marzo-Aprile 1941.) Casa Editrice Dott. A. Milani, Padua, 1941. 14 pp.

WEILL, GEORGES. Un précurseur du socialisme: Saint-Simon et son oeuvre. Paris, 1894.

———. L'école saint-simonienne. Paris, 1896.

WINSLOW, E. M. Marxian, Liberal, and Sociological Theories of Imperialism, JPE, xxxix (1931).

WRIGHT, QUINCY. A Study of War. Chicago, 1942. 2 vols.

INDEX

Accumulation, 40, 41

Agreements, trade, 159, 246

Aggression, 5, 7, 8, 12, 34, 47, 48, 52, 53, 65, 75, 93, 101, 114, 123, 179, 187, 191, 272, 286

Aggressive system, 74-78

Agriculture, 12-14, 17-23, 47, 64, 71, 131, 145-147, 150, 156-158, 234, 271 n.

Angell, 118

Arbitration, international, 48-50, 61, 62, 65, 101, 103, 197, 203 n., 244

Armaments, 61, 101, 102, 109, 123, 132, 177, 183, 187-189, 195, 273

Army, 7, 26, 57, 60, 67, 70, 74, 98, 109, 110, 123, 150, 173, 177, 179 n., 187 n., 197, 210, 224, 235, 254, 274, 275, 285; and public works, 110; as a productive body, 52, 65, 179; as an unproductive body, 12, 76, 236, 272; cost of, 181, 182; economic usefulness, 132, 181, 210; industrial or productive, 228, 229, 236-239, 243, 271 n.; international, 61; revolutionary, 272; standing, 44, 53, 74, 76, 78, 109, 110, 111 n., 132, 166, 169 n., 175 n., 177, 179, 196, 211, 258, 272, 274, 289

Arnd, 177 n.

Ashley, 202

Association, universal, 225, 226, 229, 230; *see also* Federation, universal

Athens, 5, 177

Austria, 123, 182, 183, 209, 240, 274

Autarky, 13, 14, 19, 52-56, 59, 111, 158, 165, 199, 203; *see also* Protection

Bagehot, 193

Balance of Power, 83

Bankers, 227, 228

Barbarism, 55, 97, 115, 118, 120, 126, 166, 234 n., 288, 290

Bastiat, viii, 1, 2, 60 n., 92-107, 110, 112, 117, 177, 259, 275, 282

Baudeau, 289 n.

Baudrillart, 1, 2, 107, 110-113, 282, 298

Bebel, 257

Belgium, 123, 124, 160-162

Bellicism, 14 n., 34, 49, 59 n., 65, 69, 82, 89, 104, 108, 109 n., 111, 119, 166, 179, 184, 190, 195, 199, 219, 222, 230, 235, 263, 292

Bentham, 16 n., 43, 49

Béranger, 216, 222

Biard, 214, 216, 223, 224, 228

Bidet, 92

Blanc, Louis, 214, 232-234, 239, 248, 249

Blanqui, Adolphe, 86

Bloch, 118

Boccardo, 117

Bolles, 60

Bousquet, 117

Bouvier-Ajam, 167

Brentano, 173

Brotherhood, universal, 94, 200, 234, 235, 239, 264, 267

Bücher, 173

Büsch, 12

Cabet, 239

Cairnes, 1, 2, 51, 67

Canard, 189 n.

Cancrin, 299 n.

Capital, 8, 10, 17, 18, 25, 27, 31, 37, 40, 62, 64, 65 n., 67, 71, 109, 119, 175, 178, 201, 232, 260, 261, 268

Capitalist system, 173, 252, 254, 258, 261, 269

Carballo y Wangüemert, 111 n.

Carey, 28 n., 132, 166 n.

Cattaneo, 160 n.

Cauwès, 132, 139 n.

Chalmers, 59

Chamberlain, Joseph, 202

Chaptal, 135, 149 n.

Cherbuliez, 103, 104, 109 n., 210

Chevalier, 1, 2, 100, 103, 107-110, 113, 210, 214, 216, 225-231, 282

Date Due